T0383056

HANDBOOK

THE FIRST 100 YEARS OF THE

ACLU

A COMPENDIUM OF ADVOCACY BEFORE
THE UNITED STATES SUPREME COURT

HANDBOOK

THE FIRST 100 YEARS OF THE

ACLU

A COMPENDIUM OF ADVOCACY BEFORE

THE UNITED STATES SUPREME COURT

CONCEIVED AND COMPILED BY
STEVEN C. MARKOFF

CASE SUMMARY EDITOR
JESSICA PIERUCCI

FOREWORD BY
ERWIN CHEMERINSKY

RARE BIRD

THIS IS A GENUINE BARNACLE BOOK

Rare Bird Books
6044 North Figueroa Street
Los Angeles, CA 90042
rarebirdbooks.com

For more information, address:
Rare Bird Books Subsidiary Rights Department
6044 North Figueroa Street
Los Angeles, CA 90042

Printed in the United States

10 9 8 7 6 5 4 3 2 1

Library of Congress Cataloging-in-Publication Data available upon request

The U.S. Supreme Court

The U.S. Supreme Court was organized on February 2, 1790, as written in Article III—Section 1 of the U.S. Constitution. "Each Term, approximately 7,000–8,000 new cases are filed in the [U.S.] Supreme Court. This is a substantially larger volume of cases than was presented to the [U.S. Supreme] Court in the last century. In the 1950 Term, for example, the [U.S. Supreme] Court received only

Photo credit: Commons.Wikimedia.org

1,195 new cases, and even as recently as the 1975 Term it received only 3,940. Plenary review, with oral arguments by attorneys, is currently granted in about 80 of those cases each Term, and the [U.S. Supreme] Court typically disposes of about 100 or more cases without plenary review. The publication of each Term's written opinions, including concurring opinions, dissenting opinions, and orders, can take up thousands of pages. During the drafting process, some opinions may be revised a dozen or more times before they are announced."[1]

---

[1] "The Term and Caseload - The Supreme Court at Work." Home - Supreme Court of the United States. Accessed September 17, 2019. https://www.supremecourt.gov/about/courtatwork.aspx.

This Handbook Versus the Companion Three-Volume Set

The companion to this handbook is the complete unabridged three-volume set pictured below. The sole difference between the handbook and the three-volume set is that the handbook contains a sample of three of the 1,193 cases in the three-volume set.

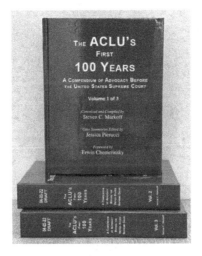

Working cover of the three-volume set, complete and unabridged

Perhaps the three sample Supreme Court cases in this handbook (beginning on page 291) will encourage your interest in more or even all the cases in the three-volume set.

TABLE OF CONTENTS

Foreword

The American Civil Liberties Union (ACLU) is unique among organizations. It exists solely to protect civil liberties and civil rights. It has done this brilliantly for a century. It has done so at the national level and the state and local levels. It has done so in the legislative and political processes and in the courts. Not surprisingly, many of these judicial battles have ended in the U.S. Supreme Court and led to crucial decisions that affect all of us, often in the most important and intimate aspects of our lives.

Surprisingly, though, no one has systematically chronicled the ACLU's history in the U.S. Supreme Court. That is the contribution of Steven Markoff and his history of the ACLU, the U.S. Constitution, and the U.S. Supreme Court. His focus is on the ACLU's involvement in the U.S. Supreme Court in the past century, from 1920 to 2020.

I must disclose that I am not an impartial observer of all of this. I have been an ACLU member my entire adult life. I served on the Board of Directors of the ACLU of Southern California for almost 15 years and on the Board of Directors of the ACLU of North Carolina for several years when I lived there. I have been directly or tangentially involved in many ACLU cases, including in the U.S. Supreme Court. I have spoken to the ACLU lawyers at their conferences for more than 30 years. One of my proudest awards (and one of the few plaques in my office) is the one naming me an honorary ACLU lawyer.

At the same time, I must confess that I do not always agree with the ACLU. I strongly disagree with its position on campaign finance and its view that spending money in election campaigns is speech. Unlike the ACLU, I regard *Citizens United v. Federal Election Commission*, which held that corporations can spend unlimited amounts of money in election campaigns, as terribly misguided.

But whether one agrees or disagrees with the ACLU in particular areas, there is no denying the importance of the ACLU as a force in the U.S.

Supreme Court and in American law. Thanks to Steven Markoff's efforts, there now is a comprehensive listing of all of the U.S. Supreme Court cases in the last century with ACLU involvement. He provides clear and concise descriptions of the cases.

I especially liked the presentation of each justice's votes and how often each sided with the ACLU. It was interesting to see that Justice Louis Brandeis voted in favor of the ACLU position 87.5% of the time, while the arch-conservative Justice James McReynolds did so only 18.18% of the time. Justice William Douglas participated in 347 ACLU cases and was with the ACLU 87.9% of the time. By contrast, Associate Justice and then Chief Justice William Rehnquist participated in 718 ACLU cases, but voted in favor of the ACLU position only 25.91% of the time.

These are just some examples of the wealth of information to be learned from Steven Markoff's terrific work. I hope that he or someone else will continually update his work. It is a wonderful wealth of information about an enormously important organization. I have found that I frequently use it as a reference tool and can see how invaluable it is in countless ways.

- *Erwin Chemerinsky, Dean and Jesse H. Choper Distinguished Professor of Law, University of California, Berkeley School of Law (August 2021)*

Background

This project began shortly after I joined the Board of the ACLU Foundation of Southern California in 1979. I knew little about the Foundation or the ACLU before I joined, given that I joined primarily to offset the negative perception of my company's gold dealing with South Africa. At that time, South Africa was broadly seen as an international pariah given its Apartheid policies of treating non-whites as second-class citizens or worse.

Shortly after I joined the Foundation Board, I found its printed marketing material more fluff than substance. As there was no "welcome to the board" information package, I started asking what the Foundation and the ACLU actually did. I was then provided the ACLU's 62-word bylaws which left many questions:

> *"The objects of the American Civil Liberties Union shall be to maintain and advance civil liberties, including the freedoms of association, press, religion, and speech, and rights to the franchised, to due process of law, and to equal protection of the laws to all people throughout the United States and its possessions. The **Union's objects shall be sought wholly without political partisanship.**"*[2]

While the ACLU's bylaws painted a comforting broad picture, I wanted to understand how the organization actually worked, what specifically it did, and how it made decisions about the various issues it was involved. I was also interested in the issues it did not pursue. Wanting a more comprehensive view of the ACLU, I asked ACLU of Southern California Executive Director Ramona Ripston to introduce me to Ira Glasser, the then-national executive director of ACLU.

---

[2] The American Civil Liberties Union Const. § 2

After a brief introduction, Mr. Glasser and I discussed the need and efficacy of a better understanding of the ACLU by its members, the media, and the general public. He agreed that a better understanding of the organization would be helpful. With my discussed donation to ACLU National, he agreed to draft a one-page description of what the ACLU did in layman's terms. Mr. Glasser then penned that draft (on page 27).

Despite my appreciation of the comprehensiveness and clarity of his draft, he was concerned that the document could somehow limit the ACLU's actions in the future. Based on that concern, he decided not to formalize his draft. His 1982 one-pager remains a draft to this day, but it's the best overall description of the ACLU I have so far encountered.

Armed with the ACLU bylaws and Mr. Glasser's one-pager, I decided to put together a modest, fact-based brochure on the ACLU, setting out who the organizers are, what they do, and an overview of various ACLU offices, its staffing, funding, and resources. In thinking about a marketing hook for the brochure, I decided to focus on the Union's legal victories and defeats in the Supreme Court of the United States (SCOTUS).

After some initial drafts of the brochure, the Southern California ACLU seemed to have little interest in it and I dropped the project. The question, though, of how the ACLU did in the U.S. Supreme Court continued to fascinate me. Although I was a bit surprised the ACLU never kept a list of all of its SCOTUS cases, I decided to collect them all. Thus began my 40-year odyssey of collecting those cases and adding case overviews and data related to those cases. This work, therefore, ended with the last SCOTUS case the ACLU was involved in, *Dep't of Commerce v. New York* decided on June 27, 2019, before the ACLU's Centennial on January 19, 2020.[3]

— *Steven C. Markoff*

---

[3] Date for establishment of the ACLU is from Samuel Walker's book *In Defense of American Liberties: A History of the ACLU* (New York: Oxford University Press, 1990). Although the ACLU was founded in 1920, its first SCOTUS case was in 1925.

I.

The ACLU – An Overview

The ACLU grew from the seeds of social activism in 1917 and was born in January 1920. Since its beginning, the ACLU has been a lightning rod for controversy, not least because the cases it has championed involve America's cherished civil rights.

Those rights have caused disagreements, fights, and litigation from the beginning of our country, and will most probably continue to do so. Those rights include freedom of the press (Is press freedom unfettered or subject to restraints?) to free speech (Who has it? When can they use it? Are there any limitations on it?) to equal protection (Who should expect equal treatment? Who should not? What is equal treatment across economic, gender, age, or racial lines?).

The ACLU was established to and has inserted itself squarely amid these and other constitutional and societal controversies.

Here is a sample of the many pros and cons about the Union[4]:

---

[4] "Top 10 Pro & Con Arguments: ACLU: ProCon.org." ProCon/Encyclopædia Britannica, February 18, 2020. https://aclu.procon.org/top-10-pro-con-arguments/#1 (with permission).

A. Pro ACLU	B. Con ACLU

1. ACLU & Defense of Individual Rights

"Over the years, the ACLU's fortunes have waxed and waned because it tends to attract or lose members following specific actions it undertakes. That waxing and waning demonstrates the organization's success at its sole endeavor, defending and preserving the individual freedoms granted through the Bill of Rights. The ACLU has challenged literary censorship, segregation, cruel and unusual punishments, gender inequality, and violations of the right to privacy and freedom of religion. The ACLU is one of the informal checks and balances protecting individuals against tyranny." *— Judy Kutulas, Ph.D., professor of history at St. Olaf College, Email to ProCon.org, October 12, 2017*	"The ACLU is trying to deprive other organizations of freedoms that it would insist upon for itself. Their work is not a defense of equality – it is an effort to impose a certain view of morality on the country by law… This organization, despite its name and origins, is now committed to a version of civil rights that cannot help but erode traditional American civil liberties. The motto of the ACLU is, 'Because Freedom Can't Defend Itself.' The irony today is that freedom needs to be defended from the ACLU." *— Carson Holloway, Ph.D., associate professor of political science, University of Nebraska, "The ACLU's Betrayal of Civil Liberties," Public Discourse, March 26, 2015*

2. ACLU & Religion

"Over the years, the ACLU has earned a reputation as the nation's foremost protector of the rights of individuals to practice their religion, as well as the chief opponent of both state aid to	"From its inception… the ACLU can be characterized as hostile to the Christian faith. In 1925, it was the ACLU that challenged the Tennessee law banning the teaching of the theory of evolution as a fact in the

A. Pro ACLU	B. Con ACLU
religion and enforcement of any religious belief by law. We support the separation of church and state for the same reason the founders of our country did: to promote and protect religious freedom by keeping the government out… We believe that the place for religious displays, as with religious events and practices, is in the private sector – the home, the religious day school, or each person's place of worship. Moreover, spirituality is undermined and religious symbols are trivialized when they are secularized in order to permit government endorsement." *— American Civil Liberties Union (ACLU), "ACLU Briefing Paper Number 3 – Church and State," lectlaw.com, (Accessed November 22, 2017)*	taxpayer-funded public schools… Since the 1960s, the ACLU has been involved in the [U.S.] Supreme Court decisions which outlawed mandated school prayer, observation of religious holidays, and Bible reading in the public schools… Current positions of the ACLU reflect this strongly secular agenda that bristles with hostility toward biblical Christianity. The organization supports same-sex marriage and the right of 'gays' to adopt children; the support of abortion rights; and the elimination of 'discrimination' against LGBTQ people." *— Steven Byas, med instructor, history & social studies education at Randall University, "ACLU Survey/Fundraising Letter Confirms Its Anti-Christian Bias," thenewamerican.com, April 19, 2016*

3. ACLU & Rights of the Minority

"I want to recognize the ACLU for its commitment to protecting our civil liberties. You have a long and proud history of standing up to defend the freedoms guaranteed to us by the	"[A] problem occurs when the ACLU wins cases that force the 'will' or viewpoint of a minority onto the will of the majority. In so doing, the ACLU uses the judicial branch of the government to undermine the rights of the majority, and thus to undermine the very foundations of our democracy,

A. Pro ACLU	B. Con ACLU
Bill of Rights and the Constitution… The ACLU seeks to prevent the 'tyranny of the majority' from destroying our fundamental liberties." *—Robert S. Mueller, III, JD, former director of the Federal Bureau of Investigation (FBI), Speech to the 2003 Inaugural ACLU Membership Conference, fbi.gov, June 13, 2003*	namely majority rule. When courts continuously side with a minority they create a society where the minority gain power over the majority, thus becoming the tyranny of the minority. This is just the opposite of a democracy." *— Charles E. Steele, industrial designer "Democratic Republic Majority Rule & the ACLU Effect on Religious Freedom," free2pray.info, June 29, 2015*

4. ACLU & Defense of Criminals

"The ACLU doesn't believe in 'going soft' on criminals. The ACLU supports just, reasonable law enforcement, even tough enforcement. However, we believe everyone is entitled to a fair trial and all rights of due process guaranteed by the Bill of Rights." *— American Civil Liberties Union "FAQ," acluohio.org, (Accessed September 28, 2017)*	"In a 1981 speech before the California Peace Officers Assn., former Attorney General Ed Meese referred to the American Civil Liberties Union (ACLU) as a 'criminals' lobby.' Lately, the American Criminal Liberties Union has been working harder than ever to justify its pejorative nickname… The ACLU has always advocated for the rights of criminals over their victims." *— Robert H. Knight, MA, senior Fellow at the American Civil Rights Union, "The ACLU Goes Hunting in Montana," Washington Times, June 24, 2017*

A. Pro ACLU	B. Con ACLU

5. ACLU & Liberal Bias

A. Pro ACLU	B. Con ACLU
"Since the ACLU was founded in 1920, there have been 17 presidents in the White House. They've come and gone, some better – and a few much worse – than others. Throughout, the ACLU has remained steadfast in our nonpartisan mission of promoting civil rights and defending civil liberties – regardless of who's in office… America needs the ACLU as an independent voice for civil rights and civil liberties, ready to meet challenges and seize opportunities to promote equal justice for all… Especially in times of tyranny, the ACLU's liberty work is paramount." *— Carol Rose, JD, executive director of the ACLU of Massachusetts, "ACLU: Defending Liberty and Democracy in an Election Year," The Docket, May 2016*	"[T]he ACLU, which bills itself as 'our nation's guardian of liberty,' would more accurately be described as the guardian of a far-left progressive agenda… It hails itself as a defender of the right of 'everyone' to free speech, but if you want to exercise that right while lawfully carrying a gun, don't rely on the ACLU. It claims to defend religious freedom, but if you're a baker whose religion does not allow you to bake a cake for a same-sex marriage celebration, you will find the ACLU on the other side of the courtroom representing the same-sex couple suing you." *— David E. Weisberg, JD, Ph.D., civil litigator and appellate lawyer, "ACLU Proves Yet Again It's a Guardian of Left-Wing Agenda," thehill.com, August 21, 2017*

6. ACLU & Communism

A. Pro ACLU	B. Con ACLU
"Throughout the organization's history and particularly during the McCarthy era, the ACLU, its members, staff and founders have been accused of being Communists. The ACLU has no political affiliations and makes no test of	"In an effort to resist the conservative agenda of President Donald Trump, the ACLU organized everything from mass rallies to weekend house parties, where thousands were reported to have gathered over the weekend.

A. Pro ACLU	B. Con ACLU
individuals' ideological leanings a condition of membership or employment. Members and staff of the national ACLU and its affiliates may be Republicans, Democrats, Communists, Federalists, Libertarians, or members of any other political party or no party at all. What the ACLU asks of its staff and officials is that they consistently defend civil liberties and the Constitution." *— American Civil Liberties Union (ACLU) "FAQs: Does the ACLU Have Communist Roots? Was Co-founder Roger Baldwin a Communist?" aclu.org, (Accessed September 11, 2017)*	Participants received a nine-point plan to resist established law and turn America into a network of 'freedom cities' that resist the Trump presidential agenda and the vote of the American people in the election of 2016. Uniting with Muslim congressman, Keith Ellison who also called for 'mass rallies' to stop Trump's conservative agenda, the ACLU hopes to turn America Democratic 'blue' by forcing its liberal Socialistic and Communistic agenda upon all America." *— Stephen Flick, Ph.D., executive director of the Christian Heritage Fellowship, "ACLU Rattles Lifeless Bones of Communism" christianheritagefellowship.com, (Accessed December 1, 2017)*

7. ACLU & Nazis' Rights

"If the ACLU allows the state to suppress the free speech rights of white nationalists or neo-Nazi groups – by refusing to defend such groups when the state tries to censor them or by allowing them to have inadequate representation – then the ACLU's ability to defend the free speech rights of groups and people that you like will be severely compromised...	"For people who see themselves as anti-racists and anti-fascists first... the insistence that free speech will save us all rings somewhat hollow after this weekend [Unite the Right violence in Charlottesville, Aug. 2017]. Given limited energy and resources, maybe [the ACLU] defending the rights of violent bigots isn't the noble choice in every case – especially when those bigots predictably use their platform to

A. Pro ACLU	B. Con ACLU
The ACLU is not defending white supremacist groups but instead is defending a principle – one that it must defend if it is going to be successful in defending free speech rights for people you support." *— Glenn Greenwald, JD, lawyer and cofounding editor of The Intercept, "The Misguided Attacks on ACLU for Defending Neo-Nazis' Free Speech Rights in Charlottesville," theintercept.com, August 13, 2017*	silence others. Free speech absolutists [such as the ACLU] insist that free speech is the foundation of anti-fascism. But maybe anti-fascism is the basis of true free speech – in which case, defending the speech of bigots can, at least in some cases, leave us all less free." *— Noah Berlatsky, MA, contributing writer for The Atlantic, "The Case Against Free Speech for Fascists," qz.com, August 15, 2017*

8. ACLU & War on Terror

"The ACLU does not undermine the War on Terror. The organization does, however, insist that government actions taken to protect Americans from terrorism be consistent with our Constitution and the rule of law. Acts of terrorism are, as the term itself indicates, intended to terrorize. Unfortunately, when people become fearful, they sometimes endorse measures that are ultimately self-defeating; the arrest of 'suspicious' people or the conduct of intrusive searches without probable cause, profiling individuals from certain ethnic groups based simply upon the way they look, 'interrogation' methods	"The ACLU has worked diligently to undermine America's stance in what was formerly known as the 'war on terror,' and has even been willing to disseminate propaganda on behalf of our jihadist enemies. If you think this is hyperbole or an exaggeration, consider a video released by the ACLU earlier this month titled 'Justice Denied: Voices from Guantanamo.' As you would expect, the video portrays Gitmo in the worst possible light. But it goes well beyond any semblance of rational criticism. As Sahab, al Qaeda's media arm, could very well have produced it.

A. Pro ACLU	B. Con ACLU
that are really torture outlawed by the Geneva conventions, and similar practices that are inconsistent with the 4th Amendment and with constitutional due process guarantees.	The short video is pure anti-American propaganda, starring men who have dedicated their lives to the jihadist cause."
Research confirms that these panicky measures ultimately make Americans less safe. Not only do they encourage lawless behavior by some law enforcement officials, but they deepen divisions within the American population. Unconstitutional tactics create resentment and discourage co-operation with the authorities, and actually hinder the search for terrorists. Worse, as members of terrorist cells operating in hostile nations learn of American behaviors inconsistent with our own rules (Abu Ghraib comes to mind), they use those behaviors as centerpieces of their propaganda, as tools to recruit more terrorists, and as an excuse to mistreat Americans they capture."	*— Thomas Joscelyn, senior Fellow at the Foundation for Defense of Democracies, "Al Qaeda's Civil Liberties Union," weeklystandard.com, November 17, 2009*
— Sheila Suess Kennedy, JD, professor and director of Public Affairs programs in the School of Public and Environmental Affairs at Indiana University-Purdue University Indianapolis,	

A. Pro ACLU	B. Con ACLU
Email to ProCon.org, October 17, 2017	

9. ACLU & Abortion

"As a journalist who has written about women's reproductive health issues for many years, I have had a front row seat at how the ACLU has continually stepped up at pivotal points to protect a woman's right to privacy, especially her right to control her own body and fertility, and to respond to the demands of her own conscience. With the pace of threats of women's access to pregnancy termination and birth control services showing no signs of abating, the ACLU's role in defending those rights is arguably more urgent than ever before." *— Angela Bonavoglia, MSW, author, journalist, and blogger, Email to ProCon.org, November 6, 2017*	"[T]he American Civil Liberties Union (the ACLU is no friend of unborn babies) is suing the Food and Drug Administration to loosen the already-liberal regulations governing the chemical abortion drug [RU486]. The ACLU wants the abortion pill to be available by prescription in commercial pharmacies without a physician visit, leaving women to abort on their own… If successful, the lawsuit would end safeguards for women as pro-abortion advocates more widely promote these drugs for profit. Think about this for a moment. The ACLU and others are literally advocating for do-it-yourself abortion which can be perilous to women's health." *— Bradley Mattes, MBS, president and CEO at the Life Issues Institute, "Silent, Deadly Abortion Tool Is Spreading," lifeissues.org, October 5, 2017*

10. ACLU & Christmas

"This year, several groups are once again introducing the Christmas	"The ACLU is at it again. With an outrageous boldness that only they

A. Pro ACLU	B. Con ACLU
season with some heated and misleading military rhetoric… One particularly bizarre charge is that there is 'a thorough and virulent anti-Christmas campaign.' Without a shred of evidence, they pretend that there is an effort afoot to remove 'God' from the Declaration of Independence. Two groups even announced that they have assembled hundreds of lawyers to protect Christmas against this imaginary threat…	could muster, the ACLU has, once again, set their sights on Christmas celebrations. In their never-ending quest to completely eradicate all things religious from public life, the ACLU's latest lawsuit is an all-out frontal attack on the freedom of speech and the free exercise of religion.
First, Christmas displays — including nativity scenes — are perfectly acceptable at homes and churches. This religious expression is a valued and protected part of the First Amendment rights guaranteed to all citizens. Second, governments should not be in the business of endorsing religious displays.	Let me ask you—when did a children's Christmas program become 'an illegal activity'? When did the nativity story and Christmas songs become unconstitutional?
	This is the outrageous and dangerous charge the ACLU has leveled against a school district in Tennessee. A children's Christmas program has been deemed to be an 'illegal act' because of the ACLU.
Religion does best when government stays out of the business of deciding which holidays and religions to promote. Religion belongs where it prospers best: with individuals, families and religious communities.	Today the American Center for Law and Justice has launched a nationwide campaign entitled 'Keep HIM in Christmas.' We want to make sure that Jesus is at the center of this holiday. We want to keep HIM in the nativity scenes, keep HIM in the music, keep HIM as the focal point—and not allow the ACLU to operate as our nationwide censor."
And finally, as a seasonal greeting to all Christians: Merry Christmas from the ACLU!"	
— T. Jeremy Gunn, Ph.D., director, ACLU Program on Freedom of	— American Center for Law and Justice,

A. Pro ACLU	B. Con ACLU
Religion and Belief, *"A Fictional 'War on Christmas',"* *USA Today, December 18, 2005*	*"The ACLU Targets Christmas,"* *ACLJ.org, November 28, 2006*

As the preceding pros and cons of the ACLU show, there are many different and conflicting views and feelings about what the ACLU is, has done, and is doing. What is indisputable is that the many SCOTUS cases the ACLU has been involved in have shaped America and our lives in many ways.

While this handbook (and its companion three-volume set) contains facts and metrics about the many ACLU/SCOTUS cases, the ACLU has always also been involved in many other issues and cases that never made it to the U.S. Supreme Court, or that did but were not accepted to be heard or not decided definitively.

In addition to the SCOTUS cases, the ACLU also handles many other issues and cases. Most of those issues are settled by research, discussion, negotiation, lobbying, and threats of litigation. When those less combative methods fail to change or modify actions or laws, the ACLU relies on the courts to try and accomplish what it couldn't accomplish by quicker, cheaper, and less combative methods.

II.

Ira Glasser's 1982 Draft Statement Describing the ACLU

The American system of government is built on two basic principles: (1) the principle of majority rule, by democratic elections of temporary representatives; and (2) the principle that even democratic majorities must be limited in order to assure individual liberties.

This second principle is codified in the Bill of Rights and in federal and state legislation implementing the Bill of Rights. While the rest of the Constitution authorizes the government to act, the Bill of Rights limits the government's Authority to Act. It sets the ground rules for individual liberty, which includes the freedoms of speech, association and religion, freedom of the press, and the right to privacy, to equal protection under the laws and to due process of law.

The ACLU exists solely to defend and secure these rights and to extend them to groups that traditionally have been excluded from their protection.

Our work can be summarily categorized as follows:

1. First Amendment—The rights of speech, free association, and assembly, freedom of the press and freedom of religion, including the strict separation of Church and State.

2. Equal Protection of the Laws—The right [to] not be discriminated against on the basis of certain classifications, such as race, sex, religion, national origin, sexual orientation, age, physical handicap, etc.

3. Due Process of Law—The right to be treated fairly, including fair procedures when facing accusation of criminal conduct or other serious accusations that can lead to results like loss of employment,

exclusion from school, denial of housing, cut-off of certain benefits or various punitive measures taken by administrative regulatory agencies.

4. Privacy—The right to a guaranteed zone of personal privacy and autonomy which cannot be penetrated by government, or by other institutions with substantial influence over one's life, such as employers.

5. Special Groups—The extension of all the right[s] described above to individuals traditionally denied the full protections of the Bill of Rights, such as mental patients, prisoners, soldiers, children in the custody of the state and other confined populations, as well as certain groups who are not confined but who nonetheless have not enjoyed full protection of the Bill of Rights: The handicapped, American Indians, homosexuals, women, and racial minorities.

Draft By Ira Glasser,
ACLU Executive Director, 1982

III.

Win/Loss Record of the ACLU at SCOTUS by Count and Decade

The following chart shows the Union's wins and losses in the 1,193 decided ACLU/SCOTUS cases in the Union's first 100 years.[5] The first case was decided by the U.S. Supreme Court on June 8, 1925, and the last on June 27, 2019.

The win and loss tallies of those 1,193 cases may be the most objective presentation of data covering the actions of the ACLU during its first 100 years of existence. Different people will surely draw different conclusions from the data from those cases, but at least those conclusions will be based on the same data and statistics.

A few numbers from the chart seem particularly worthy of notice:

- The ACLU was on the winning side 53.65% of the time in the 1,193 ACLU/SCOTUS decisions.

- The ACLU was on the winning side in 238 unanimous U.S. Supreme Court decisions while on the losing side in 122 unanimous decisions.

- 310 or 25.98% of the ACLU/SCOTUS's 1,193 decisions were 4–5 or 5–4, or 3–4 or 4–3.

---

[5] Those 1,193 cases were decided from 1925 to 2019. The ACLU had no SCOTUS cases in its first five years and none in 2020. Those cases, therefore, occurred during 94 years of the ACLU's first 100 years. Those years included powerful events in our country such as the beginning of our country's labor unions, the Great Depression, World War II, the hunt for communists in the 1950s, the Korean War, Vietnam, the civil rights upheavals of the 1960s, the Iraq wars of 1991 and 2003, 9/11, and much of the Donald J. Trump presidency.

Win / Loss Chart

From January 19, 1920, to January 19, 2020

WINS | **LOSSES**

	A.	B.	C.	D.	E.	F.	G.	H.	I.	J.	K.	L.	M.		N.
	5-4	5-3	4-2	5-1	6-0				0-6	1-5	2-4	3-5	4-5		
	4-3	6-3	5-2	6-1	7-0	Total	Total	Total	0-7	1-6	2-5	3-6	3-4		ACLU
			6-2	7-1	8-0	Wins	Cases	Losses	0-8	1-7	2-6				Decade Win %
Decade Ending Dec. 31			7-2	8-1	9-0				0-9	1-8	2-7				
1929	0	0	0	0	0	0	2	2	1	0	1	0	0		0
1939	1	0	3	1	3	8	8	0	0	0	0	0	0		100.00
1949	6	7	5	4	12	34	48	14	6	3	0	3	2		70.83
1959	4	5	5	7	14	35	53	18	2	2	0	6	8		66.04
1969	13	16	10	15	30	84	114	30	2	4	3	9	12		73.68
1979	19	25	19	20	32	115	220	105	11	14	15	39	26		52.27
1989	28	14	12	11	57	122	245	123	25	9	11	39	39		49.80
1999	20	14	12	6	44	96	182	86	22	7	14	19	24		52.75
2009	21	19	5	9	23	77	177	100	29	6	10	19	36		43.50
2019	20	14	6	6	23	69	144	75	24	2	11	7	31		47.92
Total – 100 years[6]	132	114	77	79	238	640	1,193[7]	553	122	47	65	141	178		53.65
						53.65%		46.35%							

---

[6] The first ACLU/SCOTUS case (*Gitlow v. New York*) was decided on June 8, 1925. The last ACLU/SCOTUS case (*Dep't of Commerce v. New York*) was decided on June 27, 2019. There were no ACLU/SCOTUS cases decided in 2020.

[7] 29 of the 51 justices (56.86%) who voted on the 1,193 cases were nominated by Republican presidents (on page 246).

IV.

The ACLU's Wins and Losses at SCOTUS
(Alphabetically by Case Title)

The following chart lists the 1,193 decided ACLU/SCOTUS cases alphabetically, showing where each case can be found in this handbook's companion three-volume set. For example, the case summary for *Abrams v. Johnson,* case number 2 on page 32 in Columns G / H of this handbook, is found in Vol. 2 case number 829 of the three-volume set.

During the years of putting this data together, I was asked, on numerous occasions, how many times the ACLU was a party in its SCOTUS cases. Column D, at the top of the chart on page 32, shows that the ACLU was a party in seven of the 1,193 cases. The Xs in that column mark those cases.

In addition to Columns E / F on page 32 showing which cases were considered ACLU wins or losses, the chart in columns B, C, and D also shows the ACLU's category of involvement in these 1,193 ACLU/SCOTUS cases:

- **975** cases or **81.73%** of the 1,193 cases were amicus filings

- **211** cases or **17.69%** were as "Attorney of Record / ACLU Attorney" (see footnote number 9 on page 32)

- **Seven** cases or **0.59%** were when the ACLU was a party in a case

N.B. Column C, Attorney of Record/ACLU Attorney, is probably not complete as it would take years to complete if it ever could be accurately compiled. Completing that column would entail at least tracking each lawyer listed on each SCOTUS brief and those attorneys contributing to those briefs, as well as researching which of those attorneys met this work's criteria to be counted as an ACLU attorney.

Chart: The ACLU's Wins and Losses at SCOTUS (Alphabetically by Case Title)[8]

	Case Name	ACLU's Case Involvement			Wins	Losses	Volume of Three-volume set & Case # in volume	
		Amicus	Attorney of Record / ACLU Attorney	As A Party			Vol #1, #2 or #3	Case # in Volume
	A	B	C	D	E	F	G	H
	Total	975	211[9]	7	640	553		
1	44 Liquormart, Inc. v. Rhode Island	x			x		2	797
2	Abrams v. Johnson		x			x	2	829
3	Adams v. Williams	x				x	1	272
4	Adarand Constructors, Inc. v. Mineta	x			x		3	915
5	Aday v. United States	x			x		1	194
6	Adler v. Board of Education	x				x	1	69
7	Adoptive Couple v. Baby Girl	x				x	3	1115
8	Advocate Health Care Network v. Stapleton	x				x	3	1158

---

[8] The cases in Column A are listed in alphabetical order, with cases beginning with a number being listed first. The cases that have the exact same name are listed by earliest date first. The year the case was decided is in parentheses only for the cases with the same name; full dates are added if they also share the same year and are put in order from earliest to most recent date.

[9] There are 231 cases shown with Xs for "Attorney of Record / ACLU Attorney." Twenty of those cases were with the "Amicus" or with "As a Party" cases. So as not to double the count, the 20 were grayed out in Column C for ease of viewing.

	Case Name	ACLU's Case Involvement			Wins	Losses	Volume of Three-volume set & Case # in volume	
		Amicus	Attorney of Record / ACLU Attorney	As A Party			Vol #1, #2 or #3	Case # in Volume
	A	**B**	**C**	**D**	**E**	**F**	**G**	**H**
9	Agency for Int'l Dev. v. Alliance for Open Society Int'l	x			x		3	1113
10	Agostini v. Felton	x				x	2	830
11	Aguilar v. Felton	x			x		2	570
12	Alabama State Federation of Labor v. McAdory	x				x	1	33
13	Alabama v. Pugh		x			x	1	417
14	Alabama v. White	x				x	2	704
15	Albertson v. Millard	x			x		1	76
16	Albertson v. Subversive Activities Control Board	x			x		1	170
17	Albright v. Oliver	x				x	2	767
18	Alexander v. Sandoval		x			x	3	898
19	Alexander v. United States	x				x	2	761
20	Alice Corp. v. CLS Bank Int'l	x			x		3	1124
21	Allen v. McCurry	x				x	2	459
22	Alleyne v. U.S.	x			x		3	1111
23	Alvarez v. Smith	x				x	3	1049
24	Amalgamated Food Employees Union Local 590 v. Logan Valley Plaza, Inc.	x			x		1	202

	Case Name	Amicus	Attorney of Record / ACLU Attorney	As A Party	Wins	Losses	Vol #1, #2 or #3	Case # in Volume
	A	**B**	**C**	**D**	**E**	**F**	**G**	**H**
25	American Committee for Protection of Foreign Born v. Subversive Activities Control Board	x			x		1	162
26	American Communications Ass'n v. Douds	x				x	1	61
27	American Foreign Service Ass'n v. Garfinkel	x			x		2	675
28	American Legion v. American Humanist Ass'n	x				x	3	1187
29	Anderson v. Celebrezze	x			x		2	501
30	Anderson v. City of Bessemer	x			x		2	555
31	Anderson v. Creighton	x				x	2	629
32	Ankenbrandt v. Richards	x			x		2	741
33	Apodaca v. Oregon	x				x	1	266
34	Aptheker v. Secretary of State	x			x		1	155
35	Arcara v. Cloud Books Inc.	x				x	2	599

	Case Name	ACLU's Case Involvement			Wins	Losses	Volume of Three-volume set & Case # in volume	
		Amicus	Attorney of Record / ACLU Attorney	As A Party			Vol #1, #2 or #3	Case # in Volume
	A	B	C	D	E	F	G	H
36	Arizona Christian School Tuition Organization v. Winn		x			x	3	1072
37	Arizona Governing Committee for Tax Deferred Annuity & Deferred Compensation Plans v. Norris	x			x		2	522
38	Arizona State Legislature v. Arizona Indep. Redistricting Comm'n	x			x		3	1142
39	Arizona v. Evans	x				x	2	779
40	Arizona v. Gant (2003)	x				x	3	952
41	Arizona v. Gant (2009)	x			x		3	1040
42	Arizona v. Hicks	x			x		2	607
43	Arizona v. Inter Tribal Council of Arizona		x		x		3	1110
44	Arizona v. U.S.	x			x		3	1098
45	Arizonans for Official English v. Arizona	x				x	2	817

		ACLU's Case Involvement					Volume of Three-volume set & Case # in volume	
	Case Name	Amicus	Attorney of Record / ACLU Attorney	As A Party	Wins	Losses	Vol #1, #2 or #3	Case # in Volume
	A	B	C	D	E	F	G	H
46	Arkansas Educational Television Commission v. Forbes	x				x	2	846
47	Arkansas Writers' Project, Inc. v. Ragland	x			x		2	613
48	Armstrong v. Exceptional Child Center, Inc.	x				x	3	1132
49	Ashcroft v. al-Kidd		x			x	3	1077
50	Ashcroft v. American Civil Liberties Union (2002)		x	x		x	3	922
51	Ashcroft v. American Civil Liberties Union (2004)		x	x	x		3	973
52	Ashcroft v. Free Speech Coalition	x			x		3	921
53	Ass'n for Molecular Pathology v. Myriad Genetics		x		x		3	1109
54	Associated Enterprises, Inc. v. Toltec Watershed Improvement District	x				x	1	297

| | Case Name | ACLU's Case Involvement | | | Wins | Losses | Volume of Three-volume set & Case # in volume | |
		Amicus	Attorney of Record / ACLU Attorney	As A Party			Vol #1, #2 or #3	Case # in Volume
	A	B	C	D	E	F	G	H
55	Astrup v. I.N.S.		x		x		1	246
56	Atascadero State Hospital v. Scanlon	x				x	2	568
57	Atkins v. Virginia	x			x		3	928
58	Atwater v. City of Lago Vista	x				x	3	899
59	Austin v. Michigan Chamber of Commerce	x				x	2	699
60	Austin v. United States	x			x		2	762
61	Ayestas v. Davis	x			x		3	1171
62	Ayotte v. Planned Parenthood of Northern New England		x			x	3	994
63	Babbitt v. United Farm Workers National Union	x				x	2	433
64	Baggett v. Bullitt		x		x		1	150
65	Bailey v. U.S.	x			x		3	1102
66	Baker v. McCollan	x				x	2	440
67	Ball v. James	x				x	2	466
68	Ballard v. Commissioner of Internal Revenue	x	x		x		3	981

	Case Name	ACLU's Case Involvement			Wins	Losses	Volume of Three-volume set & Case # in volume	
		Amicus	Attorney of Record / ACLU Attorney	As A Party			Vol #1, #2 or #3	Case # in Volume
	A	B	C	D	E	F	G	H
69	Bank of America Corp. v. City of Miami	x			x		3	1156
70	Bank of Nova Scotia v. United States	x				x	2	652
71	Barber v. Thomas	x				x	3	1061
72	Barefoot v. Estelle	x				x	2	521
73	Barenblatt v. United States		x			x	1	108
74	Barnes v. Glen Theatre, Inc.	x				x	2	724
75	Barrows v. Jackson	x			x		1	77
76	Bartlett v. Strickland	x				x	3	1038
77	Bartnicki v. Vopper	x			x		3	901
78	Baze v. Rees	x				x	3	1025
79	Bd. of Ed. of Indep. Sch. Dist. No. 92 of Pottawatomie Cty. v. Earls		x			x	3	933
80	Bd. of Regents of Univ. of Texas System v. New Left Education Project		x			x	1	259

	Case Name	Amicus	Attorney of Record / ACLU Attorney	As A Party	Wins	Losses	Vol #1, #2 or #3	Case # in Volume
	A	B	C	D	E	F	G	H
81	Beard v. Banks (2004)	x				x	3	967
82	Beard v. Banks (2006)	x				x	3	1006
83	Beauharnais v. Illinois		x			x	1	73
84	Beck v. Ohio	x			x		1	156
85	Bell v. Cone	x				x	3	924
86	Bell v. Hood	x	x		x		1	40
87	Bell v. Ohio	x			x		1	415
88	Bell v. Wolfish	x				x	2	428
89	Bellotti v. Baird		x		x		2	444
90	Bender v. Williamsport Area School District	x				x	2	581
91	Benisek v. Lamone	x				x	3	1177
92	Berger v. New York	x			x		1	193
93	Berghuis v. Smith	x				x	3	1054
94	Berghuis v. Thompkins	x				x	3	1060
95	Berkemer v. McCarty	x			x		2	550
96	Berry v. Doles		x		x		1	413
97	Betts v. Brady	x				x	1	16
98	Bigelow v. Virginia		x		x		1	359

		ACLU's Case Involvement						Volume of Three-volume set & Case # in volume	
	Case Name	Amicus	Attorney of Record / ACLU Attorney	As A Party	Wins	Losses	Vol #1, #2 or #3	Case # in Volume
	A	B	C	D	E	F	G	H
99	Birchfield v. North Dakota	x			x		3	1150
100	Bivens v. Six Unknown Named Agents of Federal Bureau of Narcotics	x			x		1	253
101	Black v. Cutter Laboratories	x				x	1	88
102	Blakely v. Washington	x			x		3	966
103	Blanton v. City of North Las Vegas, Nevada	x				x	2	668
104	Blessing v. Freestone	x				x	2	822
105	Blum v. Stenson	x			x		2	527
106	Board of County Commissioners, Wabaunsee County, Kansas v. Umbehr	x			x		2	809
107	Board of Curators of the University of Missouri v. Horowitz	x				x	1	403
108	Board of Directors of Rotary Int'l v. Rotary Club of Duarte	x			x		2	616

	Case Name	ACLU's Case Involvement			Wins	Losses	Volume of Three-volume set & Case # in volume	
		Amicus	Attorney of Record / ACLU Attorney	As A Party			Vol #1, #2 or #3	Case # in Volume
	A	B	C	D	E	F	G	H
109	Board of Education of Oklahoma City v. Dowell	x				x	2	712
110	Board of Education v. Pico		x		x		2	491
111	Board Of Education v. Rowley	x				x	2	492
112	Board of Estimate of New York v. Morris		x		x		2	672
113	Board of Regents of the University of Wisconsin System v. Southworth	x			x		3	878
114	Bob Jones University v. United States	x			x		2	507
115	Bolger v. Youngs Drug Products Corp.	x			x		2	514
116	Bond v. Floyd	x			x		1	180
117	Boos v. Barry	x			x		2	640
118	Booth v. Churner	x				x	3	903
119	Borough of Duryea v. Guarnieri	x				x	3	1081

	Case Name	ACLU's Case Involvement			Wins	Losses	Volume of Three-volume set & Case # in volume	
		Amicus	Attorney of Record / ACLU Attorney	As A Party			Vol #1, #2 or #3	Case # in Volume
	A	**B**	**C**	**D**	**E**	**F**	**G**	**H**
120	Bose Corp. v. Consumers Union, Inc.	x			x		2	533
121	Boston Firefighters Union, Local 718 v. Boston Chapter, NAACP	x				x	2	506
122	Boumediene v. Bush	x			x		3	1031
123	Bousley v. United States	x			x		2	844
124	Boutilier v. Immigration and Naturalization Service	x				x	1	188
125	Bowen v. City of New York	x			x		2	587
126	Bowen v. Gilliard	x				x	2	628
127	Bowen v. Kendrick		x			x	2	657
128	Boy Scouts of America v. Dale	x				x	3	888
129	Braden v. 30th Judicial Circuit Court of Kentucky	x			x		1	294
130	Bragdon v. Abbott	x			x		2	851
131	Brandenburg v. Ohio		x		x		1	221
132	Branzburg v. Hayes	x				x	1	283

		ACLU's Case Involvement					Volume of Three-volume set & Case # in volume	
	Case Name	Amicus	Attorney of Record / ACLU Attorney	As A Party	Wins	Losses	Vol #1, #2 or #3	Case # in Volume
	A	B	C	D	E	F	G	H
133	Bray v. Alexandria Women's Health Clinic	x				x	2	751
134	Brecht v. Abrahamson	x				x	2	752
135	Brendlin v. California	x			x		3	1017
136	Bridges v. California	x			x		1	14
137	Bridges v. Wixon	x			x		1	37
138	Brockington v. Rhodes		x			x	1	224
139	Browder v. Director, Department of Corrections	x			x		1	400
140	Brown v. Board of Education	x			x		1	79
141	Brown v. Chote	x			x		1	304
142	Brown v. Entertainment Merchants Ass'n	x			x		3	1083
143	Brown v. Plata	x			x		3	1075
144	Brunner v. United States		x		x		1	72

		ACLU's Case Involvement			Wins	Losses	Volume of Three-volume set & Case # in volume	
	Case Name	Amicus	Attorney of Record / ACLU Attorney	As A Party	Wins	Losses	Vol #1, #2 or #3	Case # in Volume
	A	B	C	D	E	F	G	H
145	Buckhannon Board & Care Home, Inc. v. West Virginia Department of Health & Human Resources	x				x	3	902
146	Bucklew v. Precythe	x				x	3	1183
147	Buckley v. American Constitutional Law Foundation, Inc.	x			x		3	856
148	Buckley v. Valeo		x		x		1	366
149	Burch v. Louisiana	x			x		2	426
150	Burdick v. Takushi		x			x	2	740
151	Burlington Northern & Santa Fe Ry. Co. v. White	x			x		3	1003
152	Burnett v. Grattan	x			x		2	545
153	Burns v. Reed	x			x		2	719
154	Burwell v. Hobby Lobby Stores, Inc.	x				x	3	1128
155	Bush v. Lucas	x				x	2	511
156	Bush v. Palm Beach County Canvassing Board	x				x	3	893

		ACLU's Case Involvement					Volume of Three-volume set & Case # in volume	
	Case Name	Amicus	Attorney of Record / ACLU Attorney	As A Party	Wins	Losses	Vol #1, #2 or #3	Case # in Volume
	A	B	C	D	E	F	G	H
157	Butler v. Michigan	x			x		1	91
158	Butterworth v. Smith	x			x		2	698
159	Byrd v. United States	x			x		3	1172
160	Byrne v. Karalexis	x				x	1	238
161	Caban v. Mohammed	x			x		2	427
162	Calcano-Martinez v. INS		x		x		3	910
163	Calhoon v. Harvey	x				x	1	157
164	Califano v. Goldfarb		x		x		1	382
165	Califano v. Westcott	x			x		2	438
166	California Federal Savings & Loan Association v. Guerra	x			x		2	602
167	California Medical Ass'n v. Federal Election Commission	x				x	2	479
168	California v. Brown	x				x	2	605
169	California v. Ciraolo	x				x	2	586

		ACLU's Case Involvement					Volume of Three-volume set & Case # in volume	
	Case Name	Amicus	Attorney of Record / ACLU Attorney	As A Party	Wins	Losses	Vol #1, #2 or #3	Case # in Volume
	A	B	C	D	E	F	G	H
170	California v. Krivda	x				x	1	286
171	Camara v. Municipal Court of City & County of San Francisco		x		x		1	190
172	Campbell v. Acuff-Rose Music, Inc.	x			x		2	769
173	Capital Cities Cable, Inc. v. Crisp	x			x		2	543
174	Capitol Square Review & Advisory Board v. Pinette		x		x		2	789
175	Carey v. Population Services International	x			x		1	389
176	Carlson v. California	x			x		1	11
177	Carlson v. Green	x			x		2	448
178	Carlson v. Landon		x			x	1	70
179	Carlucci v. Doe	x				x	2	660
180	Carpenter v. United States		x		x		3	1178
181	Carroll v. President & Comm'rs of Princess Anne		x		x		1	211

	Case Name	Amicus	Attorney of Record / ACLU Attorney	As A Party	Wins	Losses	Vol #1, #2 or #3	Case # in Volume
			ACLU's Case Involvement				Volume of Three-volume set & Case # in volume	
	A	B	C	D	E	F	G	H
182	Castaneda v. Partida		x		x		1	383
183	CBOCS West, Inc. v. Humphries	x			x		3	1029
184	Chamber of Commerce of U.S. v. Whiting		x			x	3	1076
185	Chandler v. Miller	x			x		2	821
186	Chappell v. Wallace	x				x	2	509
187	Chavez v. Martinez	x				x	3	941
188	Chevron U.S.A., Inc. v. Echazabal	x				x	3	925
189	Christian Legal Society v. Martinez	x			x		3	1065
190	Christopher v. Harbury	x				x	3	929
191	Church of Lukumi Babalu Aye, Inc. v. City of Hialeah		x		x		2	758
192	Church of Scientology of California v. Internal Revenue Service	x				x	2	632
193	Citizens United v. Federal Election Com'n	x			x		3	1052

	Case Name	Amicus	Attorney of Record / ACLU Attorney	As A Party	Wins	Losses	Vol #1, #2 or #3	Case # in Volume
	ACLU's Case Involvement						Volume of Three-volume set & Case # in volume	
	A	B	C	D	E	F	G	H
194	City and County of San Francisco v. Sheehan	x				x	3	1134
195	City of Akron v. Akron Center for Reproductive Health, Inc.		x		x		2	512
196	City of Boerne v. Flores	x				x	2	834
197	City of Canton, Ohio v. Harris	x				x	2	667
198	City of Chicago v. Morales		x		x		3	865
199	City of Cleburne v. Cleburne Living Center	x			x		2	571
200	City of Edmonds v. Oxford House, Inc.		x		x		2	782
201	City of Houston v. Hill	x			x		2	624
202	City of Indianapolis v. Edmond		x		x		3	892
203	City of Ladue v. Gilleo		x		x		2	773
204	City of Lakewood v. Plain Dealer Publishing Co.	x			x		2	647

| | Case Name | ACLU's Case Involvement | | | | | Volume of Three-volume set & Case # in volume | |
		Amicus	Attorney of Record / ACLU Attorney	As A Party	Wins	Losses	Vol #1, #2 or #3	Case # in Volume
	A	**B**	**C**	**D**	**E**	**F**	**G**	**H**
205	City of Los Angeles v. Preferred Communications, Inc.	x			x		2	588
206	City of Los Angeles, Department of Water and Power v. Manhart	x			x		1	406
207	City of Ontario v. Quon	x				x	3	1063
208	City of Renton v. Playtime Theatres, Inc.	x				x	2	577
209	City of Revere v. Massachusetts General Hospital	x			x		2	516
210	City of Richmond v. J.A. Croson Co.	x				x	2	663
211	City of Springfield v. Kibbe	x			x		2	606
212	Clapper v. Amnesty Int'l USA		x			x	3	1104
213	Clark v. Community for Creative Non-Violence		x			x	2	547
214	Clark v. Jeter	x			x		2	646

		ACLU's Case Involvement			Wins	Losses	Volume of Three-volume set & Case # in volume	
	Case Name	Amicus	Attorney of Record / ACLU Attorney	As A Party	Wins	Losses	Vol #1, #2 or #3	Case # in Volume
	A	B	C	D	E	F	G	H
215	Clark v. Martinez	x			x		3	977
216	Clark v. Roemer	x			x		2	721
217	Class v. United States	x			x		3	1169
218	Cleveland Board of Education v. LaFleur	x			x		1	324
219	Cleveland Board of Education v. Loudermill	x			x		2	554
220	Clinton v. Jones	x			x		2	827
221	Cohen v. California	x			x		1	249
222	Coker v. Georgia	x			x		1	398
223	Colautti v. Franklin	x			x		1	420
224	Cole v. Young		x		x		1	89
225	Coleman v. Court of Appeals of Maryland	x				x	3	1090
226	Collins v. City of Harker Heights, Texas	x				x	2	734
227	Collins v. Hardyman		x			x	1	65
228	Colorado Republican Federal Campaign Committee v. Federal Election Commission	x			x		2	808

		ACLU's Case Involvement					Volume of Three-volume set & Case # in volume	
	Case Name	Amicus	Attorney of Record / ACLU Attorney	As A Party	Wins	Losses	Vol #1, #2 or #3	Case # in Volume
	A	B	C	D	E	F	G	H
229	Colorado v. Bertine	x				x	2	603
230	Colten v. Kentucky		x			x	1	271
231	Columbus Board of Education v. Penick	x			x		2	443
232	Communist Party of Indiana v. Whitcomb		x		x		1	322
233	Communist Party of the United States v. Subversive Activities Control Board	x			x		1	87
234	Communist Party v. Subversive Activities Control Board	x				x	1	124
235	Congress of Industrial Organizations v. McAdory	x				x	1	34
236	Connecticut Dep't of Pub. Safety v. Doe		x			x	3	934
237	Connell v. Higginbotham		x		x		1	251
238	Connick v. Myers	x				x	2	502

51

		ACLU's Case Involvement					Volume of Three-volume set & Case # in volume	
	Case Name	**Amicus**	**Attorney of Record / ACLU Attorney**	**As A Party**	**Wins**	**Losses**	**Vol #1, #2 or #3**	**Case # in Volume**
	A	B	C	D	E	F	G	H
239	Connick v. Thompson	x				x	3	1071
240	Cornelius v. NAACP Legal Defense and Educational Fund, Inc.	x				x	2	572
241	Corning Glass Works v. Brennan	x			x		1	333
242	Corp. for the Presiding Bishop of the Church of Jesus Christ of Latter-Day Saints v. Amos		x			x	2	612
243	Correctional Services Corp. v. Malesko	x				x	3	914
244	Costello v. United States	x				x	1	84
245	County of Allegheny v. American Civil Liberties Union Greater Pittsburgh Chapter		x	x	x		2	690
246	County of Los Angeles v. Davis	x				x	2	423
247	County of Los Angeles v. Mendez	x				x	3	1157

	Case Name	ACLU's Case Involvement			Wins	Losses	Volume of Three-volume set & Case # in volume	
		Amicus	Attorney of Record / ACLU Attorney	As A Party			Vol #1, #2 or #3	Case # in Volume
	A	B	C	D	E	F	G	H
248	County of Riverside v. McLaughlin	x				x	2	716
249	County of Washington v. Gunther	x			x		2	475
250	Craig v. Boren	x			x		1	380
251	Crawford v. Marion County Election Bd.		x			x	3	1027
252	Crawford v. Metropolitan Government of Nashville & Davidson County, Tennessee	x			x		3	1036
253	Crawford v. Washington	x			x		3	959
254	Crawford-El v. Britton	x			x		2	842
255	Crooker v. California	x				x	1	104
256	Crosby v. United States	x			x		2	750
257	Cruzan v. Director, Missouri Department of Health		x			x	2	706
258	Cullen v. Pinholster	x				x	3	1073

		ACLU's Case Involvement					Volume of Three-volume set & Case # in volume	
	Case Name	Amicus	Attorney of Record / ACLU Attorney	As A Party	Wins	Losses	Vol #1, #2 or #3	Case # in Volume
	A	B	C	D	E	F	G	H
259	Cupp v. Murphy	x				x	1	309
260	Cutter v. Wilkinson	x			x		3	984
261	Danforth v. Minnesota	x			x		3	1024
262	Davila v. Davis	x				x	3	1166
263	Davis v. Bandemer	x				x	2	596
264	Davis v. Monroe County Board of Education	x			x		3	864
265	Davis v. Passman	x			x		2	431
266	Davis v. Scherer	x				x	2	546
267	Davis v. United States (1973)		x			x	1	302
268	Davis v. United States (1974)		x		x		1	334
269	Davis v. Washington	x				x	3	1000
270	Dawson v. Delaware	x			x		2	735
271	Dayton Board of Education v. Brinkman	x				x	1	397
272	De Jonge v. Oregon		x		x		1	6
273	De Veau v. Braisted	x				x	1	114
274	Deakins v. Monaghan	x			x		2	634
275	DeFunis v. Odegaard	x				x	1	330

		ACLU's Case Involvement					Volume of Three-volume set & Case # in volume	
	Case Name	Amicus	Attorney of Record / ACLU Attorney	As A Party	Wins	Losses	Vol #1, #2 or #3	Case # in Volume
	A	**B**	**C**	**D**	**E**	**F**	**G**	**H**
276	Delaware v. Prouse		x		x		2	424
277	Dellmuth v. Muth	x				x	2	685
278	Delta Air Lines, Inc. v. August	x			x		2	461
279	Demore v. Kim		x			x	3	939
280	Dennis v. Sparks	x			x		2	458
281	Dennis v. United States	x			x		1	179
282	Denton v. Hernandez	x				x	2	738
283	Denver Area Educational Telecommunications Consortium, Inc. v. Federal Communications Commission		x		x		2	811
284	Dep't of Commerce v. New York		x		x		3	1193
285	Dep't of Hous. & Urban Dev. v. Rucker	x				x	3	919
286	Dep't of the Air Force v. Rose		x		x		1	369
287	Department of Commerce v. United States House of Representatives	x				x	3	858

	Case Name	ACLU's Case Involvement			Wins	Losses	Volume of Three-volume set & Case # in volume	
		Amicus	Attorney of Record / ACLU Attorney	As A Party			Vol #1, #2 or #3	Case # in Volume
	A	B	C	D	E	F	G	H
288	Department of the Navy v. Egan	x				x	2	637
289	Desert Palace, Inc. v. Costa	x			x		3	942
290	DeShaney v. Winnebago County Department of Social Services	x				x	2	666
291	Dickerson v. United States	x			x		3	887
292	Diffenderfer v. Central Baptist Church of Miami		x		x		1	256
293	District Attorney's Office for the Third Judicial Dist. v. Osborne	x				x	3	1045
294	District of Columbia v. Carter		x			x	1	288
295	District of Columbia v. Wesby	x				x	3	1168
296	Doe v. Bolton		x		x		1	292
297	Doe v. Chao	x				x	3	957
298	Dombrowski v. Pfister	x			x		1	161
299	Doremus v. Board of Education	x				x	1	68

		ACLU's Case Involvement					Volume of Three-volume set & Case # in volume	
	Case Name	Amicus	Attorney of Record / ACLU Attorney	As A Party	Wins	Losses	Vol #1, #2 or #3	Case # in Volume
	A	B	C	D	E	F	G	H
300	Dorsey v. U.S.	x			x		3	1097
301	Dorszynski v. United States	x			x		1	345
302	Dothard v. Rawlinson	x			x		1	396
303	Douglas v. Independent Living Center of Southern California, Inc.	x				x	3	1089
304	Dunaway v. New York	x			x		2	430
305	Duncan v. Kahanamoku	x			x		1	39
306	Dunn v. Blumstein		x		x		1	260
307	Duren v. Missouri		x		x		1	419
308	Dyson v. Stein		x			x	1	237
309	E.E.O.C. v. Abercrombie & Fitch Stores	x			x		3	1136
310	Easley v. Cromartie	x			x		3	897
311	Eastland v. United States Servicemen's Fund		x			x	1	358
312	Edmonson v. Leesville Concrete Co.	x			x		2	720

	Case Name	ACLU's Case Involvement			Wins	Losses	Volume of Three-volume set & Case # in volume	
		Amicus	Attorney of Record / ACLU Attorney	As A Party			Vol #1, #2 or #3	Case # in Volume
	A	B	C	D	E	F	G	H
313	Edward J. DeBartolo Corp. v. Florida Gulf Coast Building & Construction Trades Council	x			x		2	643
314	Edwards v. Aguillard		x		x		2	625
315	Edwards v. Balisok	x				x	2	825
316	Edwards v. California		x		x		1	13
317	EEOC v. Waffle House, Inc.	x			x		3	916
318	Ehlert v. United States		x			x	1	243
319	Eisen v. Carlisle & Jacquelin	x				x	1	332
320	Eisenstadt v. Baird	x			x		1	262
321	Elder v. Holloway	x			x		2	768
322	Elk Grove United School District v. Newdow	x				x	3	962
323	Ellis v. Dyson		x		x		1	357
324	Elonis v. United States	x			x		3	1135
325	Employment Division v. Smith	x				x	2	700
326	Emspak v. United States	x			x		1	80
327	Engel v. Vitale		x		x		1	134

	Case Name	Amicus	Attorney of Record / ACLU Attorney	As A Party	Wins	Losses	Vol #1, #2 or #3	Case # in Volume
	A	**B**	**C**	**D**	**E**	**F**	**G**	**H**
328	Engquist v. Oregon Department of Agriculture	x				x	3	1030
329	Environmental Protection Agency v. Mink	x				x	1	290
330	Epic Systems Corp. v. Lewis	x				x	3	1173
331	Epperson v. Arkansas	x			x		1	210
332	Equal Employment Opportunity Commission v. Arabian American Oil Co.	x				x	2	714
333	Erie v. Pap's A. M.	x				x	3	881
334	Escambia County v. McMillan	x				x	2	528
335	Escobedo v. Illinois	x			x		1	154
336	Estes v. Texas	x			x		1	169
337	Evans v. Jeff D.	x				x	2	583
338	Evenwel v. Abbott	x			x		3	1145
339	Everson v. Board of Education	x				x	1	44
340	Ex parte Endo	x			x		1	31

The header also contains the spanning labels:
- "ACLU's Case Involvement" spanning Amicus, Attorney of Record / ACLU Attorney, As A Party
- "Volume of Three-volume set & Case # in volume" spanning Vol #1, #2 or #3, Case # in Volume

	Case Name	ACLU's Case Involvement			Wins	Losses	Volume of Three-volume set & Case # in volume	
		Amicus	Attorney of Record / ACLU Attorney	As A Party			Vol #1, #2 or #3	Case # in Volume
	A	**B**	**C**	**D**	**E**	**F**	**G**	**H**
341	F.C.C. v. Fox Television Stations, Inc.	x				x	3	1042
342	Falbo v. United States	x				x	1	24
343	Faragher v. City of Boca Raton	x			x		2	852
344	Farmer v. Brennan		x		x		2	772
345	Farmers Educational & Cooperative Union v. WDAY, Inc.	x			x		1	110
346	FCC v. AT&T Inc.	x			x		3	1068
347	FCC v. Fox Television Stations	x				x	3	1096
348	FCC v. League of Women Voters	x			x		2	549
349	FCC v. Midwest Video Corp.		x	x		x	2	425
350	FCC v. Pacifica Foundation	x				x	1	416
351	FEC v. Colo. Republican Fed. Campaign Comm.	x				x	3	911
352	Federal Election Commission v. Akins	x				x	2	847

	Case Name	ACLU's Case Involvement			Wins	Losses	Volume of Three-volume set & Case # in volume	
		Amicus	Attorney of Record / ACLU Attorney	As A Party			Vol #1, #2 or #3	Case # in Volume
	A	B	C	D	E	F	G	H
353	Federal Election Commission v. Massachusetts Citizens For Life, Inc.	x			x		2	601
354	Federal Election Commission v. National Conservative Political Action Committee	x			x·		2	553
355	Federal Election Commission v. Wisconsin Right to Life, Inc.	x			x		3	1019
356	Federal Trade Commission v. Superior Court Trial Lawyers Ass'n	x			x		2	693
357	Fein v. Selective Service System Local Board No. 7	x				x	1	261
358	Ferguson v. City of Charleston	x			x		3	895
359	Fernandez-Vargas v. Gonzales	x				x	3	1002
360	First Unitarian Church v. County of Los Angeles	x			x		1	107

	Case Name	Amicus	Attorney of Record / ACLU Attorney	As A Party	Wins	Losses	Vol #1, #2 or #3	Case # in Volume
		ACLU's Case Involvement					Volume of Three-volume set & Case # in volume	
	A	**B**	**C**	**D**	**E**	**F**	**G**	**H**
361	Fisher v. Univ. of Texas at Austin	x			x		3	1151
362	Fitzgerald v. Barnstable School Comm.	x			x		3	1035
363	Fitzpatrick v. Bitzer	x			x		1	375
364	Flanagan v. United States	x			x		2	524
365	Florence v. Board of Chosen Freeholders of County of Burlington	x				x	3	1094
366	Florida v. Bostick	x				x	2	723
367	Florida v. Harris	x				x	3	1103
368	Florida v. J. L.	x			x		3	880
369	Florida v. Riley	x				x	2	662
370	Flower v. United States		x		x		1	273
371	Follett v. Town of McCormick	x			x		1	25
372	Forsyth County v. Nationalist Movement	x			x		2	743
373	Fort Wayne Books, Inc. v. Indiana	x			x		2	665
374	Fox v. Vice	x			x		3	1078

| | Case Name | ACLU's Case Involvement | | | Wins | Losses | Volume of Three-volume set & Case # in volume | |
		Amicus	Attorney of Record / ACLU Attorney	As A Party			Vol #1, #2 or #3	Case # in Volume
	A	**B**	**C**	**D**	**E**	**F**	**G**	**H**
375	Frank v. Minnesota Newspaper Ass'n, Inc.	x				x	2	676
376	Franks v. Delaware	x			x		1	412
377	Frazee v. Illinois Dep't of Employment Security	x			x		2	674
378	Freedman v. Maryland	x			x		1	158
379	Freeman v. Pitts	x	x			x	2	736
380	Frew v. Hawkins	x			x		3	956
381	Friends of the Earth v. Laidlaw Environmental Services	x			x		3	875
382	Frisby v. Schultz	x				x	2	655
383	Frontiero v. Richardson	x	x		x		1	306
384	Fry v. Napoleon Community Schools		x		x		3	1153
385	Fullilove v. Klutznick	x			x		2	456
386	Furman v. Georgia	x			x		1	280

		ACLU's Case Involvement					Volume of Three-volume set & Case # in volume	
	Case Name	**Amicus**	**Attorney of Record / ACLU Attorney**	**As A Party**	**Wins**	**Losses**	**Vol #1, #2 or #3**	**Case # in Volume**
	A	B	C	D	E	F	G	H
387	Gallagher v. Crown Kosher Super Market of Massachusetts, Inc.	x				x	1	123
388	Gamble v. United States	x				x	3	1186
389	Gannett Co. v. DePasquale	x				x	2	442
390	Garcetti v. Ceballos	x				x	3	998
391	Garner v Board of Public Works	x				x	1	66
392	Garner v. Jones	x				x	3	879
393	Geduldig v. Aiello	x				x	1	336
394	Gelbard v. United States	x			x		1	278
395	General Electric Co. v. Gilbert	x				x	1	379
396	Gentile v. State Bar of Nevada	x			x		2	726
397	Georgia v. Ashcroft	x				x	3	949
398	Gideon v. Wainwright	x	x		x		1	137
399	Gill v. Whitford	x				x	3	1176
400	Gillette v. United States		x			x	1	230
401	Gilligan v. Morgan		x			x	1	311
402	Gilmore v. Taylor	x				x	2	754

		ACLU's Case Involvement					Volume of Three-volume set & Case # in volume	
	Case Name	Amicus	Attorney of Record / ACLU Attorney	As A Party	Wins	Losses	Vol #1, #2 or #3	Case # in Volume
	A	B	C	D	E	F	G	H
403	Ginsberg v. New York	x				x	1	199
404	Ginzburg v. United States	x				x	1	172
405	Girouard v. United States	x			x		1	41
406	Gitlow v. New York		x			x	1	1
407	Godinez v. Moran	x				x	2	759
408	Gojack v. United States		x		x		1	177
409	Golan v. Holder	x				x	3	1086
410	Goldberg v. Kelly		x		x		1	226
411	Goldman v. Weinberger	x				x	2	580
412	Gomez v. Perez	x			x		1	289
413	Gomez v. Toledo	x			x		2	451
414	Gomillion v. Lightfoot	x			x		1	116
415	Gonzaga Univ. v. Doe	x				x	3	927
416	Gonzales v. Carhart	x				x	3	1011
417	Gonzales v. Landon	x			x		1	82
418	Gonzales v. O Centro Espírita Beneficente União do Vegetal	x			x		3	996
419	Gonzales v. Oregon	x			x		3	993

		ACLU's Case Involvement					Volume of Three-volume set & Case # in volume	
	Case Name	Amicus	Attorney of Record / ACLU Attorney	As A Party	Wins	Losses	Vol #1, #2 or #3	Case # in Volume
	A	B	C	D	E	F	G	H
420	Good News Club v. Milford Central School	x				x	3	907
421	Gordon v. Lance	x				x	1	248
422	Gori v. United States	x				x	1	126
423	Goss v. Lopez	x			x		1	349
424	Graham v. Connor	x			x		2	669
425	Graham v. Richardson	x			x		1	252
426	Gratz v. Bollinger		x			x	3	947
427	Gravel v. United States	x				x	1	282
428	Great American Federal Savings & Loan Association v. Novotny	x				x	2	434
429	Greater New Orleans Broadcasting Ass'n, Inc. v. United States	x			x		3	867
430	Greene v. McElroy	x			x		1	109
431	Greenholtz v. Inmates of the Nebraska Penal and Correctional Complex	x				x	2	429
432	Greer v. Miller	x				x	2	630

	Case Name	Amicus	Attorney of Record / ACLU Attorney	As A Party	Wins	Losses	Vol #1, #2 or #3	Case # in Volume
	A	B	C	D	E	F	G	H
433	Greer v. Spock	x				x	1	368
434	Gregory v. City of Chicago		x		x		1	214
435	Griffin v. Wisconsin	x				x	2	631
436	Griswold v. Connecticut	x			x		1	168
437	Groppi v. Leslie	x	x		x		1	257
438	Grutter v. Bollinger	x			x		3	948
439	Guardians Ass'n v. Civil Service Commission	x				x	2	519
440	Gulf Oil Co. v. Bernard	x			x		2	472
441	Gundy v. United States	x				x	3	1188
442	Hafer v. Melo	x			x		2	727
443	Hague v. Committee for Industrial Organization			x	x		1	9
444	Halbert v. Michigan		x		x		3	987
445	Hall v. Beals	x				x	1	225
446	Hall v. Cole	x			x		1	307
447	Hamdan v. Rumsfeld	x			x		3	1007
448	Hamdi v. Rumsfeld	x			x		3	970
449	Hamling v. United States	x				x	1	339

	Case Name	Amicus	Attorney of Record / ACLU Attorney	As A Party	Wins	Losses	Vol #1, #2 or #3	Case # in Volume
	ACLU's Case Involvement						**Volume of Three-volume set & Case # in volume**	
	A	**B**	**C**	**D**	**E**	**F**	**G**	**H**
450	Hampton v. Mow Sun Wong	x			x		1	371
451	Hannegan v. Esquire, Inc.	x			x		1	38
452	Haring v. Prosise	x			x		2	510
453	Harmelin v. Michigan	x				x	2	725
454	Harper v. Virginia Board of Elections		x		x		1	173
455	Harris v. Forklift Systems, Inc.	x			x		2	763
456	Harris v. McRae		x			x	2	455
457	Hazelwood School District v. Kuhlmeier	x				x	2	635
458	Hazelwood School District v. United States	x				x	1	395
459	Healy v. James		x		x		1	279
460	Heckler v. Mathews	x				x	2	526
461	Heffron v. International Society for Krishna Consciousness, Inc.	x				x	2	476
462	Heien v. North Carolina	x				x	3	1129

		ACLU's Case Involvement					Volume of Three-volume set & Case # in volume	
	Case Name	Amicus	Attorney of Record / ACLU Attorney	As A Party	Wins	Losses	Vol #1, #2 or #3	Case # in Volume
	A	B	C	D	E	F	G	H
463	Hein v. Freedom From Religion Foundation, Inc.	x				x	3	1020
464	Hernandez v. Mesa	x			x		3	1164
465	Hernandez v. Veterans' Administration		x		x		1	325
466	Herring v. U.S.	x				x	3	1033
467	Hibbs v. Winn		x		x		3	963
468	Hiibel v. Sixth Judicial District Court of Nevada, Humboldt County	x				x	3	965
469	Hill v. Colorado	x				x	3	889
470	Hill v. Florida	x			x		1	35
471	Hilton v. Braunskill	x				x	2	619
472	Hirabayashi v. United States	x				x	1	22
473	Hishon v. King & Spalding	x			x		2	539
474	Hobby v. United States	x				x	2	548
475	Hodgson v. Minnesota		x		x		2	707
476	Hoffa v. United States	x				x	1	181
477	Hoffman Plastic Compounds, Inc. v. NLRB	x				x	3	920
478	Holbrook v. Flynn		x			x	2	582

		ACLU's Case Involvement					Volume of Three-volume set & Case # in volume	
	Case Name	Amicus	Attorney of Record / ACLU Attorney	As A Party	Wins	Losses	Vol #1, #2 or #3	Case # in Volume
	A	B	C	D	E	F	G	H
479	Holder v. Humanitarian Law Project	x				x	3	1064
480	Holland v. Florida	x			x		3	1062
481	Holland v. Illinois	x				x	2	694
482	Hollingsworth v. Perry	x			x		3	1116
483	Holt Civic Club v. City of Tuscaloosa		x			x	1	418
484	Holt v. Hobbs	x			x		3	1130
485	Holt v. Virginia		x		x		1	165
486	Hope v. Pelzer	x			x		3	931
487	Hosanna-Tabor Evangelical Lutheran Church and School v. EEOC	x				x	3	1084
488	Hoyt v. Florida	x				x	1	130
489	Hudson v. McMillian		x		x		2	733
490	Hudson v. Michigan		x			x	3	999
491	Hughes v. Superior Court	x				x	1	62
492	Hui v. Castaneda	x				x	3	1058
493	Hunt v. Cromartie	x			x		3	862
494	Hurd v. Hodge	x			x		1	51

	Case Name	Amicus	Attorney of Record / ACLU Attorney	As A Party	Wins	Losses	Vol #1, #2 or #3	Case # in Volume
	A	**B**	**C**	**D**	**E**	**F**	**G**	**H**
495	Hurley v. Irish-American Gay, Lesbian & Bisexual Group of Boston	x			x		2	788
496	Hurst v. Florida	x			x		3	1143
497	Husted v. A. Philip Randolph Institute		x			x	3	1175
498	Hustler Magazine, Inc. v. Falwell	x			x		2	639
499	Hutto v. Finney	x			x		1	411
500	Iancu v. Brunetti	x			x		3	1190
501	Idaho v. Coeur d'Alene Tribe of Idaho	x				x	2	831
502	Idaho v. Wright	x			x		2	711
503	Illinois ex rel. McCollum v. Board of Education	x			x		1	48
504	Illinois v. Caballes	x				x	3	978
505	Illinois v. Gates	x				x	2	508
506	Illinois v. Lidster	x				x	3	955
507	Illinois v. Perkins	x				x	2	702
508	Illinois v. Wardlow	x				x	3	873

The table header also includes: ACLU's Case Involvement (spanning Amicus, Attorney of Record / ACLU Attorney, As A Party) and Volume of Three-volume set & Case # in volume (spanning Vol and Case #).

		ACLU's Case Involvement					Volume of Three-volume set & Case # in volume	
	Case Name	Amicus	Attorney of Record / ACLU Attorney	As A Party	Wins	Losses	Vol #1, #2 or #3	Case # in Volume
	A	B	C	D	E	F	G	H
509	Immigration & Naturalization Service v. Cardoza-Fonseca	x			x		2	609
510	Immigration & Naturalization Service v. Delgado	x				x	2	530
511	Immigration & Naturalization Service v. Doherty	x				x	2	731
512	Immigration & Naturalization Service v. Stevic	x				x	2	542
513	Immigration and Naturalization Service v. Stanisic	x				x	1	219
514	In re Anastaplo	x				x	1	121
515	In re Gault		x		x		1	187
516	In re Griffiths		x		x		1	318
517	In re Primus		x		x		1	410
518	In re Snyder	x			x		2	565
519	Independent Federation of Flight Attendants v. Zipes	x				x	2	687
520	INS v. St. Cyr		x		x		3	909

	Case Name	Amicus	Attorney of Record / ACLU Attorney	As A Party	Wins	Losses	Vol #1, #2 or #3	Case # in Volume
			ACLU's Case Involvement				Volume of Three-volume set & Case # in volume	
	A	**B**	**C**	**D**	**E**	**F**	**G**	**H**
521	International Society for Krishna Consciousness, Inc. v. Lee	x				x	2	747
522	Interstate Circuit, Inc. v. City of Dallas	x			x		1	200
523	J.D.B. v. North Carolina	x			x		3	1079
524	J.E.B. v. Alabama ex rel. T.B.	x			x		2	770
525	Jackson v. Birmingham Bd. of Educ.	x			x		3	983
526	Jacobellis v. Ohio	x			x		1	153
527	Jacobson v. United States	x			x		2	737
528	Janus v. American Federation of State, County, and Municipal Employees, Council 31	x				x	3	1180
529	Jean v. Nelson	x				x	2	567
530	Jennings v. Rodriguez		x			x	3	1170

	Case Name	Amicus	Attorney of Record / ACLU Attorney	As A Party	Wins	Losses	Vol #1, #2 or #3	Case # in Volume
				ACLU's Case Involvement			Volume of Three-volume set & Case # in volume	
	A	B	C	D	E	F	G	H
531	Jimmy Swaggart Ministries v. Board of Equalization of California	x			x		2	692
532	Johnson v. Avery	x			x		1	212
533	Johnson v. California (February 23, 2005)	x			x		3	979
534	Johnson v. California (June 13, 2005)	x			x		3	985
535	Johnson v. New Jersey	x				x	1	178
536	Johnson v. Transportation Agency	x			x		2	610
537	Jones v. Alfred H. Mayer Co.	x			x		1	208
538	Jones v. Bock	x			x		3	1009
539	Jones v. City of Opelika		x		x		1	17
540	Jones v. United States	x				x	2	517
541	Joseph Burstyn, Inc. v. Wilson	x			x		1	74
542	Justices of Boston Municipal Court v. Lydon	x				x	2	531

	Case Name	ACLU's Case Involvement					Volume of Three-volume set & Case # in volume	
		Amicus	Attorney of Record / ACLU Attorney	As A Party	Wins	Losses	Vol #1, #2 or #3	Case # in Volume
	A	B	C	D	E	F	G	H
543	Kadrmas v. Dickinson Public Schools	x				x	2	654
544	Kahn v. Shevin		x			x	1	331
545	Kansas v. Cheever	x				x	3	1118
546	Kansas v. Crane	x				x	3	917
547	Kansas v. Hendricks	x				x	2	832
548	Karcher v. May		x		x		2	633
549	Kastigar v. United States	x				x	1	267
550	Keller v. State Bar of California	x			x		2	701
551	Kennedy v. Louisiana	x			x		3	1032
552	Kennedy v. Mendoza-Martinez	x			x		1	136
553	Kent v. Dulles	x			x		1	103
554	Kentucky v. Stincer	x				x	2	627
555	Ker v. California	x				x	1	140
556	Kerry v. Din	x				x	3	1137
557	Keyes v. School District No. 1	x			x		1	315
558	Keyishian v. Board of Regents	x			x		1	185
559	Kimberlin v. Quinlan	x			x		2	786
560	Kimbrough v. U.S.	x			x		3	1022

	Case Name	Amicus	Attorney of Record / ACLU Attorney	As A Party	Wins	Losses	Vol #1, #2 or #3	Case # in Volume
	A	**B**	**C**	**D**	**E**	**F**	**G**	**H**
561	Kimmelman v. Morrison	x			x		2	591
562	King v. Smith		x		x		1	207
563	Kingsley Books, Inc. v. Brown	x				x	1	96
564	Kingsley v. Hendrickson	x			x		3	1139
565	Kiobel v. Royal Dutch Petroleum Co.	x				x	3	1105
566	Kirchberg v. Feenstra	x			x		2	462
567	Kiyemba v. Obama	x			x		3	1053
568	Kleindienst v. Mandel	x				x	1	284
569	Klopfer v. North Carolina	x			x		1	186
570	Knowles v. Iowa	x			x		2	855
571	Kolender v. Lawson	x			x		2	505
572	Kolstad v. American Dental Ass'n	x			x		3	870
573	Konigsberg v. State Bar of California (1957)	x			x		1	93
574	Konigsberg v. State Bar of California (1961)	x				x	1	120
575	Korematsu v. United States	x				x	1	30

The ACLU's Case Involvement header spans columns Amicus, Attorney of Record / ACLU Attorney, As A Party. The header "Volume of Three-volume set & Case # in volume" spans columns G and H.

	Case Name	Amicus	Attorney of Record / ACLU Attorney	As A Party	Wins	Losses	Vol #1, #2 or #3	Case # in Volume
	A	B	C	D	E	F	G	H
576	Kovacs v. Cooper	x				x	1	56
577	Kowalski v. Tesmer		x			x	3	976
578	Kucana v. Holder	x			x		3	1050
579	Kunz v. New York		x		x		1	64
580	Kush v. Rutledge	x			x		2	500
581	Kyllo v. United States	x			x		3	905
582	Labine v. Vincent	x				x	1	241
583	Lafler v. Cooper	x			x		3	1093
584	Laird v. Tatum		x			x	1	277
585	Lamb's Chapel v. Center Moriches Union Free School District	x			x		2	756
586	Lamont v. Postmaster General of the United States	x			x		1	166
587	Landmark Communications, Inc. v. Virginia	x			x		1	407
588	Lane v. Franks	x			x		3	1125
589	Lane v. Pena		x			x	2	803
590	Larkin v. Grendel's Den, Inc.	x			x		2	497
591	Larson v. Valente	x			x		2	486

The table header reads:

ACLU's Case Involvement spanning Amicus / Attorney of Record / ACLU Attorney / As A Party / Wins / Losses columns.

Volume of Three-volume set & Case # in volume spanning Vol #1, #2 or #3 / Case # in Volume.

	Case Name	Amicus	Attorney of Record / ACLU Attorney	As A Party	Wins	Losses	Vol #1, #2 or #3	Case # in Volume
	ACLU's Case Involvement						Volume of Three-volume set & Case # in volume	
	A	B	C	D	E	F	G	H
592	Lassiter v. Department of Social Services	x				x	2	470
593	Lawrence v. Florida	x				x	3	1010
594	Lawrence v. Texas	x			x		3	950
595	Leary v. United States	x			x		1	218
596	Lebron v. National Railroad Passenger Corp.	x			x		2	776
597	Ledbetter v. Goodyear Tire & Rubber Co.	x				x	3	1013
598	Lee v. Washington		x		x		1	198
599	Lee v. Weisman	x	x		x		2	746
600	Lefkowitz v. Cunningham	x			x		1	390
601	Legal Services Corp. v. Velazquez	x			x		3	894
602	Lehman v. City of Shaker Heights		x			x	1	343
603	Lemon v. Kurtzman		x			x	1	301
604	Leocal v. Ashcroft	x			x		3	975
605	Lerner v. Casey	x				x	1	105
606	Levy v. Louisiana		x		x		1	201
607	Lewis v. Casey		x			x	2	806

	Case Name	Amicus	Attorney of Record / ACLU Attorney	As A Party	Wins	Losses	Vol #1, #2 or #3	Case # in Volume
	A	B	C	D	E	F	G	H
608	Lewis v. City of Chicago	x			x		3	1059
609	Lewis v. United States	x				x	2	805
610	Liberty Mutual Insurance Co. v. Wetzel	x				x	1	367
611	Lightfoot v. United States	x			x		1	98
612	Lilly v. Virginia	x			x		3	866
613	Lindahl v. Office of Personnel Management	x			x		2	556
614	Linmark Associates, Inc. v. Township of Willingboro	x			x		1	386
615	Little v. Streater	x			x		2	469
616	Lloyd Corp. v. Tanner		x			x	1	276
617	Locke v. Davey	x			x		3	958
618	Lockyer v. Andrade		x			x	3	935
619	Long Island Care at Home, Ltd. v. Coke	x				x	3	1016
620	Lopez v. Gonzales	x			x		3	1008
621	Lopez v. Monterey County, California	x			x		2	812

	Case Name	Amicus	Attorney of Record / ACLU Attorney	As A Party	Wins	Losses	Vol #1, #2 or #3	Case # in Volume
			ACLU's Case Involvement					Volume of Three-volume set & Case # in volume
	A	B	C	D	E	F	G	H
622	Lorillard Tobacco Co. v. Reilly	x			x		3	912
623	Lovell v. City of Griffin	x			x		1	8
624	Loving v. United States	x				x	2	800
625	Loving v. Virginia		x		x		1	192
626	Lowe v. Securities & Exchange Commission	x			x		2	561
627	Lynch v. Donnelly		x			x	2	525
628	Lynch v. Overholser	x			x		1	132
629	Lyng v. Northwest Indian Cemetery Protective Ass'n	x				x	2	641
630	Lyons v. Oklahoma	x				x	1	26
631	M. L. B. v. S. L. J.		x		x		2	814
632	Maine v. Thiboutot	x			x		2	454
633	Maleng v. Cook	x			x		2	678
634	Malley v. Briggs	x			x		2	578
635	Malloy v. Hogan	x			x		1	152
636	Manhattan Community Access Corp. v. Halleck	x				x	3	1185

	Case Name	ACLU's Case Involvement			Wins	Losses	Volume of Three-volume set & Case # in volume	
		Amicus	Attorney of Record / ACLU Attorney	As A Party			Vol #1, #2 or #3	Case # in Volume
	A	B	C	D	E	F	G	H
637	Maples v. Thomas	x			x		3	1085
638	Mapp v. Ohio	x	x		x		1	129
639	Marek v. Chesny	x				x	2	573
640	Marshall v. Barlow's, Inc.	x			x		1	409
641	Martin v. City of Struthers	x			x		1	18
642	Martin v. Hadix	x				x	3	868
643	Martin v. Wilks	x				x	2	680
644	Martinez v. Bynum	x				x	2	504
645	Maryland v. King	x				x	3	1108
646	Maryland v. Macon	x				x	2	563
647	Maryland v. Pringle	x				x	3	954
648	Massachusetts Bd. of Retirement v. Murgia	x				x	1	373
649	Massachusetts v. Painten	x			x		1	197
650	Masterpiece Cakeshop, Ltd. v. Colorado Civil Rights Comm'n		x			x	3	1174
651	Matal v. Tam	x			x		3	1161
652	Mathews v. Diaz	x				x	1	370
653	Maxwell v. Bishop	x			x		1	231

	Case Name	Amicus	Attorney of Record / ACLU Attorney	As A Party	Wins	Losses	Vol #1, #2 or #3	Case # in Volume
	A	**B**	**C**	**D**	**E**	**F**	**G**	**H**
654	Mayo Collaborative Services v. Prometheus Laboratories, Inc.	x			x		3	1091
655	McBurney v. Young	x				x	3	1107
656	McConnell v. Federal Election Comm'n		x	x		x	3	953
657	McCreary County v. American Civil Liberties Union of Kentucky		x		x		3	989
658	McCullen v. Coakley	x				x	3	1127
659	McDaniel v. Paty	x			x		1	405
660	McDaniel v. Sanchez	x			x		2	474
661	McDonald v. Smith	x				x	2	564
662	McDonough v. Smith	x			x		3	1189
663	McFarland v. Scott	x			x		2	774
664	McGautha v. California	x				x	1	244
665	McIntyre v. Ohio Elections Commission		x		x		2	781

The header above the table (spanning columns B–D) reads "ACLU's Case Involvement" and the header spanning columns G–H reads "Volume of Three-volume set & Case # in volume".

	Case Name	Amicus	Attorney of Record / ACLU Attorney	As A Party	Wins	Losses	Vol #1, #2 or #3	Case # in Volume
			ACLU's Case Involvement				**Volume of Three-volume set & Case # in volume**	
	A	**B**	**C**	**D**	**E**	**F**	**G**	**H**
666	McLaurin v. Oklahoma State Regents for Higher Education	x			x		1	63
667	McLucas v. DeChamplain	x				x	1	353
668	McMann v. Richardson	x				x	1	230
669	McMillian v. Monroe County, Alabama	x				x	2	828
670	McNeese v. Board of Education	x			x		1	139
671	Medical Board of California v. Hason		x		x		3	938
672	Meek v. Pittenger	x			x		1	356
673	Meese v. Keene	x				x	2	614
674	Members of the City Council of Los Angeles v. Taxpayers for Vincent	x				x	2	537
675	Mempa v. Rhay		x		x		1	195
676	Memphis Community School District v. Stachura	x				x	2	590
677	Messerschmidt v. Millender	x				x	3	1088

83

	Case Name	Amicus	Attorney of Record / ACLU Attorney	As A Party	Wins	Losses	Vol #1, #2 or #3	Case # in Volume
	A	**B**	**C**	**D**	**E**	**F**	**G**	**H**
678	Metro Broadcasting, Inc. v. FCC	x			x		2	708
679	Metro-Goldwyn-Mayer Studios, Inc. v. Grokster, Ltd.	x				x	3	990
680	Metromedia, Inc. v. City of San Diego	x			x		2	481
681	Meyer v. Grant	x			x		2	645
682	Miami Herald Publishing Co. v. Tornillo	x			x		1	341
683	Michael H. v. Gerald D.	x				x	2	683
684	Michael M. v. Superior Court of Sonoma County	x				x	2	463
685	Michigan v. DeFillippo	x				x	2	437
686	Michigan v. Harvey	x				x	2	697
687	Michigan v. Summers	x				x	2	477
688	Middlesex County Ethics Committee v. Garden State Bar Association	x				x	2	489

ACLU's Case Involvement

Volume of Three-volume set & Case # in volume

	Case Name	ACLU's Case Involvement			Wins	Losses	Volume of Three-volume set & Case # in volume	
		Amicus	Attorney of Record / ACLU Attorney	As A Party			Vol #1, #2 or #3	Case # in Volume
	A	**B**	**C**	**D**	**E**	**F**	**G**	**H**
689	Migra v. Warren City School District Board of Education	x			x		2	523
690	Milkovich v. Lorain Journal Co.	x				x	2	705
691	Miller v. Albright	x				x	2	841
692	Miller v. California	x				x	1	312
693	Miller v. Fenton	x			x		2	574
694	Miller v. Florida	x			x		2	623
695	Miller v. French		x			x	3	886
696	Miller v. Johnson		x			x	2	791
697	Mills v. Alabama	x			x		1	174
698	Milner v. Dep't of Navy	x			x		3	1070
699	Minersville School District v. Gobitis	x				x	1	12
700	Minneapolis Star & Tribune Co. v. Minnesota Commissioner of Revenue	x			x		2	498
701	Minnesota v. Carter	x				x	2	854
702	Minnesota v. Dickerson	x			x		2	755

	Case Name	Amicus	Attorney of Record / ACLU Attorney	As A Party	Wins	Losses	Vol #1, #2 or #3	Case # in Volume
	A	B	C	D	E	F	G	H
703	Minnick v. California Department of Corrections	x			x		2	473
704	Miranda v. Arizona	x			x		1	176
705	Mississippi Univ. for Women v. Hogan		x		x		2	494
706	Missouri v. Frye	x			x		3	1092
707	Missouri v. Jenkins	x				x	2	785
708	Missouri v. McNeely		x		x		3	1106
709	Missouri v. Seibert	x			x		3	971
710	Mitchell v. Donovan		x			x	1	233
711	Mitchell v. Helms	x				x	3	890
712	Mitchell v. Wisconsin	x				x	3	1192
713	Montejo v. Louisiana	x				x	3	1043
714	Montgomery v. Louisiana	x			x		3	1144
715	Moore v. City of East Cleveland, Ohio	x			x		1	387
716	Moore v. Illinois	x			x		1	285
717	Moore v. Texas	x			x		3	1155
718	Morgan v. Illinois	x			x		2	742

The table has a top spanning header: "ACLU's Case Involvement" over columns Amicus, Attorney of Record / ACLU Attorney, As A Party; and "Volume of Three-volume set & Case # in volume" over columns Vol #1, #2 or #3, Case # in Volume.

	Case Name	ACLU's Case Involvement			Wins	Losses	Volume of Three-volume set & Case # in volume	
		Amicus	Attorney of Record / ACLU Attorney	As A Party			Vol #1, #2 or #3	Case # in Volume
	A	**B**	**C**	**D**	**E**	**F**	**G**	**H**
719	Morgan v. Virginia	x			x		1	43
720	Morrissey v. Brewer	x			x		1	281
721	Morse v. Frederick		x			x	3	1018
722	Morse v. Republican Party of Virginia	x			x		2	795
723	Muehler v. Mena	x				x	3	982
724	Mulloy v. United States	x			x		1	232
725	Munro v. Socialist Workers Party	x				x	2	600
726	Murphy v. Hunt	x				x	2	484
727	Murray v. Carrier	x				x	2	592
728	Murray v. Giarratano	x				x	2	688
729	Murray v. United States	x			x		2	656
730	Musser v. Utah	x			x		1	47
731	NAACP v. Claiborne Hardware Co.	x			x		2	496
732	Nashville Gas Co. v. Satty	x			x		1	399
733	National Aeronautics and Space Administration v. Nelson	x				x	3	1066

87

		ACLU's Case Involvement					Volume of Three-volume set & Case # in volume	
	Case Name	Amicus	Attorney of Record / ACLU Attorney	As A Party	Wins	Losses	Vol #1, #2 or #3	Case # in Volume
	A	B	C	D	E	F	G	H
734	National Broadcasting Co. v. United States	x			x		1	19
735	National Cable and Television Communications Ass'n v. Brand X Internet Services	x				x	3	991
736	National Collegiate Athletic Ass'n v. Smith	x				x	3	859
737	National Endowment for the Arts v. Finley		x			x	2	850
738	National Fed'n of Indep. Business v. Sebelius	x			x		3	1099
739	National Labor Relations Board v. Sears, Roebuck & Co.	x				x	1	354
740	National Labor Relations Board v. Town & Country Electric, Inc.	x			x		2	792
741	National Organization for Women, Inc. v. Scheidler	x			x		2	766

	Case Name	ACLU's Case Involvement			Wins	Losses	Volume of Three-volume set & Case # in volume	
		Amicus	Attorney of Record / ACLU Attorney	As A Party			Vol #1, #2 or #3	Case # in Volume
	A	B	C	D	E	F	G	H
742	National Socialist Party of America v. Village of Skokie		x		x		1	392
743	National Treasury Employees Union v. Von Raab	x				x	2	671
744	Nebraska Press Association v. Stuart	x			x		1	376
745	Neil v. Biggers	x				x	1	287
746	Nelson v. Los Angeles County		x			x	1	112
747	Nevada Dep't of Human Res. v. Hibbs	x			x		3	940
748	New Jersey v. T.L.O.	x				x	2	552
749	New Mexico v. Earnest	x				x	2	594
750	New York State Bd. of Elections v. Lopez Torres	x				x	3	1023
751	New York State Club Ass'n v. City of New York	x			x		2	648
752	New York Times Co. v. Sullivan	x			x		1	144

	Case Name	ACLU's Case Involvement					Volume of Three-volume set & Case # in volume	
		Amicus	Attorney of Record / ACLU Attorney	As A Party	Wins	Losses	Vol #1, #2 or #3	Case # in Volume
	A	**B**	**C**	**D**	**E**	**F**	**G**	**H**
753	New York Times Co. v. United States	x			x		1	254
754	New York v. Belton	x				x	2	480
755	New York v. Burger	x				x	2	626
756	New York v. Ferber	x				x	2	495
757	New York v. Uplinger	x			x		2	541
758	Nguyen v. INS		x			x	3	906
759	Nichols v. United States	x				x	2	771
760	Nielsen v. Preap		x			x	3	1182
761	Nieves v. Bartlett	x				x	3	1184
762	Nijhawan v. Holder	x				x	3	1044
763	Nike, Inc. v. Kasky	x				x	3	951
764	Nixon v. Shrink Missouri Government PAC	x				x	3	876
765	Nken v. Holder	x			x		3	1041
766	NLRB v. Catholic Bishop of Chicago	x			x		1	422
767	Norman v. Reed	x			x		2	730
768	North Carolina v. Pearce	x			x		1	223
769	North v. Russell	x				x	1	374

	Case Name	Amicus	Attorney of Record / ACLU Attorney	As A Party	Wins	Losses	Vol #1, #2 or #3	Case # in Volume
	ACLU's Case Involvement						Volume of Three-volume set & Case # in volume	
	A	B	C	D	E	F	G	H
770	Northwest Austin Mun. Utility Dist. No. One v. Holder		x			x	3	1046
771	O'Connor v. Donaldson		x		x		1	363
772	O'Connor v. Ortega	x				x	2	611
773	O'Hare Truck Service, Inc. v. City of Northlake		x		x		2	810
774	O'Lone v. Estate of Shabazz	x				x	2	622
775	O'Neal v. McAninch	x			x		2	777
776	Obergefell v. Hodges		x		x		3	1141
777	Ohio Adult Parole Authority v. Woodard	x				x	2	839
778	Ohio Civil Rights Commission v. Dayton Christian Schools, Inc.	x			x		2	593
779	Ohio Mun. Judges Ass'n v. Davis	x				x	1	300
780	Ohio v. Robinette	x				x	2	813
781	Oklahoma City v. Tuttle	x				x	2	559

| | Case Name | ACLU's Case Involvement | | | Wins | Losses | Volume of Three-volume set & Case # in volume | |
		Amicus	Attorney of Record / ACLU Attorney	As A Party			Vol #1, #2 or #3	Case # in Volume
	A	B	C	D	E	F	G	H
782	Old Dominion Branch No. 496 v. Austin	x			x		1	342
783	Oliver v. United States	x				x	2	529
784	Olmstead v. L.C. ex rel. Zimring	x			x		3	871
785	Oncale v. Sundowner Offshore Services, Inc.	x			x		2	838
786	Oregon v. Kennedy	x				x	2	487
787	Oregon v. Mitchell	x			x		1	235
788	Org. for a Better Austin v. Keefe		x		x		1	245
789	Ornelas v. United States	x			x		2	799
790	Orr v. Orr	x			x		1	421
791	Overton v. Bazzetta	x				x	3	944
792	Owen v. City of Independence	x			x		2	447
793	Owens v. Okure		x		x		2	661
794	Oyama v. California	x	x		x		1	46
795	Packingham v. North Carolina	x			x		3	1160
796	Palmer v. City of Euclid		x		x		1	247
797	Palmore v. Sidoti	x			x		2	532

	Case Name	ACLU's Case Involvement					Volume of Three-volume set & Case # in volume	
		Amicus	Attorney of Record / ACLU Attorney	As A Party	Wins	Losses	Vol #1, #2 or #3	Case # in Volume
	A	B	C	D	E	F	G	H
798	Papish v. Bd. of Curators of Univ. of Missouri		x		x		1	295
799	Parents Involved in Community Schools v. Seattle School Dist. No. 1	x				x	3	1021
800	Parker v. Levy		x			x	1	337
801	Parratt v. Taylor	x				x	2	468
802	Patterson v. Alabama		x		x		1	5
803	Patterson v. McLean Credit Union	x				x	2	684
804	Pearson v. Callahan	x				x	3	1034
805	Pembaur v. City of Cincinnati	x			x		2	579
806	Pena-Rodriguez v. Colorado	x			x		3	1154
807	Pennekamp v. Florida	x			x		1	42
808	Pennell v. City of San Jose	x			x		2	638
809	Pennsylvania Board of Probation & Parole v. Scott	x				x	2	849

| | Case Name | ACLU's Case Involvement | | | Wins | Losses | Volume of Three-volume set & Case # in volume | |
		Amicus	Attorney of Record / ACLU Attorney	As A Party			Vol #1, #2 or #3	Case # in Volume
	A	B	C	D	E	F	G	H
810	Pennsylvania Department of Corrections v. Yeskey	x			x		2	848
811	Pennsylvania ex rel. Herman v. Claudy		x		x		1	83
812	Pennsylvania State Police v. Suders	x				x	3	964
813	Pennsylvania v. Finley	x				x	2	617
814	Pennsylvania v. Nelson	x			x		1	85
815	Penson v. Ohio	x			x		2	659
816	Perdue v. Kenny A.	x				x	3	1056
817	Personnel Administrator of Massachusetts v. Feeney		x			x	2	432
818	Peters v. Hobby	x			x		1	81
819	Philadelphia Newspapers, Inc. v. Hepps	x			x		2	584
820	Phillips v. Martin Marietta Corp.	x			x		1	236
821	Pickering v. Board of Education	x			x		1	204

	Case Name	Amicus	Attorney of Record / ACLU Attorney	As A Party	Wins	Losses	Vol #1, #2 or #3	Case # in Volume
	ACLU's Case Involvement						Volume of Three-volume set & Case # in volume	
	A	B	C	D	E	F	G	H
822	Pipefitters Local Union No. 562 v. United States	x			x		1	275
823	Pittsburgh Press Co. v. Pittsburg Commission on Human Relations	x			x		1	316
824	Planned Parenthood of Southeastern Pennsylvania v. Casey		x		x		2	748
825	Poe v. Ullman	x				x	1	128
826	Pollard v. E. I. du Pont de Nemours & Co.	x			x		3	904
827	Pope v. Illinois	x			x		2	615
828	Posadas de Puerto Rico Associates v. Tourism Company of Puerto Rico	x				x	2	597
829	Powell v. Alabama		x		x		1	4
830	Powell v. McCormack	x			x		1	222
831	Powell v. Texas	x	x			x	1	209
832	Powers v. Ohio	x			x		2	715
833	Preiser v. Newkirk	x				x	1	362

	Case Name	Amicus	Attorney of Record / ACLU Attorney	As A Party	Wins	Losses	Vol #1, #2 or #3	Case # in Volume
	A	B	C	D	E	F	G	H
834	Preiser v. Rodriguez		x			x	1	305
835	Press-Enterprise Co. v. Superior Court	x			x		2	595
836	Price v. Johnston	x			x		1	53
837	Price-Waterhouse v. Hopkins	x				x	2	677
838	Procunier v. Navarette	x				x	1	402
839	PruneYard Shopping Center v. Robins	x			x		2	453
840	Pugach v. Dollinger	x				x	1	118
841	Pulliam v. Allen	x			x		2	534
842	Quinn v. Millsap	x			x		2	682
843	R.A.V. v. City of St. Paul	x			x		2	745
844	Railway Mail Ass'n. v. Corsi	x			x		1	36
845	Randall v. Sorrell		x		x		3	1005
846	Rasul v. Bush	x			x		3	969
847	Red Lion Broadcasting Co. v. FCC	x			x		1	220
848	Reed v. Reed		x		x		1	255
849	Reeves v. Sanderson Plumbing Products, Inc.	x			x		3	884

The table has a header spanning "ACLU's Case Involvement" over Amicus, Attorney of Record / ACLU Attorney, As A Party; and "Volume of Three-volume set & Case # in volume" over Vol #1, #2 or #3, and Case # in Volume.

| | Case Name | ACLU's Case Involvement | | | | | Volume of Three-volume set & Case # in volume | |
		Amicus	Attorney of Record / ACLU Attorney	As A Party	Wins	Losses	Vol #1, #2 or #3	Case # in Volume
	A	B	C	D	E	F	G	H
850	Regents of the University of California v. Bakke	x				x	1	414
851	Reichle v. Howards	x				x	3	1095
852	Reitman v. Mulkey	x			x		1	189
853	Renegotiation Board v. Grunmman Aircraft Engineering Corp.	x				x	1	355
854	Renne v. Geary	x				x	2	722
855	Reno v. American Civil Liberties Union			x	x		2	837
856	Reno v. American-Arab Anti-Discrimination Committee		x			x	3	860
857	Reno v. Bossier Parish School Board	x				x	2	826
858	Reno v. Condon	x			x		3	874
859	Republican Party of Minnesota v. White	x			x		3	932
860	Reynolds v. Sims		x		x		1	151

		ACLU's Case Involvement					Volume of Three-volume set & Case # in volume	
	Case Name	Amicus	Attorney of Record / ACLU Attorney	As A Party	Wins	Losses	Vol #1, #2 or #3	Case # in Volume
	A	B	C	D	E	F	G	H
861	Ricci v. DeStefano	x				x	3	1048
862	Ricci v. Village of Arlington Heights	x				x	2	843
863	Richards v. Wisconsin	x				x	2	824
864	Richardson v. McKnight	x			x		2	833
865	Richardson v. Ramirez	x				x	1	338
866	Richmond Newspapers, Inc. v. Virginia	x			x		2	457
867	Riley v. California	x			x		3	1126
868	Riley v. Kennedy	x				x	3	1028
869	Rios v. United States	x			x		1	115
870	Rizzo v. Goode	x				x	1	365
871	Roberts v. Galen of Virginia, Inc.	x			x		3	857
872	Roberts v. United States	x				x	2	446
873	Roberts v. United States Jaycees	x			x		2	551
874	Robinson v. Shell Oil Co.	x			x		2	815
875	Rochin v. California	x			x		1	67
876	Roe v. Wade		x		x		1	291

	Case Name	ACLU's Case Involvement			Wins	Losses	Volume of Three-volume set & Case # in volume	
		Amicus	Attorney of Record / ACLU Attorney	As A Party			Vol #1, #2 or #3	Case # in Volume
	A	B	C	D	E	F	G	H
877	Rogers v. United States	x			x		1	360
878	Romer v. Evans		x		x		2	798
879	Roper v. Simmons	x			x		3	980
880	Rosado v. Wyman	x			x		1	228
881	Rosario v. Rockefeller		x			x	1	298
882	Rose v. Clark	x				x	2	598
883	Rosenberger v. Rector & Visitors of the University of Virginia	x				x	2	790
884	Rosenblatt v. Baer	x			x		1	171
885	Ross v. Oklahoma	x				x	2	651
886	Rostker v. Goldberg		x			x	2	478
887	Roth v. United States	x				x	1	97
888	Rucho v. Common Cause	x				x	3	1191
889	Rufo v. Inmates of the Suffolk County Jail	x				x	2	732
890	Rumsfeld v. Forum for Academic & Institutional Rights, Inc.	x				x	3	997

	Case Name	Amicus	Attorney of Record / ACLU Attorney	As A Party	Wins	Losses	Vol #1, #2 or #3	Case # in Volume
		ACLU's Case Involvement					Volume of Three-volume set & Case # in volume	
	A	**B**	**C**	**D**	**E**	**F**	**G**	**H**
891	Rumsfeld v. Padilla	x				x	3	968
892	Rusk v. Cort	x			x		1	131
893	Russell v. United States	x			x		1	133
894	Rust v. Sullivan		x			x	2	717
895	Ryan v. Gonzales	x				x	3	1101
896	Saenz v. Roe		x		x		3	861
897	Safford Unified School Dist. No. 1 v. Redding		x		x		3	1047
898	Salazar v. Buono		x			x	3	1057
899	Saldana v. United States	x			x		1	119
900	Salinas v. Texas	x				x	3	1112
901	Salyer Land Co. v. Tulare Lake Basin Water Storage District	x				x	1	296
902	Samson v. California	x				x	3	1001
903	San Antonio Independent School District v. Rodriguez	x				x	1	299
904	Sandin v. Conner	x				x	2	787
905	Santa Clara Pueblo v. Martinez	x				x	1	408

	Case Name	ACLU's Case Involvement			Wins	Losses	Volume of Three-volume set & Case # in volume	
		Amicus	Attorney of Record / ACLU Attorney	As A Party			Vol #1, #2 or #3	Case # in Volume
	A	B	C	D	E	F	G	H
906	Santa Fe Independent School District v. Doe		x		x		3	885
907	Santosky v. Kramer	x			x		2	485
908	Sarno v. Illinois Crime Investigating Commission	x				x	1	269
909	Saucier v. Katz	x				x	3	908
910	Scales v. United States (1957)	x			x		1	99
911	Scales v. United States (1961)	x				x	1	125
912	Schad v. Borough of Mount Ephraim	x			x		2	471
913	Schenck v. Pro-Choice Network of Western New York	x			x		2	816
914	Scheuer v. Rhodes		x		x		1	329
915	Schlanger v. Seamans	x				x	1	240
916	Schlesinger v. Councilman	x				x	1	352
917	Schlesinger v. Holtzman		x		x		1	319
918	Schneckloth v. Bustamonte	x				x	1	308

		ACLU's Case Involvement					Volume of Three-volume set & Case # in volume	
	Case Name	Amicus	Attorney of Record / ACLU Attorney	As A Party	Wins	Losses	Vol #1, #2 or #3	Case # in Volume
	A	B	C	D	E	F	G	H
919	Schneider v. New Jersey	x	x		x		1	10
920	Schneider v. Rusk	x			x		1	149
921	School District of Abington Township v. Schempp		x		x		1	142
922	Schroeder v. City of New York	x			x		1	135
923	Schuette v. Coalition to Defend Affirmative Action	x				x	3	1120
924	Schware v. Bd. of Bar Exam'rs of N. M.		x		x		1	92
925	Schweiker v. Chilicky	x				x	2	653
926	Scott v. Harris	x				x	3	1012
927	Seattle Times Co. v. Rhinehart	x				x	2	538
928	Secretary of State of Maryland. v. Joseph H. Munson Co.	x			x		2	544
929	See v. City of Seattle		x		x		1	191
930	Sell v. United States	x				x	3	945

| | Case Name | ACLU's Case Involvement | | | Wins | Losses | Volume of Three-volume set & Case # in volume | |
		Amicus	Attorney of Record / ACLU Attorney	As A Party			Vol #1, #2 or #3	Case # in Volume
	A	**B**	**C**	**D**	**E**	**F**	**G**	**H**
931	Senn v. Tile Layers Protective Union	x			x		1	7
932	Sessions v. Morales-Santana	x			x		3	1159
933	Shapiro v. Thompson	x			x		1	216
934	Shaw v. Delta Air Lines, Inc.	x			x		2	515
935	Shaw v. Hunt	x				x	2	802
936	Shaw v. Murphy	x				x	3	896
937	Shelby County v. Holder		x			x	3	1114
938	Shelley v. Kraemer	x			x		1	50
939	Sheppard v. Maxwell	x			x		1	175
940	Sibron v. New York	x				x	1	206
941	Siegert v. Gilley	x				x	2	718
942	Simmons v. Himmelreich	x			x		3	1147
943	Simon & Schuster, Inc. v. Members of the New York State Crime Victims Board	x			x		2	728
944	Sinclair v. United States	x			x		1	59

	Case Name	ACLU's Case Involvement					Volume of Three-volume set & Case # in volume	
		Amicus	Attorney of Record / ACLU Attorney	As A Party	Wins	Losses	Vol #1, #2 or #3	Case # in Volume
	A	B	C	D	E	F	G	H
945	Sipuel v. Board of Regents of University of Oklahoma	x			x		1	45
946	Skinner v. Railway Labor Executives' Ass'n	x				x	2	670
947	Slochower v. Board of Higher Education	x			x		1	86
948	Smalis v. Pennsylvania	x			x		2	585
949	Smith v. Allwright	x			x		1	27
950	Smith v. California (1959)	x			x		1	111
951	Smith v. California (1963)	x			x		1	143
952	Smith v. Daily Mail Publishing Co.	x			x		2	439
953	Smith v. Doe	x				x	3	936
954	Smith v. Goguen		x		x		1	326
955	Smith v. Org. of Foster Families for Equality & Reform		x			x	1	391
956	Smith v. Pennsylvania	x			x		1	145
957	Smith v. Phillips	x				x	2	483
958	Snyder v. Phelps	x			x		3	1069
959	Soldal v. Cook County, Illinois	x			x		2	749

		ACLU's Case Involvement			Wins	Losses	Volume of Three-volume set & Case # in volume	
	Case Name	Amicus	Attorney of Record / ACLU Attorney	As A Party	Wins	Losses	Vol #1, #2 or #3	Case # in Volume
	A	B	C	D	E	F	G	H
960	Sole v. Wyner		x			x	3	1015
961	Sosa v. Alvarez-Machain		x			x	3	974
962	Sossamon v. Texas	x				x	3	1074
963	Southeastern Community College v. Davis	x				x	2	435
964	Spallone v. United States	x				x	2	691
965	Speiser v. Randall	x	x		x		1	106
966	Spence v. Washington		x		x		1	344
967	Spevack v. Klein	x			x		1	183
968	Staats v. American Civil Liberties Union aka ACLU v. Jennings, 365 F. Supp. 1041 (D.D.C. 1973)	x				x	1	361
969	Stainback v. Mo Hock Ke Lok Po	x				x	1	57
970	Staub v. City of Baxley	x			x		1	100
971	Steagald v. United States	x			x		2	465
972	Steele v. Louisville & Nashville Railroad Co.	x			x		1	28

	Case Name	Amicus	Attorney of Record / ACLU Attorney	As A Party	Wins	Losses	Vol #1, #2 or #3	Case # in Volume
	ACLU's Case Involvement						**Volume of Three-volume set & Case # in volume**	
	A	B	C	D	E	F	G	H
973	Stenberg v. Carhart	x			x		3	891
974	Stewart v. Martinez-Villareal	x			x		2	845
975	Stone v. Powell	x				x	1	377
976	Stoner v. California	x			x		1	146
977	Storer v. Brown		x		x		1	327
978	Strait v. Laird		x		x		1	265
979	Street v. New York		x		x		1	215
980	Stromberg v. California		x		x		1	3
981	Stump v. Sparkman	x				x	1	404
982	Superior Films, Inc. v. Department of Education	x			x		1	78
983	Supreme Court of Virginia v. Consumers Union of the United States, Inc.	x				x	2	452
984	Susan B. Anthony List v. Driehaus	x			x		3	1123
985	Sutton v. United Air Lines, Inc.	x				x	3	869

	Case Name	ACLU's Case Involvement			Wins	Losses	Volume of Three-volume set & Case # in volume	
		Amicus	Attorney of Record / ACLU Attorney	As A Party			Vol #1, #2 or #3	Case # in Volume
	A	B	C	D	E	F	G	H
986	Swierkiewicz v. Sorema N. A.	x			x		3	918
987	Swint v. Chambers County Commission	x				x	2	780
988	Takahashi v. Fish and Game Commission	x			x		1	54
989	Talley v. California		x		x		1	113
990	Taylor v. Alabama	x			x		2	490
991	Taylor v. Hayes	x			x		1	346
992	Taylor v. Mississippi	x			x		1	20
993	Terminiello v. City of Chicago	x			x		1	58
994	Terry v. Ohio	x				x	1	205
995	Texas Dept. of Housing and Community Affairs v. Inclusive Communities Project, Inc.	x			x		3	1140
996	Texas Monthly, Inc. v. Bullock	x			x		2	664
997	Texas v. Johnson	x			x		2	686
998	Texas v. United States	x			x		2	840

	Case Name	Amicus	Attorney of Record / ACLU Attorney	As A Party	Wins	Losses	Vol #1, #2 or #3	Case # in Volume
			ACLU's Case Involvement					Volume of Three-volume set & Case # in volume
	A	B	C	D	E	F	G	H
999	Thomas v. Collins	x			x		1	32
1000	Thomas v. Review Board of the Indiana Employment Security Division	x			x		2	464
1001	Thompson v. North American Stainless, LP	x			x		3	1067
1002	Thornburgh v. American College of Obstetricians and Gynecologists	x			x		2	589
1003	Thornton v. United States	x				x	3	961
1004	Tillman v. Wheaton-Haven Recreation Assn.		x		x		1	293
1005	Timbs v. Indiana	x			x		3	1181
1006	Times Film Corp. v. Chicago	x				x	1	117
1007	Timmons v. Twin Cities Area New Party	x				x	2	823
1008	Tinker v. Des Moines Independent Community School District		x		x		1	213

| | Case Name | ACLU's Case Involvement | | | Wins | Losses | Volume of Three-volume set & Case # in volume | |
		Amicus	Attorney of Record / ACLU Attorney	As A Party			Vol #1, #2 or #3	Case # in Volume
	A	B	C	D	E	F	G	H
1009	Tony and Susan Alamo Foundation v. Secretary of Labor	x			x		2	557
1010	Torcaso v. Watkins		x		x		1	127
1011	Torres v. Puerto Rico	x			x		2	436
1012	Town of Castle Rock v. Gonzales	x				x	3	988
1013	Town of Greece v. Galloway	x				x	3	1121
1014	Town of Newton v. Rumery	x				x	2	608
1015	Trans World Airlines, Inc. v. Hardison	x				x	1	393
1016	Travis v. United States		x		x		1	182
1017	Traynor v. Turnage		x			x	2	642
1018	Trbovich v. United Mine Workers of America	x			x		1	258
1019	Trimble v. Gordon	x			x		1	384
1020	Trinity Lutheran Church of Columbia, Inc. v. Comer	x				x	3	1165

	Case Name	ACLU's Case Involvement			Wins	Losses	Volume of Three-volume set & Case # in volume	
		Amicus	Attorney of Record / ACLU Attorney	As A Party			Vol #1, #2 or #3	Case # in Volume
	A	B	C	D	E	F	G	H
1021	Trop v. Dulles		x		x		1	102
1022	Troxel v. Granville	x			x		3	883
1023	Trump v. Hawaii	x				x	3	1179
1024	Trump v. Int'l Refugee Assistance Project		x			x	3	1167
1025	Tuilaepa v. California	x				x	2	775
1026	Tunstall v. Brotherhood of Locomotive Firemen	x			x		1	29
1027	Turner v. Dep't of Employment Security of Utah		x		x		1	364
1028	Turner v. Rogers	x			x		3	1082
1029	Two Guys from Harrison-Allentown, Inc. v. McGinley	x				x	1	122
1030	U.S. Civil Service Comm'n v. Nat'l Ass'n of Letter Carriers		x			x	1	317
1031	U.S. Term Limits, Inc. v. Thornton	x			x		2	783
1032	U.S. v. Alvarez	x			x		3	1100

		ACLU's Case Involvement					Volume of Three-volume set & Case # in volume	
	Case Name	Amicus	Attorney of Record / ACLU Attorney	As A Party	Wins	Losses	Vol #1, #2 or #3	Case # in Volume
	A	B	C	D	E	F	G	H
1033	U.S. v. American Library Ass'n, Inc.		x			x	3	946
1034	U.S. v. Apel		x			x	3	1119
1035	U.S. v. Georgia	x			x		3	992
1036	U.S. v. Jones	x			x		3	1087
1037	U.S. v. Oakland Cannabis Buyers' Coop.	x				x	3	900
1038	U.S. v. Stevens	x			x		3	1055
1039	U.S. v. Windsor		x		x		3	1117
1040	UAW v. Johnson Controls, Inc.	x			x		2	713
1041	Ungar v. Sarafite	x	x			x	1	147
1042	United Brotherhood of Carpenters v. Scott	x	x			x	2	520
1043	United States Catholic Conference v. Abortion Rights Mobilization, Inc.	x				x	2	650
1044	United States Department of Justice v. Reporters Committee for Freedom of the Press	x			x		2	673

	Case Name	ACLU's Case Involvement			Wins	Losses	Volume of Three-volume set & Case # in volume	
		Amicus	Attorney of Record / ACLU Attorney	As A Party			Vol #1, #2 or #3	Case # in Volume
	A	B	C	D	E	F	G	H
1045	United States Department of State v. Ray	x				x	2	729
1046	United States ex rel. Knauff v. Shaughnessy	x				x	1	60
1047	United States Postal Service Board of Governors v. Aikens	x				x	2	499
1048	United States v. 12 200-Foot Reels of Super 8mm. Film	x				x	1	313
1049	United States v. Albertini		x			x	2	566
1050	United States v. Armstrong	x				x	2	796
1051	United States v. Barnett	x				x	1	148
1052	United States v. Biswell	x				x	1	264
1053	United States v. Brown	x			x		1	167
1054	United States v. Burke	x				x	2	739
1055	United States v. Calandra	x				x	1	321
1056	United States v. Chadwick	x			x		1	394

	Case Name	Amicus	Attorney of Record / ACLU Attorney	As A Party	Wins	Losses	Vol #1, #2 or #3	Case # in Volume
	ACLU's Case Involvement						**Volume of Three-volume set & Case # in volume**	
	A	**B**	**C**	**D**	**E**	**F**	**G**	**H**
1057	United States v. Chesapeake & Potomac Telephone Co. of Virginia	x				x	2	793
1058	United States v. Congress of Industrial Organizations	x			x		1	55
1059	United States v. Cronic	x				x	2	535
1060	United States v. DiFrancesco	x				x	2	460
1061	United States v. Edge Broadcasting Co.	x				x	2	760
1062	United States v. Eichman	x			x		2	703
1063	United States v. Gouveia	x				x	2	540
1064	United States v. Grace	x			x		2	503
1065	United States v. Hohri	x				x	2	621
1066	United States v. James Daniel Good Real Property	x			x		2	764
1067	United States v. Kokinda	x				x	2	710
1068	United States v. Lanier	x			x		2	819

	Case Name	Amicus	Attorney of Record / ACLU Attorney	As A Party	Wins	Losses	Vol #1, #2 or #3	Case # in Volume
	ACLU's Case Involvement						**Volume of Three-volume set & Case # in volume**	
	A	B	C	D	E	F	G	H
1069	United States v. Martinez-Fuerte	x				x	1	378
1070	United States v. Mendenhall	x				x	2	450
1071	United States v. Mendoza-Lopez	x			x		2	620
1072	United States v. Midwest Video Corp.	x				x	1	270
1073	United States v. Mississippi	x			x		1	159
1074	United States v. National Treasury Employees Union		x		x		2	778
1075	United States v. New Jersey State Lottery Commission	x				x	1	350
1076	United States v. Nixon	x			x		1	348
1077	United States v. Orito	x				x	1	314
1078	United States v. Paramount Pictures, Inc	x				x	1	52
1079	United States v. Patane	x				x	3	972
1080	United States v. Place	x			x		2	513

	Case Name	ACLU's Case Involvement			Wins	Losses	Volume of Three-volume set & Case # in volume	
		Amicus	Attorney of Record / ACLU Attorney	As A Party			Vol #1, #2 or #3	Case # in Volume
	A	**B**	**C**	**D**	**E**	**F**	**G**	**H**
1081	United States v. Providence Journal Co.	x			x		2	644
1082	United States v. Ramsey	x				x	1	388
1083	United States v. Richardson		x			x	1	340
1084	United States v. Robel	x			x		1	196
1085	United States v. Robinson	x				x	1	320
1086	United States v. Russell	x				x	1	303
1087	United States v. Salerno	x				x	2	618
1088	United States v. Seeger	x			x		1	160
1089	United States v. Sells Engineering, Inc.	x			x		2	518
1090	United States v. Sisson	x			x		1	234
1091	United States v. Spector		x			x	1	71
1092	United States v. United States District Court for the Eastern District of Michigan	x			x		1	274
1093	United States v. Ursery	x				x	2	804

	Case Name	ACLU's Case Involvement			Wins	Losses	Volume of Three-volume set & Case # in volume	
		Amicus	Attorney of Record / ACLU Attorney	As A Party			Vol #1, #2 or #3	Case # in Volume
	A	B	C	D	E	F	G	H
1094	United States v. Verdugo-Urquidez	x				x	2	696
1095	United States v. Virginia	x			x		2	807
1096	United States v. Vuitch	x	x			x	1	242
1097	United States v. Weatherhead	x				x	3	872
1098	United Steelworkers of America v. Weber	x			x		2	441
1099	United Steelworkers v. Sadlowski	x				x	2	488
1100	University of Texas v. Camenisch	x			x		2	467
1101	Utah v. Strieff	x				x	3	1149
1102	Uttecht v. Brown	x				x	3	1014
1103	Vacco v. Quill	x				x	2	836
1104	Vachon v. New Hampshire		x		x		1	323
1105	Valentine v. Chrestensen	x				x	1	15
1106	Van de Kamp v. Goldstein	x				x	3	1037

| | Case Name | ACLU's Case Involvement | | | Wins | Losses | Volume of Three-volume set & Case # in volume | |
		Amicus	Attorney of Record / ACLU Attorney	As A Party			Vol #1, #2 or #3	Case # in Volume
	A	B	C	D	E	F	G	H
1107	Verizon Maryland, Inc. v. Pub. Serv. Comm'n of Maryland	x			x		3	923
1108	Vermont v. Brillon	x				x	3	1039
1109	Veterans of the Abraham Lincoln Brigade v. Subversive Activities Control Board	x			x		1	163
1110	Vieth v. Jubelirer	x				x	3	960
1111	Village of Belle Terre v. Boraas		x			x	1	328
1112	Village of Willowbrook v. Olech	x			x		3	877
1113	Virginia v. American Booksellers Ass'n, Inc.	x				x	2	636
1114	Virginia v. Black		x		x		3	937
1115	Virginia v. Hicks	x				x	3	943
1116	Virginia v. Moore	x				x	3	1026
1117	Vlandis v. Kline	x			x		1	310
1118	Wainwright v. Greenfield	x			x		2	575
1119	Wal-Mart Stores, Inc. v. Dukes	x				x	3	1080

	Case Name	ACLU's Case Involvement					Volume of Three-volume set & Case # in volume	
		Amicus	Attorney of Record / ACLU Attorney	As A Party	Wins	Losses	Vol #1, #2 or #3	Case # in Volume
	A	B	C	D	E	F	G	H
1120	Walker v. City of Hutchinson		x		x		1	90
1121	Walker v. Texas Div., Sons of Confederate Veterans, Inc.	x				x	3	1138
1122	Wallace v. Jaffree	x			x		2	560
1123	Walters v. National Ass'n of Radiation Survivors	x				x	2	569
1124	Walton v. Arizona	x				x	2	709
1125	Walz v. Tax Commission	x				x	1	229
1126	Wards Cove Packing Co. v. Atonio	x				x	2	679
1127	Washington v. Chrisman	x				x	2	482
1128	Washington v. Glucksberg	x				x	2	835
1129	Washington v. Seattle School District No. 1		x		x		2	493
1130	Washington v. Washington State Commercial Passenger Fishing Vessel Ass'n	x			x		2	445

	Case Name	Amicus	Attorney of Record / ACLU Attorney	As A Party	Wins	Losses	Vol #1, #2 or #3	Case # in Volume
	ACLU's Case Involvement						**Volume of Three-volume set & Case # in volume**	
	A	B	C	D	E	F	G	H
1131	Watchtower Bible & Tract Soc'y of New York, Inc. v. Village of Stratton	x			x		3	926
1132	Watkins v. United States	x			x		1	94
1133	Watson v. Fort Worth Bank & Trust	x			x		2	658
1134	Watts v. United States	x			x		1	217
1135	Weatherford v. Bursey		x			x	1	381
1136	Weaver v. Massachusetts	x				x	3	1163
1137	Weber v. Aetna Casualty & Surety Co.	x			x		1	263
1138	Webster v. Reproductive Health Services	x				x	2	689
1139	Weinberger v. Wiesenfeld		x		x		1	351
1140	Weiss v. United States	x				x	2	765
1141	Welsh v. Wisconsin	x			x		2	536
1142	Wengler v. Druggists Mutual Insurance Co.	x			x		2	449
1143	West v. Atkins	x			x		2	649

	Case Name	ACLU's Case Involvement			Wins	Losses	Volume of Three-volume set & Case # in volume	
		Amicus	Attorney of Record / ACLU Attorney	As A Party			Vol #1, #2 or #3	Case # in Volume
	A	B	C	D	E	F	G	H
1144	West Virginia State Board of Education v. Barnette	x			x		1	21
1145	Western Air Lines, Inc. v. Criswell	x			x		2	562
1146	Wheeler v. Barrera	x				x	1	335
1147	Wheeler v. Montgomery	x			x		1	227
1148	Whitcomb v. Chavis	x				x	1	250
1149	White v. Maryland		x		x		1	138
1150	Whitney v. California		x			x	1	2
1151	Whitus v. Georgia		x		x		1	184
1152	Whole Woman's Health v. Hellerstedt	x			x		3	1152
1153	Whren v. United States	x				x	2	801
1154	Wieman v. Updegraff	x			x		1	75
1155	Wilkinson v. Austin		x			x	3	986
1156	Will v. Michigan Department of State Police		x			x	2	681
1157	Williams v. Pennsylvania	x			x		3	1148

	Case Name	ACLU's Case Involvement					Volume of Three-volume set & Case # in volume	
		Amicus	Attorney of Record / ACLU Attorney	As A Party	Wins	Losses	Vol #1, #2 or #3	Case # in Volume
	A	**B**	**C**	**D**	**E**	**F**	**G**	**H**
1158	Williams v. Taylor	x			x		3	882
1159	Williams-Yulee v. Florida Bar	x				x	3	1133
1160	Wilson v. Arkansas	x			x		2	784
1161	Wilson v. Layne		x			x	3	863
1162	Wilson v. Loew's, Inc.	x				x	1	101
1163	Wimberly v. Labor and Industrial Relations Commission of Missouri	x				x	2	604
1164	Winters v. New York	x			x		1	49
1165	Wisconsin Right to Life, Inc. v. Federal Election Commission	x			x		3	995
1166	Wisconsin v. City of New York	x				x	2	794
1167	Wisconsin v. Mitchell	x			x		2	757
1168	Witherspoon v. Illinois	x			x		1	203
1169	Withrow v. Williams	x			x		2	753

| | Case Name | ACLU's Case Involvement | | | Wins | Losses | Volume of Three-volume set & Case # in volume | |
		Amicus	Attorney of Record / ACLU Attorney	As A Party	Wins	Losses	Vol #1, #2 or #3	Case # in Volume
	A	B	C	D	E	F	G	H
1170	Witters v. Washington Department of Services for the Blind	x				x	2	576
1171	Wolff v. McDonnell	x				x	1	347
1172	Wood v. Allen	x				x	3	1051
1173	Wood v. Moss		x			x	3	1122
1174	Woodford v. Ngo	x				x	3	1004
1175	Wooley v. Maynard		x		x		1	385
1176	Wright v. Universal Maritime Service Corp.	x			x		2	853
1177	Wright v. West	x				x	2	744
1178	Yasui v. United States	x				x	1	23
1179	Yates v. United States	x			x		1	95
1180	Yellin v. United States	x			x		1	141
1181	Young v. American Mini Theatres, Inc.	x				x	1	372
1182	Young v. Fordice		x		x		2	820
1183	Young v. Harper		x		x		2	818
1184	Young v. United Parcel Service, Inc.	x			x		3	1131

	Case Name	ACLU's Case Involvement					Volume of Three-volume set & Case # in volume	
		Amicus	Attorney of Record / ACLU Attorney	As A Party	Wins	Losses	Vol #1, #2 or #3	Case # in Volume
	A	**B**	**C**	**D**	**E**	**F**	**G**	**H**
1185	Zablocki v. Redhail	x			x		1	401
1186	Zadvydas v. Davis	x			x		3	913
1187	Zauderer v. Office of Disciplinary Counsel	x			x		2	558
1188	Zelman v. Simmons-Harris		x			x	3	930
1189	Zemel v. Rusk	x				x	1	164
1190	Zicarelli v. New Jersey State Commission of Investigation	x				x	1	268
1191	Ziglar v. Abbasi	x				x	3	1162
1192	Zinermon v. Burch	x			x		2	695
1193	Zubik v. Burwell	x				x	3	1146
	Total	**975**	**211**	**7**	**640**	**553**		

V.

Votes of Each Justice on Each ACLU/SCOTUS Case from 1925 to 2019 (by Date)

The following 118-page chart shows how each of the 51 U.S. Supreme Court justices voted on each of the 1,193 cases. Their votes brought out some interesting facts and information.

In addition, in assembling this work I learned about *per curiam* cases, which translated from Latin means *by the Court*. Many *per curiam* decisions do not show how the justices voted on those cases. However, in unanimous *per curiam* decisions, or when there is a concurring or dissenting *per curiam* opinion, it's generally easy to see which justice voted which way.

Per curiam tie votes, 3–3 and 4–4, are published by the U.S. Supreme Court without disclosing how the justices voted (see Methodology on page 283). In such tie votes, the U.S. Supreme Court does, however, usually include the name(s) of the justice(s) not voting on such cases and publishes which prior justice's seat may be vacant at that time.

In part because it is not clear which justices voted on which side of the 3–3 and 4–4 *per curiam* decisions, and in part because the split decisions are inconclusive of the U.S. Supreme Court's mind, the nine such cases[10]—one 3–3 vote and eight 4–4 votes—are not included in this work.

---

[10] Those nine cases are 1. *Hyun v. Landon* (350 U.S. 990); 2. *School Board of the City of Richmond, Virginia v. State Board of Education* (412 U.S. 92); 3. *Common Cause v. Schmitt* (455 U.S. 129); 4. *Reagan v. Abourezk* (484 U.S. 1), the only 3–3 *per curiam* vote located; 5. *Tompkins v. Texas* (490 U.S. 754); 6. *Flores-Villar v. United States* (564 U.S. 210); 7. *Friedrichs v. California Teachers Ass'n* (136 S.Ct. 1083; 578 U.S. _); 8. *Dollar General Corp. v. Mississippi Band of Choctaw Indians* (136 S.Ct. 2159; 579 U.S. _); and 9. *United States v. Texas* (136 S.Ct. 2271; 579 U.S. _).

Chart: Votes of Each Justice on Each ACLU/SCOTUS Case from 1925 to 2019 (by Date)[11]

	Case Name	Date Decided	Case #	Justices and Their Votes (W = ACLU Win; L = ACLU Loss)								
A	B	C	D	E	F	G	H	I	J	K	L	M
				Holmes	Brandeis	Sanford	Taft	Van Devanter	McReynolds	Sutherland	Butler	Stone
1	Gitlow v. New York	June 8, 1925	268 U.S. 652	W	W	L	L	L	L	L	L	L
2	Whitney v. California	May 16, 1927	274 U.S. 357	L	L	L	L	L	L	L	L	L
3	Stromberg v. California	May 18, 1931	283 U.S. 359	W	W	Roberts, O. W	Hughes W	W	L	W	L	W
4	Powell v. Alabama	November 7, 1932	287 U.S. 45	Cardozo W	W	W	W	W	L	W	L	W
5	Patterson v. Alabama	April 1, 1935	294 U.S. 600	W	W	W	W	W	Took no part in the decision	W	W	W
6	De Jonge v. Oregon	January 4, 1937	299 U.S. 353	W	W	W	W	W	W	W	W	Took no part in the decision
7	Senn v. Tile Layers Protective Union	May 24, 1937	301 U.S. 468	W	W	W	W	L	L	L	L	W
8	Lovell v. City of Griffin	March 28, 1938	303 U.S. 444	Took no part in the decision	W	W	W	Black W	W	Reed W	W	W

[11] These cases are listed in "Date Decided" order in Column C, with the earliest cases first. If there are cases with the same date, then they will be listed by Case number in Column D, from lowest to highest case number.

A	B Case Name	C Date Decided	D Case #	E Cardozo	F Brandeis	G Roberts, O.	H Hughes	I Black	J McReynolds	K Reed	L Butler	M Stone
						Justices and Their Votes (W = ACLU Win; L = ACLU Loss)						
9	Hague v. Committee for Industrial Organization	June 5, 1939	307 U.S. 496	Frankfurter Took no part in the decision	Douglas Took no part in the decision	W	W	W	L	W	L	W
10	Schneider v. New Jersey	November 22, 1939	308 U.S. 147	W	W	W	W	W	L	W	VACANT SEAT	W
11	Carlson v. California	April 22, 1940	310 U.S. 106	W	W	W	W	W	L	W	Murphy W	W
12	Minersville School District v. Gobitis	June 3, 1940	310 U.S. 586	L	L	L	L	L	L	L	L	W
13	Edwards v. California	November 24, 1941	314 U.S. 160	W	W	W	Jackson W	W	Byrnes W	W	W	W
14	Bridges v. California	December 8, 1941	314 U.S. 252	L	W	L	W	W	L	W	W	L
15	Valentine v. Chrestensen	April 13, 1942	316 U.S. 52	L	L	L	L	L	L	L	L	L
16	Betts v. Brady	June 1, 1942	316 U.S. 455	L	W	L	L	W	L	L	W	L
17	Jones v. City of Opelika	May 3, 1943	319 U.S. 105	L	W	L	L	W	Rutledge W	L	W	W
18	Martin v. City of Struthers	May 3, 1943	319 U.S. 141	L	W	L	L	W	W	L	W	W

A	B	C	D	E	F	G	H	I	J	K	L	M
	Case Name	**Date Decided**	**Case #**	**Justices and Their Votes** (W = ACLU Win; L = ACLU Loss)								
				Frankfurter	Douglas	Roberts, O.	Jackson	Black	Rutledge	Reed	Murphy	Stone
19	National Broadcasting Co. v. United States	May 10, 1943	319 U.S. 190	W	W	L	W	Took no part in the decision	Took no part in the decision	W	L	W
20	Taylor v. Mississippi	June 14, 1943	319 U.S. 583	W	W	W	W	W	W	W	W	W
21	West Virginia State Board of Education v. Barnette	June 14, 1943	319 U.S. 624	L	W	L	W	W	W	L	W	W
22	Hirabayashi v. United States	June 21, 1943	320 U.S. 81	L	L	L	L	L	L	L	L	L
23	Yasui v. United States	June 21, 1943	320 U.S. 115	L	L	L	L	L	L	L	L	L
24	Falbo v. United States	January 3, 1944	320 U.S. 549	L	L	L	L	L	L	L	W	L
25	Follett v. Town of McCormick	March 27, 1944	321 U.S. 573	L	W	L	L	W	W	W	W	W
26	Lyons v. Oklahoma	June 5, 1944	322 U.S. 596	L	L	L	L	W	W	L	W	L
27	Smith v. Allwright	June 12, 1944, As Amended (April 3, 1944)	321 U.S. 649	W	W	L	W	W	W	W	W	W
28	Steele v. Louisville & Nashville Railroad Co.	December 18, 1944	323 U.S. 192	W	W	W	W	W	W	W	W	W

A	B	C	D	E Frankfurter	F Douglas	G Roberts, O.	H Jackson	I Black	J Rutledge	K Reed	L Murphy	M Stone
Case Name	Date Decided	Case #				Justices and Their Votes (W = ACLU Win; L = ACLU Loss)						
29	Tunstall v. Brotherhood of Locomotive Firemen	December 18, 1944	323 U.S. 210	W	W	W	W	W	W	W	W	W
30	Korematsu v. United States	December 18, 1944	323 U.S. 214	L	L	W	W	L	L	L	W	L
31	Ex parte Endo	December 18, 1944	323 U.S. 283	W	W	W	W	W	W	W	W	W
32	Thomas v. Collins	January 8, 1945	323 U.S. 516	L	W	L	W	W	W	L	W	L
33	Alabama State Federation of Labor v. McAdory	June 11, 1945	325 U.S. 450	L	L	L	L	L	L	L	L	L
34	Congress of Industrial Organizations v. McAdory	June 11, 1945	325 U.S. 472	L	L	L	L	L	L	L	L	L
35	Hill v. Florida	June 11, 1945	325 U.S. 538	L	W	L	W	W	W	W	W	W
36	Railway Mail Ass'n. v. Corsi	June 18, 1945	326 U.S. 88	W	W	W	W	W	W	W	W	W
37	Bridges v. Wixon	June 18, 1945	326 U.S. 135	L	W	L	Took no part in the decision	W	W	W	W	L
38	Hannegan v. Esquire, Inc.	February 4, 1946	327 U.S. 146	W	W	Burton W	Took no part in the decision	W	W	W	W	W

	Case Name	Date Decided	Case #	Justices and Their Votes (W = ACLU Win; L = ACLU Loss)								
A	B	C	D	E	F	G	H	I	J	K	L	M
				Frankfurter	Douglas	Burton	Jackson	Black	Rutledge	Reed	Murphy	Stone
39	Duncan v. Kahanamoku	February 25, 1946	327 U.S. 304	L	W	L	Took no part in the decision	W	W	W	W	W
40	Bell v. Hood	April 1, 1946	327 U.S. 678	W	W	L	Took no part in the decision	W	W	W	W	L
41	Girouard v. United States	April 22, 1946	328 U.S. 61	L	W	W	Took no part in the decision	W	W	L	W	L
42	Pennekamp v. Florida	June 3, 1946	328 U.S. 331	W	W	W	Took no part in the decision	W	W	W	W	VACANT SEAT
43	Morgan v. Virginia	June 3, 1946	328 U.S. 373	W	W	L	Took no part in the decision	W	W	W	W	VACANT SEAT
44	Everson v. Board of Education	February 10, 1947	330 U.S. 1	W	L	W	W	L	W	L	L	Vinson L
45	Sipuel v. Board of Regents of University of Oklahoma	January 12, 1948	332 U.S. 631	W	W	W	W	W	W	W	W	W
46	Oyama v. California	January 19, 1948	332 U.S. 633	W	W	L	L	W	W	L	W	W
47	Musser v. Utah	February 9, 1948	333 U.S. 95	W	L	W	W	W	L	W	L	W

	Case Name	Date Decided	Case #	Justices and Their Votes (W = ACLU Win; L = ACLU Loss)								
A	B	C	D	E Frankfurter	F Douglas	G Burton	H Jackson	I Black	J Rutledge	K Reed	L Murphy	M Vinson
48	Illinois ex rel. McCollum v. Board of Education	March 8, 1948	333 U.S. 203	W	W	W	W	W	W	L	W	W
49	Winters v. New York	March 29, 1948	333 U.S. 507	L	W	L	L	W	W	W	W	W
50	Shelley v. Kraemer	May 3, 1948	334 U.S. 1	W	W	W	Took no part in the decision	W	Took no part in the decision	Took no part in the decision	W	W
51	Hurd v. Hodge	May 3, 1948	334 U.S. 24	W	W	W	Took no part in the decision	W	Took no part in the decision	Took no part in the decision	W	W
52	United States v. Paramount Pictures, Inc	May 3, 1948	334 U.S. 131	W	L	L	Took no part in the decision	L	L	L	L	L
53	Price v. Johnston	May 24, 1948	334 U.S. 266	L	W	W	L	W	W	L	W	L
54	Takahashi v. Fish and Game Commission	June 7, 1948	334 U.S. 410	W	W	W	L	W	W	L	W	W
55	United States v. Congress of Industrial Organizations	June 21, 1948	335 U.S. 106	W	W	W	W	W	W	W	W	W
56	Kovacs v. Cooper	January 31, 1949	336 U.S. 77	L	W	L	L	W	W	L	W	L
57	Stainback v. Mo Hock Ke Lok Po	March 14, 1949	336 U.S. 368	L	L	L	L	L	L	L	L	L

	Case Name	Date Decided	Case #	Justices and Their Votes (W = ACLU Win; L = ACLU Loss)								
A	B	C	D	E	F	G	H	I	J	K	L	M
				Frankfurter	Douglas	Burton	Jackson	Black	Rutledge	Reed	Murphy	Vinson
58	Terminiello v. City of Chicago	May 16, 1949	337 U.S. 1	L	W	L	L	W	W	W	W	L
59	Sinclair v. United States	January 9, 1950	338 U.S. 908	W	W	W	W	W	Clark W	W	Minton W	W
60	United States ex rel. Knauff v. Shaughnessy	January 16, 1950	338 U.S. 537	W	Took no part in the decision	L	W	W	Took no part in the decision	L	L	L
61	American Communications Ass'n v. Douds	May 8, 1950	339 U.S. 382	L	Took no part in the decision	L	L	W	Took no part in the decision	L	Took no part in the decision	L
62	Hughes v. Superior Court	May 8, 1950	339 U.S. 460	L	Took no part in the decision	L	L	L	L	L	L	L
63	McLaurin v. Oklahoma State Regents for Higher Education	June 5, 1950	339 U.S. 637	W	W	W	W	W	W	W	W	W
64	Kunz v. New York	January 15, 1951	340 U.S. 290	W	W	W	L	W	W	W	W	W
65	Collins v. Hardyman	June 4, 1951	341 U.S. 651	L	W	W	L	W	L	L	L	L
66	Garner v Board of Public Works	June 4, 1951	341 U.S. 716	W	W	W	L	W	L	L	L	L
67	Rochin v. California	January 2, 1952	342 U.S. 165	W	W	W	W	W	W	W	Took no part in the decision	W

	Case Name	Date Decided	Case #	Justices and Their Votes (W = ACLU Win; L = ACLU Loss)								
A	B	C	D	E	F	G	H	I	J	K	L	M
				Frankfurter	Douglas	Burton	Jackson	Black	Clark	Reed	Minton	Vinson
68	Doremus v. Board of Education	March 3, 1952	342 U.S. 429	L	W	W	L	L	L	W	L	L
69	Adler v. Board of Education	March 3, 1952	342 U.S. 485	W	W	L	L	W	L	L	L	L
70	Carlson v. Landon	March 10, 1952	342 U.S. 524	W	W	W	L	W	L	L	L	L
71	United States v. Spector	April 7, 1952	343 U.S. 169	W	L	L	W	W	Took no part in the decision	L	L	L
72	Brunner v. United States	April 7, 1952	343 U.S. 918	Took no part in the decision	L	W	W	W	W	L	W	W
73	Beauharnais v. Illinois	April 28, 1952	343 U.S. 250	L	W	L	W	W	L	W	L	L
74	Joseph Burstyn, Inc. v. Wilson	May 26, 1952	343 U.S. 495	W	W	W	W	W	W	W	W	W
75	Wieman v. Updegraff	December 15, 1952	344 U.S. 183	W	W	W	Took no part in the decision	W	W	W	W	W
76	Albertson v. Millard	March 16, 1953	345 U.S. 242	W	L	W	W	L	W	W	W	W
77	Barrows v. Jackson	June 15, 1953	346 U.S. 249	W	W	W	Took no part in the decision	W	W	Took no part in the decision	W	L

	Case Name	Date Decided	Case #	Justices and Their Votes (W = ACLU Win; L = ACLU Loss)								
A	B	C	D	E	F	G	H	I	J	K	L	M
				Frankfurter	Douglas	Burton	Jackson	Black	Clark	Reed	Minton	Vinson
78	Superior Films, Inc. v. Department of Education	January 18, 1954	346 U.S. 587	W	W	W	W	W	W	W	W	Warren W
79	Brown v. Board of Education	May 17, 1954	347 U.S. 483	W	W	W	W	W	W	W	W	W
80	Emspak v. United States	May 23, 1955	349 U.S. 190	W	W	W	Harlan L	W	W	L	L	W
81	Peters v. Hobby	June 6, 1955	349 U.S. 331	W	W	L	W	W	W	L	W	W
82	Gonzales v. Landon	December 12, 1955	350 U.S. 920	W	W	W	W	W	W	W	W	W
83	Pennsylvania ex rel. Herman v. Claudy	January 9, 1956	350 U.S. 116	W	W	W	W	W	W	W	W	W
84	Costello v. United States	March 5, 1956	350 U.S. 359	L	L	L	Took no part in the decision	L	Took no part in the decision	L	L	L
85	Pennsylvania v. Nelson	April 2, 1956	350 U.S. 497	W	W	L	W	W	W	L	L	W
86	Slochower v. Board of Higher Education	April 9, 1956	350 U.S. 551	W	W	L	L	W	W	L	L	W
87	Communist Party of the United States v. Subversive Activities Control Board	April 30, 1956	351 U.S. 115	W	W	W	W	W	L	L	L	W

	Case Name	Date Decided	Case #	Justices and Their Votes (W = ACLU Win; L = ACLU Loss)								
A	B	C	D	E	F	G	H	I	J	K	L	M
				Frankfurter	Douglas	Burton	Harlan	Black	Clark	Reed	Minton	Warren
88	Black v. Cutter Laboratories	June 4, 1956	351 U.S. 292	L	W	L	L	W	L	L	L	W
89	Cole v. Young	June 11, 1956	351 U.S. 536	W	W	W	W	W	L	L	L	W
90	Walker v. City of Hutchinson	December 10, 1956	352 U.S. 112	L	W	L	W	W	W	W	Brennan Took no part in the decision	W
91	Butler v. Michigan	February 25, 1957	352 U.S. 380	W	W	W	W	W	W	W	W	W
92	Schware v. Bd. of Bar Exam'rs of N. M.	May 6, 1957	353 U.S. 232	W	W	W	W	W	W	Whittaker Took no part in the decision	W	W
93	Konigsberg v. State Bar of California	May 6, 1957	353 U.S. 252	L	W	W	L	W	L	Took no part in the decision	W	W
94	Watkins v. United States	June 17, 1957	354 U.S. 178	W	W	Took no part in the decision	W	W	L	Took no part in the decision	W	W

A	B	C	D	E	F	G	H	I	J	K	L	M
	Case Name	**Date Decided**	**Case #**	**Justices and Their Votes** (W = ACLU Win; L = ACLU Loss)								
				Frankfurter	Douglas	Burton	Harlan	Black	Clark	Whittaker	Brennan	Warren
95	Yates v. United States	June 17, 1957	354 U.S. 298	W	W	W	W	W	L	Took no part in the decision	Took no part in the decision	W
96	Kingsley Books, Inc. v. Brown	June 24, 1957	354 U.S. 436	L	W	L	L	W	L	L	W	W
97	Roth v. United States	June 24, 1957	354 U.S. 476	L	W	L	W	W	L	L	L	L
98	Lightfoot v. United States	October 14, 1957	355 U.S. 2	W	W	W	W	W	W	W	W	W
99	Scales v. United States	October 15, 1957	355 U.S. 1	W	W	W	W	W	W	W	W	W
100	Staub v. City of Baxley	January 13, 1958	355 U.S. 313	L	W	W	W	W	L	W	W	W
101	Wilson v. Loew's, Inc.	March 3, 1958	355 U.S. 597	L	W	L	L	L	L	L	L	L
102	Trop v. Dulles	March 31, 1958	356 U.S. 86	L	W	L	L	W	L	W	W	W
103	Kent v. Dulles	June 16, 1958	357 U.S. 116	W	W	L	L	W	L	L	W	W
104	Crooker v. California	June 30, 1958	357 U.S. 433	L	W	L	L	W	L	L	W	W
105	Lerner v. Casey	June 30, 1958	357 U.S. 468	L	W	L	L	W	L	L	W	W
106	Speiser v. Randall	June 30, 1958	357 U.S. 513	W	W	W	W	W	L	W	W	Took no part in the decision

A	B	C	D	E	F	G	H	I	J	K	L	M
	Case Name	Date Decided	Case #	Justices and Their Votes (W = ACLU Win; L = ACLU Loss)								
				Frankfurter	Douglas	Burton	Harlan	Black	Clark	Whittaker	Brennan	Warren
107	First Unitarian Church v. County of Los Angeles	June 30, 1958	357 U.S. 545	W	W	W	W	W	L	W	W	Took no part in the decision
108	Barenblatt v. United States	June 8, 1959	360 U.S. 109	L	W	Stewart L	L	W	L	L	W	W
109	Greene v. McElroy	June 29, 1959	360 U.S. 474	W	W	W	W	W	L	W	W	W
110	Farmers Educational & Cooperative Union v. WDAY, Inc.	June 29, 1959	360 U.S. 525	L	W	L	L	W	W	L	W	W
111	Smith v. California	December 14, 1959	361 U.S. 147	W	W	W	W	W	W	W	W	W
112	Nelson v. Los Angeles County	February 29, 1960	362 U.S. 1	L	W	L	L	W	L	L	W	Took no part in the decision
113	Talley v. California	March 7, 1960	362 U.S. 60	L	W	W	W	W	L	L	W	W
114	De Veau v. Braisted	June 6, 1960	363 U.S. 144	L	W	L	Took no part in the decision	W	L	L	L	W
115	Rios v. United States	June 27, 1960	364 U.S. 253	L	W	W	L	W	L	L	W	W
116	Gomillion v. Lightfoot	November 14, 1960	364 U.S. 339	W	W	W	W	W	W	W	W	W

	Case Name	Date Decided	Case #	Justices and Their Votes (W = ACLU Win; L = ACLU Loss)								
A	B	C	D	E	F	G	H	I	J	K	L	M
				Frankfurter	Douglas	Stewart	Harlan	Black	Clark	Whittaker	Brennan	Warren
117	Times Film Corp. v. Chicago	January 23, 1961	365 U.S. 43	L	W	L	L	W	L	L	W	W
118	Pugach v. Dollinger	February 27, 1961	365 U.S. 458	L	W	L	L	L	L	L	L	W
119	Saldana v. United States	April 3, 1961	365 U.S. 646	W	W	W	W	W	W	W	W	W
120	Konigsberg v. State Bar of California	April 24, 1961	366 U.S. 36	L	W	L	L	W	L	L	W	W
121	In re Anastaplo	April 24, 1961	366 U.S. 82	L	W	L	L	W	L	L	W	W
122	Two Guys from Harrison-Allentown, Inc. v. McGinley	May 29, 1961	366 U.S. 582	L	W	L	L	L	L	L	L	L
123	Gallagher v. Crown Kosher Super Market of Massachusetts, Inc.	May 29, 1961	366 U.S. 617	L	W	W	L	L	L	L	W	L
124	Communist Party v. Subversive Activities Control Board	June 5, 1961	367 U.S. 1	L	W	L	L	W	L	L	W	W
125	Scales v. United States	June 5, 1961	367 U.S. 203	L	W	L	L	W	L	L	W	W
126	Gori v. United States	June 12, 1961	367 U.S. 364	L	W	L	L	W	L	L	W	W
127	Torcaso v. Watkins	June 19, 1961	367 U.S. 488	W	W	W	W	W	W	W	W	W

A	B	C	D	Justices and Their Votes (W = ACLU Win; L = ACLU Loss)								
	Case Name	Date Decided	Case #	Frankfurter	Douglas	Stewart	Harlan	Black	Clark	Whittaker	Brennan	Warren
				E	F	G	H	I	J	K	L	M
128	Poe v. Ullman	June 19, 1961	367 U.S. 497	L	W	W	W	W	L	L	L	L
129	Mapp v. Ohio	June 19, 1961	367 U.S. 643	L	W	W	L	W	W	L	W	W
130	Hoyt v. Florida	November 20, 1961	368 U.S. 57	L	L	L	L	L	L	L	L	L
131	Rusk v. Cort	April 2, 1962	369 U.S. 367	L	W	W	L	W	L	White W	W	W
132	Lynch v. Overholser	May 21, 1962	369 U.S. 705	Took no part in the decision	W	W	W	W	L	Took no part in the decision	W	W
133	Russell v. United States	May 21, 1962	369 U.S. 749	Took no part in the decision	W	W	L	W	L	Took no part in the decision	W	W
134	Engel v. Vitale	June 25, 1962	370 U.S. 421	Took no part in the decision	W	L	W	W	W	Took no part in the decision	W	W
135	Schroeder v. City of New York	December 17, 1962	371 U.S. 208	Goldberg W	W	W	W	W	W	W	W	W
136	Kennedy v. Mendoza-Martinez	February 18, 1963	372 U.S. 144	W	W	L	L	W	L	L	W	W

A	B	C	D	E	F	G	H	I	J	K	L	M
	Case Name	**Date Decided**	**Case #**	Goldberg	Douglas	Stewart	Harlan	Black	Clark	White	Brennan	Warren
137	Gideon v. Wainwright	March 18, 1963	372 U.S. 335	W	W	W	W	W	W	W	W	W
138	White v. Maryland	April 29, 1963	373 U.S. 59	W	W	W	W	W	W	W	W	W
139	McNeese v. Board of Education	June 3, 1963	373 U.S. 668	W	W	W	L	W	W	W	W	W
140	Ker v. California	June 10, 1963	374 U.S. 23	W	W	L	L	L	L	L	W	W
141	Yellin v. United States	June 17, 1963	374 U.S. 109	W	W	L	L	W	L	L	W	W
142	School District of Abington Township v. Schempp	June 17, 1963	374 U.S. 203	W	W	L	W	W	W	W	W	W
143	Smith v. California	December 16, 1963	375 U.S. 259	W	W	W	W	W	W	W	W	W
144	New York Times Co. v. Sullivan	March 9, 1964	376 U.S. 254	W	W	W	W	W	W	W	W	W
145	Smith v. Pennsylvania	March 9, 1964	376 U.S. 354	W	W	W	W	W	W	W	W	W
146	Stoner v. California	March 23, 1964	376 U.S. 483	W	W	W	L	W	W	W	W	W
147	Ungar v. Sarafite	March 30, 1964	376 U.S. 575	W	W	L	L	W	L	L	L	L
148	United States v. Barnett	April 6, 1964	376 U.S. 681	W	W	L	L	W	L	L	L	W

Justices and Their Votes

(W = ACLU Win; L = ACLU Loss)

	Case Name	Date Decided	Case #	Justices and Their Votes (W = ACLU Win; L = ACLU Loss)								
A	B	C	D	E	F	G	H	I	J	K	L	M
				Goldberg	Douglas	Stewart	Harlan	Black	Clark	White	Brennan	Warren
149	Schneider v. Rusk	May 18, 1964	377 U.S. 163	W	W	W	L	W	L	L	Took no part in the decision	W
150	Baggett v. Bullitt	June 1, 1964	377 U.S. 360	W	W	W	L	W	L	W	W	W
151	Reynolds v. Sims	June 15, 1964	377 U.S. 533	W	W	W	L	W	W	W	W	W
152	Malloy v. Hogan	June 15, 1964	378 U.S. 1	W	W	L	L	W	L	L	W	W
153	Jacobellis v. Ohio	June 22, 1964	378 U.S. 184	W	W	W	L	W	L	W	W	L
154	Escobedo v. Illinois	June 22, 1964	378 U.S. 478	W	W	L	L	W	L	L	W	W
155	Aptheker v. Secretary of State	June 22, 1964	378 U.S. 500	W	W	W	L	W	L	L	W	W
156	Beck v. Ohio	November 23, 1964	379 U.S. 89	W	W	W	L	L	L	W	W	W
157	Calhoon v. Harvey	December 7, 1964	379 U.S. 134	L	W	L	L	L	L	L	L	L
158	Freedman v. Maryland	March 1, 1965	380 U.S. 51	W	W	W	W	W	W	W	W	W
159	United States v. Mississippi	March 8, 1965	380 U.S. 128	W	W	W	W	W	W	W	W	W
160	United States v. Seeger	March 8, 1965	380 U.S. 163	W	W	W	W	W	W	W	W	W

	Case Name	Date Decided	Case #	Justices and Their Votes (W = ACLU Win; L = ACLU Loss)								
A	B	C	D	E	F	G	H	I	J	K	L	M
				Goldberg	Douglas	Stewart	Harlan	Black	Clark	White	Brennan	Warren
161	Dombrowski v. Pfister	April 26, 1965	380 U.S. 479	W	W	Took no part in the decision	L	Took no part in the decision	L	W	W	W
162	American Committee for Protection of Foreign Born v. Subversive Activities Control Board	April 26, 1965	380 U.S. 503	W	L	W	L	L	W	Took no part in the decision	W	W
163	Veterans of the Abraham Lincoln Brigade v. Subversive Activities Control Board	April 26, 1965	380 U.S. 513	W	L	W	L	L	W	Took no part in the decision	W	W
164	Zemel v. Rusk	May 3, 1965	381 U.S. 1	W	W	L	L	W	L	L	L	L
165	Holt v. Virginia	May 17, 1965	381 U.S. 131	W	W	W	L	W	W	W	W	W
166	Lamont v. Postmaster General of the United States	May 24, 1965	381 U.S. 301	W	W	W	W	W	W	Took no part in the decision	W	W
167	United States v. Brown	June 7, 1965	381 U.S. 437	W	W	L	L	W	L	L	W	W
168	Griswold v. Connecticut	June 7, 1965	381 U.S. 479	W	W	L	W	L	W	W	W	W
169	Estes v. Texas	June 7, 1965	381 U.S. 532	W	W	L	W	L	W	L	L	W

	Case Name	Date Decided	Case #	Justices and Their Votes (W = ACLU Win; L = ACLU Loss)								
A	B	C	D	E	F	G	H	I	J	K	L	M
				Goldberg	Douglas	Stewart	Harlan	Black	Clark	White	Brennan	Warren
170	Albertson v. Subversive Activities Control Board	November 15, 1965	382 U.S. 70	Fortas W	W	W	W	W	W	Took no part in the decision	W	W
171	Rosenblatt v. Baer	February 21, 1966	383 U.S. 75	L	W	W	W	W	W	W	W	W
172	Ginzburg v. United States	March 21, 1966	383 U.S. 463	L	W	W	W	W	L	L	L	L
173	Harper v. Virginia Board of Elections	March 24, 1966	383 U.S. 663	W	W	L	L	L	W	W	W	W
174	Mills v. Alabama	May 23, 1966	384 U.S. 214	W	W	W	W	W	W	W	W	W
175	Sheppard v. Maxwell	June 6, 1966	384 U.S. 333	W	W	W	W	L	W	W	W	W
176	Miranda v. Arizona	June 13, 1966	384 U.S. 436	W	W	L	L	W	L	L	W	W
177	Gojack v. United States	June 13, 1966	384 U.S. 702	W	W	W	W	W	W	W	W	W
178	Johnson v. New Jersey	June 20, 1966	384 U.S. 719	L	W	L	L	W	L	L	L	L
179	Dennis v. United States	June 20, 1966	384 U.S. 855	W	L	W	W	L	W	W	W	W
180	Bond v. Floyd	December 5, 1966	385 U.S. 116	W	W	W	W	W	W	W	W	W
181	Hoffa v. United States	December 12, 1966	385 U.S. 293	Took no part in the decision	W	L	L	L	W	Took no part in the decision	L	W

	Case Name	Date Decided	Case #	Fortas	Douglas	Stewart	Harlan	Black	Clark	White	Brennan	Warren
A	B	C	D	E	F	G	H	I	J	K	L	M
182	Travis v. United States	January 10, 1967	385 U.S. 491	W	W	W	W	W	W	W	W	W
183	Spevack v. Klein	January 16, 1967	385 U.S. 511	W	W	L	L	W	L	L	W	W
184	Whitus v. Georgia	January 23, 1967	385 U.S. 545	W	W	W	W	W	W	W	W	W
185	Keyishian v. Board of Regents	January 23, 1967	385 U.S. 589	W	W	L	L	W	L	L	W	W
186	Klopfer v. North Carolina	March 13, 1967	386 U.S. 213	W	W	W	W	W	W	W	W	W
187	In re Gault	May 15, 1967	387 U.S. 1	W	W	L	W	W	W	W	W	W
188	Boutilier v. Immigration and Naturalization Service	May 22, 1967	387 U.S. 118	W	W	L	L	L	L	L	W	L
189	Reitman v. Mulkey	May 29, 1967	387 U.S. 369	W	W	L	L	L	L	W	W	W
190	Camara v. Municipal Court of City & County of San Francisco	June 5, 1967	387 U.S. 523	W	W	L	L	W	L	W	W	W
191	See v. City of Seattle	June 5, 1967	387 U.S. 541	W	W	L	L	W	L	W	W	W
192	Loving v. Virginia	June 12, 1967	388 U.S. 1	W	W	W	W	W	W	W	W	W
193	Berger v. New York	June 12, 1967	388 U.S. 41	W	W	W	L	L	W	L	W	W

	Case Name	Date Decided	Case #	Justices and Their Votes (W = ACLU Win; L = ACLU Loss)								
A	B	C	D	E	F	G	H	I	J	K	L	M
				Fortas	Douglas	Stewart	Harlan	Black	Clark	White	Brennan	Warren
194	Aday v. United States	June 12, 1967	388 U.S. 447	W	W	W	W	W	L	W	W	W
195	Mempa v. Rhay	November 13, 1967	389 U.S. 128	W	W	W	W	W	Marshall W	W	W	W
196	United States v. Robel	December 11, 1967	389 U.S. 258	W	W	W	L	W	Took no part in the decision	L	W	W
197	Massachusetts v. Painten	January 15, 1968	389 U.S. 560	W	W	L	L	W	W	L	W	W
198	Lee v. Washington	March 11, 1968	390 U.S. 333	W	W	W	W	W	W	W	W	W
199	Ginsberg v. New York	April 22, 1968	390 U.S. 629	W	W	L	L	W	L	L	L	L
200	Interstate Circuit, Inc. v. City of Dallas	April 22, 1968	390 U.S. 676	W	W	W	L	W	W	W	W	W
201	Levy v. Louisiana	May 20, 1968	391 U.S. 68	W	W	W	L	W	W	W	W	W
202	Amalgamated Food Employees Union Local 590 v. Logan Valley Plaza, Inc.	May 20, 1968	391 U.S. 308	W	W	W	L	L	W	L	W	W
203	Witherspoon v. Illinois	June 3, 1968	391 U.S. 510	W	W	W	L	L	W	L	W	W
204	Pickering v. Board of Education	June 3, 1968	391 U.S. 563	W	W	W	W	W	W	L	W	W

	Case Name	Date Decided	Case #	Justices and Their Votes (W = ACLU Win; L = ACLU Loss)								
A	B	C	D	E	F	G	H	I	J	K	L	M
				Fortas	Douglas	Stewart	Harlan	Black	Marshall	White	Brennan	Warren
205	Terry v. Ohio	June 10, 1968	392 U.S. 1	L	W	L	L	L	L	L	L	L
206	Sibron v. New York	June 10, 1968	392 U.S. 40	L	L	L	L	W	L	L	L	L
207	King v. Smith	June 17, 1968	392 U.S. 309	W	W	W	W	W	W	W	W	W
208	Jones v. Alfred H. Mayer Co.	June 17, 1968	392 U.S. 409	W	W	W	L	W	W	L	W	W
209	Powell v. Texas	June 17, 1968	392 U.S. 514	W	W	W	L	L	L	L	W	L
210	Epperson v. Arkansas	November 12, 1968	393 U.S. 97	W	W	W	W	W	W	W	W	W
211	Carroll v. President & Comm'rs of Princess Anne	November 19, 1968	393 U.S. 175	W	W	W	W	W	W	W	W	W
212	Johnson v. Avery	February 24, 1969	393 U.S. 483	W	W	W	W	L	W	L	W	W
213	Tinker v. Des Moines Independent Community School District	February 24, 1969	393 U.S. 503	W	W	W	L	L	W	W	W	W
214	Gregory v. City of Chicago	March 10, 1969	394 U.S. 111	W	W	W	W	W	W	W	W	W
215	Street v. New York	April 21, 1969	394 U.S. 576	L	W	W	W	L	W	L	W	L
216	Shapiro v. Thompson	April 21, 1969	394 U.S. 618	W	W	W	L	L	W	W	W	L

146

	Case Name	Date Decided	Case #	Justices and Their Votes (W = ACLU Win; L = ACLU Loss)								
A	B	C	D	E	F	G	H	I	J	K	L	M
				Fortas	Douglas	Stewart	Harlan	Black	Marshall	White	Brennan	Warren
217	Watts v. United States	April 21, 1969	394 U.S. 705	L	W	L	L	W	W	L	W	W
218	Leary v. United States	May 19, 1969	395 U.S. 6	VACANT SEAT	W	W	W	W	W	W	W	W
219	Immigration and Naturalization Service v. Stanisic	May 19, 1969	395 U.S. 62	VACANT SEAT	W	L	L	W	W	L	L	L
220	Red Lion Broadcasting Co. v. FCC	June 9, 1969	395 U.S. 367	VACANT SEAT	Took no part in the decision	W	W	W	W	W	W	W
221	Brandenburg v. Ohio	June 9, 1969	395 U.S. 444	VACANT SEAT	W	W	W	W	W	W	W	W
222	Powell v. McCormack	June 16, 1969	395 U.S. 486	VACANT SEAT	W	L	W	W	W	W	W	W
223	North Carolina v. Pearce	June 23, 1969	395 U.S. 711	Burger W	W	W	L	L	W	W	W	W
224	Brockington v. Rhodes	November 24, 1969	396 U.S. 41	L	L	L	L	L	L	L	L	VACANT SEAT
225	Hall v. Beals	November 24, 1969	396 U.S. 45	L	L	L	L	L	W	L	W	VACANT SEAT
226	Goldberg v. Kelly	March 23, 1970	397 U.S. 254	L	W	L	W	L	W	W	W	VACANT SEAT
227	Wheeler v. Montgomery	March 23, 1970	397 U.S. 280	L	W	L	W	L	W	W	W	VACANT SEAT

	Case Name	Date Decided	Case #	Justices and Their Votes (W = ACLU Win; L = ACLU Loss)								
A	B	C	D	E	F	G	H	I	J	K	L	M
				Burger	Douglas	Stewart	Harlan	Black	Marshall	White	Brennan	Warren
228	Rosado v. Wyman	April 6, 1970	397 U.S. 397	L	W	W	W	L	W	W	W	Blackmun Took no part in the decision
229	Walz v. Tax Commission	May 4, 1970	397 U.S. 664	L	W	L	L	L	L	L	L	Took no part in the decision
230	McMann v. Richardson	May 4, 1970	397 U.S. 759	L	W	L	L	L	W	L	W	Took no part in the decision
231	Maxwell v. Bishop	June 1, 1970	398 U.S. 262	W	W	W	W	L	Took no part in the decision	W	W	Took no part in the decision
232	Mulloy v. United States	June 15, 1970	398 U.S. 410	W	W	W	W	W	W	W	W	Took no part in the decision
233	Mitchell v. Donovan	June 15, 1970	398 U.S. 427	L	W	L	L	L	L	L	L	Took no part in the decision
234	United States v. Sisson	June 29, 1970	399 U.S. 267	L	L	W	W	W	W	L	W	Took no part in the decision

A	B	C	D					Justices and Their Votes				
	Case Name	Date Decided	Case #				(W = ACLU Win; L = ACLU Loss)					
				E	F	G	H	I	J	K	L	M
				Burger	Douglas	Stewart	Harlan	Black	Marshall	White	Brennan	Blackmun
235	Oregon v. Mitchell	December 21, 1970	400 U.S. 112	L	W	L	L	W	W	W	W	L
236	Phillips v. Martin Marietta Corp.	January 25, 1971	400 U.S. 542	W	W	W	W	W	W	W	W	W
237	Dyson v. Stein	February 23, 1971	401 U.S. 200	L	W	L	L	L	L	L	L	L
238	Byrne v. Karalexis	February 23, 1971	401 U.S. 216	L	Took no part in the decision	L	L	L	W	W	W	L
239	Gillette v. United States	March 8, 1971	401 U.S. 437	L	W	L	L	L	L	L	L	L
240	Schlanger v. Seamans	March 23, 1971	401 U.S. 487	L	L	W	L	L	L	L	L	L
241	Labine v. Vincent	March 29, 1971	401 U.S. 532	L	W	L	L	L	W	W	W	L
242	United States v. Vuitch	April 21, 1971	402 U.S. 62	L	W	W	L	L	W	L	W	L
243	Ehlert v. United States	April 21, 1971	402 U.S. 99	L	W	L	L	L	W	L	W	L
244	McGautha v. California	May 3, 1971	402 U.S. 183	L	W	L	L	L	W	L	W	L
245	Org. for a Better Austin v. Keefe	May 17, 1971	402 U.S. 415	W	W	W	L	W	W	W	W	W
246	Astrup v. I.N.S.	May 24, 1971	402 U.S. 509	W	W	W	W	W	W	W	W	W
247	Palmer v. City of Euclid	May 24, 1971	402 U.S. 544	W	W	W	W	W	W	W	W	W

A	B Case Name	C Date Decided	D Case #	E Burger	F Douglas	G Stewart	H Harlan	I Black	J Marshall	K White	L Brennan	M Blackmun
								Justices and Their Votes (W = ACLU Win; L = ACLU Loss)				
248	Gordon v. Lance	June 7, 1971	403 U.S. 1	L	L	L	L	L	W	L	W	L
249	Cohen v. California	June 7, 1971	403 U.S. 15	L	W	W	W	L	W	L	W	L
250	Whitcomb v. Chavis	June 7, 1971	403 U.S. 124	L	W	L	L	L	W	L	W	L
251	Connell v. Higginbotham	June 7, 1971	403 U.S. 207	W	W	W	W	W	W	W	W	W
252	Graham v. Richardson	June 14, 1971	403 U.S. 365	W	W	W	W	W	W	W	W	W
253	Bivens v. Six Unknown Named Agents of Federal Bureau of Narcotics	June 21, 1971	403 U.S. 388	L	W	W	W	L	W	W	W	L
254	New York Times Co. v. United States	June 30, 1971	403 U.S. 713	L	W	W	L	W	W	W	W	L
255	Reed v. Reed	November 22, 1971	404 U.S. 71	W	W	W	W	W	W	W	W	W
256	Diffenderfer v. Central Baptist Church of Miami	January 10, 1972	404 U.S. 412	W	L	W	Rehnquist Took no part in the decision	Powell Took no part in the decision	W	W	W	W

A	B	C	D	E	F	G	H	I	J	K	L	M
	Case Name	**Date Decided**	**Case #**	**Justices and Their Votes** (W = ACLU Win; L = ACLU Loss)								
				Burger	Douglas	Stewart	Rehnquist	Powell	Marshall	White	Brennan	Blackmun
257	Groppi v. Leslie	January 13, 1972	404 U.S. 496	W	W	W	Took no part in the decision	Took no part in the decision	W	W	W	W
258	Trbovich v. United Mine Workers of America	January 17, 1972	404 U.S. 528	W	L	W	Took no part in the decision	Took no part in the decision	W	W	W	W
259	Bd. of Regents of Univ. of Texas System v. New Left Education Project	January 24, 1972	404 U.S. 541	L	W	L	Took no part in the decision	Took no part in the decision	L	L	L	L
260	Dunn v. Blumstein	March 21, 1972	405 U.S. 330	L	W	W	Took no part in the decision	Took no part in the decision	W	W	W	W
261	Fein v. Selective Service System Local Board No. 7	March 21, 1972	405 U.S. 365	L	W	W	Took no part in the decision	Took no part in the decision	W	L	L	L
262	Eisenstadt v. Baird	March 22, 1972	405 U.S. 438	L	W	W	Took no part in the decision	Took no part in the decision	W	W	W	W
263	Weber v. Aetna Casualty & Surety Co.	April 24, 1972	406 U.S. 164	W	W	W	L	W	W	W	W	W
264	United States v. Biswell	May 15, 1972	406 U.S. 311	L	W	L	L	L	L	L	L	L
265	Strait v. Laird	May 22, 1972	406 U.S. 341	L	W	W	L	L	W	W	L	W

A	B	C	D									
	Case Name	**Date Decided**	**Case #**	**Justices and Their Votes** (W = ACLU Win; L = ACLU Loss)								
A	B	C	D	E	F	G	H	I	J	K	L	M
				Burger	Douglas	Stewart	Rehnquist	Powell	Marshall	White	Brennan	Blackmun
266	Apodaca v. Oregon	May 22, 1972	406 U.S. 404	L	W	W	L	L	W	L	W	L
267	Kastigar v. United States	May 22, 1972	406 U.S. 441	L	W	L	Took no part in the decision	L	W	L	Took no part in the decision	L
268	Zicarelli v. New Jersey State Commission of Investigation	May 22, 1972	406 U.S. 472	L	W	L	Took no part in the decision	L	W	L	Took no part in the decision	L
269	Sarno v. Illinois Crime Investigating Commission	May 22, 1972	406 U.S. 482	L	W	L	Took no part in the decision	L	W	L	Took no part in the decision	L
270	United States v. Midwest Video Corp.	June 7, 1972	406 U.S. 649	L	W	W	W	W	L	L	L	L
271	Colten v. Kentucky	June 12, 1972	407 U.S. 104	L	W	L	L	L	W	L	L	L
272	Adams v. Williams	June 12, 1972	407 U.S. 143	L	W	L	L	L	W	L	W	L
273	Flower v. United States	June 12, 1972	407 U.S. 197	L	W	W	L	W	W	W	W	L
274	United States v. United States District Court for the Eastern District of Michigan	June 19, 1972	407 U.S. 297	W	W	W	Took no part in the decision	W	W	W	W	W

	Case Name	Date Decided	Case #	Justices and Their Votes (W = ACLU Win; L = ACLU Loss)								
A	B	C	D	E	F	G	H	I	J	K	L	M
				Burger	Douglas	Stewart	Rehnquist	Powell	Marshall	White	Brennan	Blackmun
275	Pipefitters Local Union No. 562 v. United States	June 22, 1972	407 U.S. 385	L	W	W	W	L	W	W	W	Took no part in the decision
276	Lloyd Corp. v. Tanner	June 22, 1972	407 U.S. 551	L	W	W	L	L	W	L	W	L
277	Laird v. Tatum	June 26, 1972	408 U.S. 1	L	W	W	L	L	W	L	W	L
278	Gelbard v. United States	June 26, 1972	408 U.S. 41	L	W	W	L	L	W	W	W	L
279	Healy v. James	June 26, 1972	408 U.S. 169	W	W	W	W	W	W	W	W	W
280	Furman v. Georgia	June 29, 1972	408 U.S. 238	L	W	W	L	L	W	W	W	L
281	Morrissey v. Brewer	June 29, 1972	408 U.S. 471	W	W	W	W	W	W	W	W	W
282	Gravel v. United States	June 29, 1972	408 U.S. 606	L	W	W	L	L	W	L	W	L
283	Branzburg v. Hayes	June 29, 1972	408 U.S. 665	L	W	W	L	L	W	L	W	L
284	Kleindienst v. Mandel	June 29, 1972	408 U.S. 753	L	W	L	L	L	W	L	W	L
285	Moore v. Illinois	June 29, 1972	408 U.S. 786	W	L	L	W	L	L	W	W	W
286	California v. Krivda	October 24, 1972	409 U.S. 33	L	L	L	L	L	L	L	L	L

A	B	C	D	E	F	G	H	I	J	K	L	M
	Case Name	Date Decided	Case #	Justices and Their Votes (W = ACLU Win; L = ACLU Loss)								
				Burger	Douglas	Stewart	Rehnquist	Powell	Marshall	White	Brennan	Blackmun
287	Neil v. Biggers	December 6, 1972	409 U.S. 188	L	W	W	L	L	Took no part in the decision	L	W	L
288	District of Columbia v. Carter	January 10, 1973	409 U.S. 418	L	L	L	L	L	L	L	L	L
289	Gomez v. Perez	January 17, 1973	409 U.S. 535	W	W	L	L	W	W	W	W	W
290	Environmental Protection Agency v. Mink	January 22, 1973	410 U.S. 73	L	W	L	Took no part in the decision	L	W	L	W	L
291	Roe v. Wade	January 22, 1973	410 U.S. 113	W	W	W	L	W	W	L	W	W
292	Doe v. Bolton	January 22, 1973	410 U.S. 179	W	W	W	L	W	W	L	W	W
293	Tillman v. Wheaton-Haven Recreation Assn.	February 27, 1973	410 U.S. 431	W	W	W	W	W	W	W	W	W
294	Braden v. 30th Judicial Circuit Court of Kentucky	February 28, 1973	410 U.S. 484	L	W	W	L	L	W	W	W	W
295	Papish v. Bd. of Curators of Univ. of Missouri	March 19, 1973	410 U.S. 667	L	W	W	L	W	W	W	W	L
296	Salyer Land Co. v. Tulare Lake Basin Water Storage District	March 20, 1973	410 U.S. 719	L	W	L	L	L	W	L	W	L

	Case Name	Date Decided	Case #	Justices and Their Votes (W = ACLU Win; L = ACLU Loss)								
A	B	C	D	E	F	G	H	I	J	K	L	M
				Burger	Douglas	Stewart	Rehnquist	Powell	Marshall	White	Brennan	Blackmun
297	Associated Enterprises, Inc. v. Toltec Watershed Improvement District	March 20, 1973	410 U.S. 743	L	W	L	L	L	W	L	W	L
298	Rosario v. Rockefeller	March 21, 1973	410 U.S. 752	L	W	L	L	W	W	L	W	L
299	San Antonio Independent School District v. Rodriguez	March 21, 1973	411 U.S. 1	L	W	L	L	L	W	W	W	L
300	Ohio Mun. Judges Ass'n v. Davis	March 26, 1973	411 U.S. 144	L	L	L	L	L	L	L	L	L
301	Lemon v. Kurtzman	April 2, 1973	411 U.S. 192	L	W	W	L	L	Took no part in the decision	L	W	L
302	Davis v. United States	April 17, 1973	411 U.S. 233	L	W	L	L	L	W	L	W	L
303	United States v. Russell	April 24, 1973	411 U.S. 423	L	W	W	L	L	W	L	W	L
304	Brown v. Chote	May 7, 1973	411 U.S. 452	W	W	W	W	W	W	W	W	W
305	Preiser v. Rodriguez	May 7, 1973	411 U.S. 475	L	W	L	L	L	W	L	W	L
306	Frontiero v. Richardson	May 14, 1973	411 U.S. 677	W	W	W	L	W	W	W	W	W

A	B	C	D	E	F	G	H	I	J	K	L	M
	Case Name	**Date Decided**	**Case #**	**Justices and Their Votes** (W = ACLU Win; L = ACLU Loss)								
				Burger	Douglas	Stewart	Rehnquist	Powell	Marshall	White	Brennan	Blackmun
307	Hall v. Cole	May 21, 1973	412 U.S. 1	W	W	W	L	W	Took no part in the decision	L	W	W
308	Schneckloth v. Bustamonte	May 29, 1973	412 U.S. 218	L	W	L	L	L	W	L	W	L
309	Cupp v. Murphy	May 29, 1973	412 U.S. 291	L	W	L	L	L	L	L	W	L
310	Vlandis v. Kline	June 11, 1973	412 U.S. 441	L	L	W	L	W	W	W	W	W
311	Gilligan v. Morgan	June 21, 1973	413 U.S. 1	L	W	W	L	L	W	L	W	L
312	Miller v. California	June 21, 1973	413 U.S. 15	L	W	W	L	L	W	L	W	L
313	United States v. 12 200-Foot Reels of Super 8mm. Film	June 21, 1973	413 U.S. 123	L	W	W	L	L	W	L	W	L
314	United States v. Orito	June 21, 1973	413 U.S. 139	L	W	W	L	L	W	L	W	L
315	Keyes v. School District No. 1	June 21, 1973	413 U.S. 189	W	W	W	L	W	W	Took no part in the decision	W	W
316	Pittsburgh Press Co. v. Pittsburg Commission on Human Relations	June 21, 1973	413 U.S. 376	L	L	L	W	W	W	W	W	L

A	B Case Name	C Date Decided	D Case #	E Burger	F Douglas	G Stewart	H Rehnquist	I Powell	J Marshall	K White	L Brennan	M Blackmun
317	U.S. Civil Service Comm'n v. Nat'l Ass'n of Letter Carriers	June 25, 1973	413 U.S. 548	L	W	L	L	L	W	L	W	L
318	In re Griffiths	June 25, 1973	413 U.S. 717	L	W	W	L	W	W	W	W	W
319	Schlesinger v. Holtzman	August 4, 1973	414 U.S. 1321	W	L	W	W	W	W	W	W	W
320	United States v. Robinson	December 11, 1973	414 U.S. 218	L	W	L	L	L	W	L	W	L
321	United States v. Calandra	January 8, 1974	414 U.S. 338	L	W	L	L	L	W	L	W	L
322	Communist Party of Indiana v. Whitcomb	January 9, 1974	414 U.S. 441	W	W	W	W	W	W	W	W	W
323	Vachon v. New Hampshire	January 14, 1974	414 U.S. 478	L	W	W	L	W	W	L	W	W
324	Cleveland Board of Education v. LaFleur	January 21, 1974	414 U.S. 632	L	W	W	L	W	W	W	W	W
325	Hernandez v. Veterans' Administration	March 4, 1974	415 U.S. 391	W	W	W	W	W	W	W	W	W
326	Smith v. Goguen	March 25, 1974	415 U.S. 566	L	W	W	L	W	W	W	W	L
327	Storer v. Brown	March 26, 1974	415 U.S. 724	W	L	W	W	W	L	W	L	W
328	Village of Belle Terre v. Boraas	April 1, 1974	416 U.S. 1	L	L	L	L	L	W	L	W	L

A	B Case Name	C Date Decided	D Case #	E Burger	F Douglas	G Stewart	H Rehnquist	I Powell	J Marshall	K White	L Brennan	M Blackmun
329	Scheuer v. Rhodes	April 17, 1974	416 U.S. 232	W	Took no part in the decision	W	W	W	W	W	W	W
330	DeFunis v. Odegaard	April 23, 1974	416 U.S. 312	L	W	L	L	L	W	W	W	L
331	Kahn v. Shevin	April 24, 1974	416 U.S. 351	L	L	L	L	L	W	W	W	L
332	Eisen v. Carlisle & Jacquelin	May 28, 1974	417 U.S. 156	L	W	L	L	L	W	L	W	L
333	Corning Glass Works v. Brennan	June 3, 1974	417 U.S. 188	L	W	Took no part in the decision	L	W	W	W	W	L
334	Davis v. United States	June 10, 1974	417 U.S. 333	W	W	W	L	L	W	W	W	W
335	Wheeler v. Barrera	June 10, 1974	417 U.S. 402	L	W	L	L	L	L	L	L	L
336	Geduldig v. Aiello	June 17, 1974	417 U.S. 484	L	W	L	L	L	W	L	W	L
337	Parker v. Levy	June 19, 1974	417 U.S. 733	L	W	W	L	L	Took no part in the decision	L	W	L
338	Richardson v. Ramirez	June 24, 1974	418 U.S. 24	L	W	L	L	L	W	L	W	L
339	Hamling v. United States	June 24, 1974	418 U.S. 87	L	W	W	L	L	W	L	W	L

	Case Name	Date Decided	Case #	Justices and Their Votes (W = ACLU Win; L = ACLU Loss)								
A	B	C	D	E	F	G	H	I	J	K	L	M
				Burger	Douglas	Stewart	Rehnquist	Powell	Marshall	White	Brennan	Blackmun
340	United States v. Richardson	June 25, 1974	418 U.S. 166	L	W	W	L	L	W	L	W	L
341	Miami Herald Publishing Co. v. Tornillo	June 25, 1974	418 U.S. 241	W	W	W	W	W	W	W	W	W
342	Old Dominion Branch No. 496 v. Austin	June 25, 1974	418 U.S. 264	L	W	W	L	L	W	W	W	W
343	Lehman v. City of Shaker Heights	June 25, 1974	418 U.S. 298	L	L	W	L	W	W	L	W	L
344	Spence v. Washington	June 25, 1974	418 U.S. 405	L	W	W	L	W	W	L	W	W
345	Dorszynski v. United States	June 26, 1974	418 U.S. 424	W	W	W	W	W	W	W	W	W
346	Taylor v. Hayes	June 26, 1974	418 U.S. 488	W	W	W	L	W	W	W	W	W
347	Wolff v. McDonnell	June 26, 1974	418 U.S. 539	L	W	L	L	L	W	L	W	L
348	United States v. Nixon	July 24, 1974	418 U.S. 683	W	W	W	Took no part in the decision	W	W	W	W	W
349	Goss v. Lopez	January 22, 1975	419 U.S. 565	L	W	W	L	L	W	W	W	L
350	United States v. New Jersey State Lottery Commission	February 25, 1975	420 U.S. 371	Took no part in the decision	W	L	L	L	L	L	L	L

A	B	C	D	E	F	G	H	I	J	K	L	M
	Case Name	**Date Decided**	**Case #**	**Justices and Their Votes** (W = ACLU Win; L = ACLU Loss)								
				Burger	Douglas	Stewart	Rehnquist	Powell	Marshall	White	Brennan	Blackmun
351	Weinberger v. Wiesenfeld	March 19, 1975	420 U.S. 636	W	Took no part in the decision	W	W	W	W	W	W	W
352	Schlesinger v. Councilman	March 25, 1975	420 U.S. 738	L	W	L	L	L	W	L	W	L
353	McLucas v. DeChamplain	April 15, 1975	421 U.S. 21	L	L	L	L	L	L	L	L	L
354	National Labor Relations Board v. Sears, Roebuck & Co.	April 28, 1975	421 U.S. 132	L	L	L	L	Took no part in the decision	L	L	L	L
355	Renegotiation Board v. Grunmman Aircraft Engineering Corp.	April 28, 1975	421 U.S. 168	L	W	L	L	Took no part in the decision	L	L	L	L
356	Meek v. Pittenger	May 19, 1975	421 U.S. 349	L	W	W	L	W	W	L	W	W
357	Ellis v. Dyson	May 19, 1975	421 U.S. 426	L	W	L	W	L	W	W	W	W
358	Eastland v. United States Servicemen's Fund	May 27, 1975	421 U.S. 491	L	W	L	L	L	L	L	L	L
359	Bigelow v. Virginia	June 16, 1975	421 U.S. 809	W	W	W	L	W	W	L	W	W
360	Rogers v. United States	June 17, 1975	422 U.S. 35	W	W	W	W	W	W	W	W	W

	Case Name	Date Decided	Case #	Justices and Their Votes (W = ACLU Win; L = ACLU Loss)								
A	B	C	D	E	F	G	H	I	J	K	L	M
				Burger	Douglas	Stewart	Rehnquist	Powell	Marshall	White	Brennan	Blackmun
361	Staats v. American Civil Liberties Union aka ACLU v. Jennings, 365 F. Supp. 1041 (D.D.C. 1973)	June 23, 1975	422 U.S. 1030	L	Took no part in the decision	L	L	L	L	L	L	L
362	Preiser v. Newkirk	June 25, 1975	422 U.S. 395	L	W	L	L	L	L	L	L	L
363	O'Connor v. Donaldson	June 26, 1975	422 U.S. 563	W	W	W	W	W	W	W	W	W
364	Turner v. Dep't of Employment Security of Utah	November 17, 1975	423 U.S. 44	L	W	W	L	W	W	W	W	L
365	Rizzo v. Goode	January 21, 1976	423 U.S. 362	L	Stevens Took no part in the decision	L	L	L	W	L	W	W
366	Buckley v. Valeo	January 30, 1976	424 U.S. 1	L	Took no part in the decision	W	W	W	W	W	W	W
367	Liberty Mutual Insurance Co. v. Wetzel	March 23, 1976	424 U.S. 737	L	L	L	L	L	L	L	L	Took no part in the decision
368	Greer v. Spock	March 24, 1976	424 U.S. 828	L	Took no part in the decision	L	L	L	W	L	W	L

	Case Name	Date Decided	Case #	Justices and Their Votes (W = ACLU Win; L = ACLU Loss)								
A	B	C	D	E	F	G	H	I	J	K	L	M
				Burger	Stevens	Stewart	Rehnquist	Powell	Marshall	White	Brennan	Blackmun
369	Dep't of the Air Force v. Rose	April 21, 1976	425 U.S. 352	L	Took no part in the decision	W	L	W	W	W	W	L
370	Mathews v. Diaz	June 1, 1976	426 U.S. 67	L	L	L	L	L	L	L	L	L
371	Hampton v. Mow Sun Wong	June 1, 1976	426 U.S. 88	L	W	W	L	W	W	L	W	L
372	Young v. American Mini Theatres, Inc.	June 24, 1976	427 U.S. 50	L	L	W	L	L	W	L	W	W
373	Massachusetts Bd. of Retirement v. Murgia	June 25, 1976	427 U.S. 307	L	Took no part in the decision	L	L	L	W	L	L	L
374	North v. Russell	June 28, 1976	427 U.S. 328	L	Took no part in the decision	W	L	L	W	L	L	L
375	Fitzpatrick v. Bitzer	June 28, 1976	427 U.S. 445	W	W	W	W	W	W	W	W	W
376	Nebraska Press Association v. Stuart	June 30, 1976	427 U.S. 539	W	W	W	W	W	W	W	W	W
377	Stone v. Powell	July 6, 1976	428 U.S. 465	L	L	L	L	L	W	W	W	L
378	United States v. Martinez-Fuerte	July 6, 1976	428 U.S. 543	L	L	L	L	L	W	L	W	L
379	General Electric Co. v. Gilbert	December 7, 1976	429 U.S. 125	L	W	L	L	L	W	L	W	L

	Case Name	Date Decided	Case #	Justices and Their Votes (W = ACLU Win; L = ACLU Loss)								
A	B	C	D	E	F	G	H	I	J	K	L	M
				Burger	Stevens	Stewart	Rehnquist	Powell	Marshall	White	Brennan	Blackmun
380	Craig v. Boren	December 20, 1976	429 U.S. 190	L	W	W	L	W	W	W	W	W
381	Weatherford v. Bursey	February 22, 1977	429 U.S. 545	L	L	L	L	L	W	L	W	L
382	Califano v. Goldfarb	March 2, 1977	430 U.S. 199	L	W	L	L	W	W	W	W	L
383	Castaneda v. Partida	March 23, 1977	430 U.S. 482	L	W	L	L	L	W	W	W	W
384	Trimble v. Gordon	April 26, 1977	430 U.S. 762	L	W	L	L	W	W	W	W	L
385	Wooley v. Maynard	April 30, 1977	430 U.S. 705	W	W	W	L	W	W	L	W	L
386	Linmark Associates, Inc. v. Township of Willingboro	May 2, 1977	431 U.S. 85	W	W	W	Took no part in the decision	W	W	W	W	W
387	Moore v. City of East Cleveland, Ohio	May 31, 1977	431 U.S. 494	L	W	L	L	W	W	L	W	W
388	United States v. Ramsey	June 6, 1977	431 U.S. 606	L	W	L	L	L	W	L	W	L
389	Carey v. Population Services International	June 9, 1977	431 U.S. 678	L	W	W	L	W	W	W	W	W
390	Lefkowitz v. Cunningham	June 13, 1977	431 U.S. 801	W	L	W	Took no part in the decision	W	W	W	W	W

A	Case Name (B)	Date Decided (C)	Case # (D)	Burger (E)	Stevens (F)	Stewart (G)	Rehnquist (H)	Powell (I)	Marshall (J)	White (K)	Brennan (L)	Blackmun (M)
391	Smith v. Org. of Foster Families for Equality & Reform	June 13, 1977	431 U.S. 816	L	L	L	L	L	L	L	L	L
392	National Socialist Party of America v. Village of Skokie	June 14, 1977	432 U.S. 43	L	W	L	L	W	W	L	W	W
393	Trans World Airlines, Inc. v. Hardison	June 16, 1977	432 U.S. 63	L	L	L	L	L	W	L	W	L
394	United States v. Chadwick	June 21, 1977	433 U.S. 1	W	W	W	L	W	W	W	W	L
395	Hazelwood School District v. United States	June 27, 1977	433 U.S. 299	L	W	L	L	L	L	L	L	L
396	Dothard v. Rawlinson	June 27, 1977	433 U.S. 321	W	W	W	W	W	L	L	L	W
397	Dayton Board of Education v. Brinkman	June 27, 1977	433 U.S. 406	L	L	L	L	L	Took no part in the decision	L	L	L
398	Coker v. Georgia	June 29, 1977	433 U.S. 584	L	W	W	L	W	W	W	W	W
399	Nashville Gas Co. v. Satty	December 6, 1977	434 U.S. 136	W	W	W	W	W	W	W	W	W
400	Browder v. Director, Department of Corrections	January 10, 1978	434 U.S. 257	W	W	W	W	W	W	W	W	W

Justices and Their Votes (W = ACLU Win; L = ACLU Loss)

	Case Name	Date Decided	Case #	Justices and Their Votes (W = ACLU Win; L = ACLU Loss)								
A	B	C	D	E	F	G	H	I	J	K	L	M
				Burger	Stevens	Stewart	Rehnquist	Powell	Marshall	White	Brennan	Blackmun
401	Zablocki v. Redhail	January 18, 1978	434 U.S. 374	W	W	W	L	W	W	W	W	W
402	Procunier v. Navarette	February 22, 1978	434 U.S. 555	W	W	L	L	L	L	L	L	L
403	Board of Curators of the University of Missouri v. Horowitz	March 1, 1978	435 U.S. 78	L	L	L	L	L	W	L	W	W
404	Stump v. Sparkman	March 28, 1978	435 U.S. 349	L	L	W	L	W	W	L	Took no part in the decision	L
405	McDaniel v. Paty	April 19, 1978	435 U.S. 618	W	W	W	W	W	W	W	W	Took no part in the decision
406	City of Los Angeles, Department of Water and Power v. Manhart	April 25, 1978	435 U.S. 702	L	W	W	L	W	W	W	Took no part in the decision	W
407	Landmark Communications, Inc. v. Virginia	May 1, 1978	435 U.S. 829	W	W	W	W	Took no part in the decision	W	W	Took no part in the decision	W
408	Santa Clara Pueblo v. Martinez	May 15, 1978	436 U.S. 49	L	L	L	L	L	L	W	L	Took no part in the decision

	Case Name	Date Decided	Case #	Justices and Their Votes (W = ACLU Win; L = ACLU Loss)								
A	B	C	D	E	F	G	H	I	J	K	L	M
				Burger	Stevens	Stewart	Rehnquist	Powell	Marshall	White	Brennan	Blackmun
409	Marshall v. Barlow's, Inc.	May 23, 1978	436 U.S. 307	W	L	W	L	W	W	W	Took no part in the decision	L
410	In re Primus	May 30, 1978	436 U.S. 412	W	W	W	L	W	W	W	Took no part in the decision	W
411	Hutto v. Finney	June 23, 1978	437 U.S. 678	L	W	W	L	L	W	L	W	W
412	Franks v. Delaware	June 26, 1978	438 U.S. 154	L	W	W	L	W	W	W	W	W
413	Berry v. Doles	June 26, 1978	438 U.S. 190	W	L	W	L	W	W	W	W	W
414	Regents of the University of California v. Bakke	June 28, 1978	438 U.S. 265	W	W	W	W	L	L	L	L	L
415	Bell v. Ohio	July 3, 1978	438 U.S. 637	W	W	W	L	W	W	W	Took no part in the decision	W
416	FCC v. Pacifica Foundation	July 3, 1978	438 U.S. 726	L	L	W	L	L	W	W	W	L
417	Alabama v. Pugh	July 3, 1978	438 U.S. 781	L	W	L	L	L	W	L	W	L
418	Holt Civic Club v. City of Tuscaloosa	November 28, 1978	439 U.S. 60	L	L	L	L	L	W	W	W	L
419	Duren v. Missouri	January 9, 1979	439 U.S. 357	W	W	W	L	W	W	W	W	W

	Case Name	Date Decided	Case #	Justices and Their Votes (W = ACLU Win; L = ACLU Loss)								
A	B	C	D	E	F	G	H	I	J	K	L	M
				Burger	Stevens	Stewart	Rehnquist	Powell	Marshall	White	Brennan	Blackmun
420	Colautti v. Franklin	January 9, 1979	439 U.S. 379	L	W	W	L	W	W	L	W	W
421	Orr v. Orr	March 5, 1979	440 U.S. 268	L	W	W	L	L	W	W	W	W
422	NLRB v. Catholic Bishop of Chicago	March 21, 1979	440 U.S. 490	W	W	W	W	W	L	L	L	L
423	County of Los Angeles v. Davis	March 27, 1979	440 U.S. 625	W	L	W	W	W	L	L	L	L
424	Delaware v. Prouse	March 27, 1979	440 U.S. 648	W	W	W	L	W	W	W	W	W
425	FCC v. Midwest Video Corp.	April 2, 1979	440 U.S. 689	L	W	L	L	L	W	L	W	L
426	Burch v. Louisiana	April 17, 1979	441 U.S. 130	W	W	W	W	W	W	W	W	W
427	Caban v. Mohammed	April 24, 1979	441 U.S. 380	L	L	L	L	W	W	W	W	W
428	Bell v. Wolfish	May 14, 1979	441 U.S. 520	L	W	L	L	L	W	L	W	L
429	Greenholtz v. Inmates of the Nebraska Penal and Correctional Complex	May 29, 1979	442 U.S. 1	L	W	L	L	W	W	L	W	L
430	Dunaway v. New York	June 5, 1979	442 U.S. 200	L	W	W	L	Took no part in the decision	W	W	W	W

	Case Name	Date Decided	Case #	Justices and Their Votes (W = ACLU Win; L = ACLU Loss)								
A	B	C	D	E	F	G	H	I	J	K	L	M
				Burger	Stevens	Stewart	Rehnquist	Powell	Marshall	White	Brennan	Blackmun
431	Davis v. Passman	June 5, 1979	442 U.S. 228	L	W	L	L	L	W	W	W	W
432	Personnel Administrator of Massachusetts v. Feeney	June 5, 1979	442 U.S. 256	L	L	L	L	L	W	L	W	L
433	Babbitt v. United Farm Workers National Union	June 5, 1979	442 U.S. 289	L	L	L	L	L	W	L	W	L
434	Great American Federal Savings & Loan Association v. Novotny	June 11, 1979	442 U.S. 366	L	L	L	L	L	W	W	W	L
435	Southeastern Community College v. Davis	June 11, 1979	442 U.S. 397	L	L	L	L	L	L	L	L	L
436	Torres v. Puerto Rico	June 18, 1979	442 U.S. 465	W	W	W	W	W	W	W	W	W
437	Michigan v. DeFillippo	June 25, 1979	443 U.S. 31	L	W	L	L	L	W	L	W	L
438	Califano v. Westcott	June 25, 1979	443 U.S. 76	L	W	L	L	L	W	W	W	W
439	Smith v. Daily Mail Publishing Co.	June 26, 1979	443 U.S. 97	W	W	W	W	Took no part in the decision	W	W	W	W
440	Baker v. McCollan	June 26, 1979	443 U.S. 137	L	W	L	L	L	W	L	W	L

	Case Name	Date Decided	Case #	Justices and Their Votes (W = ACLU Win; L = ACLU Loss)								
A	B	C	D	E	F	G	H	I	J	K	L	M
				Burger	Stevens	Stewart	Rehnquist	Powell	Marshall	White	Brennan	Blackmun
441	United Steelworkers of America v. Weber	June 27, 1979	443 U.S. 193	L	Took no part in the decision	W	L	Took no part in the decision	W	W	W	W
442	Gannett Co. v. DePasquale	July 2, 1979	443 U.S. 368	L	L	L	L	L	W	W	W	W
443	Columbus Board of Education v. Penick	July 2, 1979	443 U.S. 449	W	W	W	L	L	W	W	W	W
444	Bellotti v. Baird	July 2, 1979	443 U.S. 622	W	W	W	W	W	W	L	W	W
445	Washington v. Washington State Commercial Passenger Fishing Vessel Ass'n	July 2, 1979	443 U.S. 658	W	W	L	L	L	W	W	W	W
446	Roberts v. United States	April 15, 1980	445 U.S. 552	L	L	L	L	L	W	L	L	L
447	Owen v. City of Independence	April 16, 1980	445 U.S. 622	L	W	L	L	L	W	W	W	W
448	Carlson v. Green	April 22, 1980	446 U.S. 14	L	W	W	L	W	W	W	W	W
449	Wengler v. Druggists Mutual Insurance Co.	April 22, 1980	446 U.S. 142	W	W	W	L	W	W	W	W	W
450	United States v. Mendenhall	May 27, 1980	446 U.S. 544	L	W	L	L	L	W	W	W	L
451	Gomez v. Toledo	May 27, 1980	446 U.S. 635	W	W	W	W	W	W	W	W	W

	Case Name	Date Decided	Case #	Justices and Their Votes (W = ACLU Win; L = ACLU Loss)								
A	B	C	D	E	F	G	H	I	J	K	L	M
				Burger	Stevens	Stewart	Rehnquist	Powell	Marshall	White	Brennan	Blackmun
452	Supreme Court of Virginia v. Consumers Union of the United States, Inc.	June 2, 1980	446 U.S. 719	L	L	L	L	Took no part in the decision	L	L	L	L
453	PruneYard Shopping Center v. Robins	June 9, 1980	447 U.S. 74	W	W	W	W	W	W	W	W	W
454	Maine v. Thiboutot	June 25, 1980	448 U.S. 1	L	W	W	L	L	W	W	W	W
455	Harris v. McRae	June 30, 1980	448 U.S. 297	L	W	L	L	L	W	L	W	W
456	Fullilove v. Klutznick	July 2, 1980	448 U.S. 448	W	L	L	L	W	W	W	W	W
457	Richmond Newspapers, Inc. v. Virginia	July 2, 1980	448 U.S. 555	W	W	W	L	Took no part in the decision	W	W	W	W
458	Dennis v. Sparks	November 17, 1980	449 U.S. 24	W	W	W	W	W	W	W	W	W
459	Allen v. McCurry	December 9, 1980	449 U.S. 90	L	L	L	L	L	W	L	W	W
460	United States v. DiFrancesco	December 9, 1980	449 U.S. 117	L	W	L	L	L	W	W	W	L
461	Delta Air Lines, Inc. v. August	March 9, 1981	450 U.S. 346	L	W	L	L	W	W	W	W	W
462	Kirchberg v. Feenstra	March 23, 1981	450 U.S. 455	W	W	W	W	W	W	W	W	W

	Case Name	Date Decided	Case #	Justices and Their Votes (W = ACLU Win; L = ACLU Loss)								
A	B	C	D	E Burger	F Stevens	G Stewart	H Rehnquist	I Powell	J Marshall	K White	L Brennan	M Blackmun
463	Michael M. v. Superior Court of Sonoma County	March 23, 1981	450 U.S. 464	L	W	L	L	L	W	W	W	L
464	Thomas v. Review Board of the Indiana Employment Security Division	April 6, 1981	450 U.S. 707	W	W	W	L	W	W	W	W	W
465	Steagald v. United States	April 21, 1981	451 U.S. 204	W	W	W	L	W	W	L	W	W
466	Ball v. James	April 29, 1981	451 U.S. 355	L	L	L	L	L	W	W	W	W
467	University of Texas v. Camenisch	April 29, 1981	451 U.S. 390	W	W	W	W	W	W	W	W	W
468	Parratt v. Taylor	May 18, 1981	451 U.S. 527	L	L	L	L	L	W	L	L	L
469	Little v. Streater	June 1, 1981	452 U.S. 1	W	W	W	W	W	W	W	W	W
470	Lassiter v. Department of Social Services	June 1, 1981	452 U.S. 18	L	W	L	L	L	W	L	W	W
471	Schad v. Borough of Mount Ephraim	June 1, 1981	452 U.S. 61	L	W	W	L	W	W	W	W	W
472	Gulf Oil Co. v. Bernard	June 1, 1981	452 U.S. 89	W	W	W	W	W	W	W	W	W
473	Minnick v. California Department of Corrections	June 1, 1981	452 U.S. 105	W	W	L	W	W	W	W	W	W

A	B	C	D	E	F	G	H	I	J	K	L	M
	Case Name	Date Decided	Case #	Justices and Their Votes (W = ACLU Win; L = ACLU Loss)								
				Burger	Stevens	Stewart	Rehnquist	Powell	Marshall	White	Brennan	Blackmun
474	McDaniel v. Sanchez	June 1, 1981	452 U.S. 130	W	W	L	L	W	W	W	W	W
475	County of Washington v. Gunther	June 8, 1981	452 U.S. 161	L	W	L	L	L	W	W	W	W
476	Heffron v. International Society for Krishna Consciousness, Inc.	June 22, 1981	452 U.S. 640	L	W	L	L	L	W	L	W	W
477	Michigan v. Summers	June 22, 1981	452 U.S. 692	L	L	W	L	L	W	L	W	L
478	Rostker v. Goldberg	June 25, 1981	453 U.S. 57	L	L	L	L	L	W	W	W	L
479	California Medical Ass'n v. Federal Election Commission	June 26, 1981	453 U.S. 182	W	L	W	W	W	L	L	L	L
480	New York v. Belton	July 1, 1981	453 U.S. 454	L	L	L	L	L	W	W	W	L
481	Metromedia, Inc. v. City of San Diego	July 2, 1981	453 U.S. 490	L	L	W	L	W	W	W	W	W
482	Washington v. Chrisman	January 13, 1982	455 U.S. 1	L	L	O'Connor L	L	L	W	W	W	L
483	Smith v. Phillips	January 25, 1982	455 U.S. 209	L	W	L	L	L	W	L	W	L

A	B	C	D	E Burger	F Stevens	G O'Connor	H Rehnquist	I Powell	J Marshall	K White	L Brennan	M Blackmun
	Case Name	**Date Decided**	**Case #**	**Justices and Their Votes** (W = ACLU Win; L = ACLU Loss)								
484	Murphy v. Hunt	March 2, 1982	455 U.S. 478	L	L	L	L	L	L	W	L	L
485	Santosky v. Kramer	March 24, 1982	455 U.S. 745	L	W	L	L	W	W	L	W	W
486	Larson v. Valente	April 21, 1982	456 U.S. 228	L	W	L	L	W	W	L	W	W
487	Oregon v. Kennedy	May 24, 1982	456 U.S. 667	L	L	L	L	L	L	L	L	L
488	United Steelworkers v. Sadlowski	June 14, 1982	457 U.S. 102	W	L	L	L	L	L	W	W	W
489	Middlesex County Ethics Committee v. Garden State Bar Association	June 21, 1982	457 U.S. 423	L	L	L	L	L	L	L	L	L
490	Taylor v. Alabama	June 23, 1982	457 U.S. 687	L	W	L	L	L	W	W	W	W
491	Board of Education v. Pico	June 25, 1982	457 U.S. 853	L	W	L	L	L	W	W	W	W
492	Board Of Education v. Rowley	June 28, 1982	458 U.S. 176	L	L	L	L	L	W	W	W	L
493	Washington v. Seattle School District No. 1	June 30, 1982	458 U.S. 457	L	W	L	L	L	W	W	W	W
494	Mississippi Univ. for Women v. Hogan	July 1, 1982	458 U.S. 718	L	W	W	L	L	W	W	W	L
495	New York v. Ferber	July 2, 1982	458 U.S. 747	L	L	L	L	L	L	L	L	L

	Case Name	Date Decided	Case #	Justices and Their Votes (W = ACLU Win; L = ACLU Loss)								
A	B	C	D	E	F	G	H	I	J	K	L	M
				Burger	Stevens	O'Connor	Rehnquist	Powell	Marshall	White	Brennan	Blackmun
496	NAACP v. Claiborne Hardware Co.	July 2, 1982	458 U.S. 886	W	W	W	W	W	Took no part in the decision	W	W	W
497	Larkin v. Grendel's Den, Inc.	December 13, 1982	459 U.S. 116	W	W	W	L	W	W	W	W	W
498	Minneapolis Star & Tribune Co. v. Minnesota Commissioner of Revenue	March 29, 1983	460 U.S. 575	W	W	W	L	W	W	W	W	W
499	United States Postal Service Board of Governors v. Aikens	April 4, 1983	460 U.S. 711	L	L	L	L	L	L	L	L	L
500	Kush v. Rutledge	April 4, 1983	460 U.S. 719	W	W	W	W	W	W	W	W	W
501	Anderson v. Celebrezze	April 19, 1983	460 U.S. 780	W	W	L	L	L	W	L	W	W
502	Connick v. Myers	April 20, 1983	461 U.S. 138	L	W	L	L	L	W	L	W	W
503	United States v. Grace	April 20, 1983	461 U.S. 171	W	L	W	W	W	L	W	W	W
504	Martinez v. Bynum	May 2, 1983	461 U.S. 321	L	L	L	L	L	W	L	L	L
505	Kolender v. Lawson	May 2, 1983	461 U.S. 352	W	W	W	L	W	W	L	W	W

	Case Name	Date Decided	Case #	Justices and Their Votes (W = ACLU Win; L = ACLU Loss)								
A	B	C	D	E	F	G	H	I	J	K	L	M
				Burger	Stevens	O'Connor	Rehnquist	Powell	Marshall	White	Brennan	Blackmun
506	Boston Firefighters Union, Local 718 v. Boston Chapter, NAACP	May 16, 1983	461 U.S. 477	L	L	L	L	L	Took no part in the decision	L	L	L
507	Bob Jones University v. United States	May 24, 1983	461 U.S. 574	W	W	W	L	W	W	W	W	W
508	Illinois v. Gates	June 8, 1983	462 U.S. 213	L	W	L	L	L	W	L	W	L
509	Chappell v. Wallace	June 13, 1983	462 U.S. 296	L	L	L	L	L	L	L	L	L
510	Haring v. Prosise	June 13, 1983	462 U.S. 306	W	W	W	W	W	W	W	W	W
511	Bush v. Lucas	June 13, 1983	462 U.S. 367	L	L	L	L	L	L	L	L	L
512	City of Akron v. Akron Center for Reproductive Health, Inc.	June 15, 1983	462 U.S. 416	W	W	L	L	W	W	L	W	W
513	United States v. Place	June 20, 1983	462 U.S. 696	W	W	W	W	W	W	W	W	W
514	Bolger v. Youngs Drug Products Corp.	June 24, 1983	463 U.S. 60	W	W	W	W	W	W	W	Took no part in the decision	W
515	Shaw v. Delta Air Lines, Inc.	June 24, 1983	463 U.S. 85	W	W	W	W	W	W	W	W	W

	Case Name	Date Decided	Case #	Justices and Their Votes (W = ACLU Win; L = ACLU Loss)								
A	B	C	D	E	F	G	H	I	J	K	L	M
				Burger	Stevens	O'Connor	Rehnquist	Powell	Marshall	White	Brennan	Blackmun
516	City of Revere v. Massachusetts General Hospital	June 27, 1983	463 U.S. 239	W	W	W	W	W	W	W	W	W
517	Jones v. United States	June 29, 1983	463 U.S. 354	L	W	L	L	L	W	L	W	W
518	United States v. Sells Engineering, Inc.	June 30, 1983	463 U.S. 418	L	W	L	L	L	W	W	W	W
519	Guardians Ass'n v. Civil Service Commission	July 1, 1983	463 U.S. 582	L	W	L	L	L	W	L	W	W
520	United Brotherhood of Carpenters v. Scott	July 5, 1983	463 U.S. 825	L	L	W	L	L	W	L	W	W
521	Barefoot v. Estelle	July 6, 1983	463 U.S. 880	L	L	L	L	L	W	L	W	W
522	Arizona Governing Committee for Tax Deferred Annuity & Deferred Compensation Plans v. Norris	July 16, 1983	463 U.S. 1073	L	W	W	L	L	W	W	W	L
523	Migra v. Warren City School District Board of Education	January 23, 1984	465 U.S. 75	W	W	W	W	W	W	W	W	W
524	Flanagan v. United States	February 21, 1984	465 U.S. 259	W	W	W	W	W	W	W	W	W
525	Lynch v. Donnelly	March 5, 1984	465 U.S. 668	L	W	L	L	L	W	L	W	W

176

	Case Name	Date Decided	Case #	Justices and Their Votes (W = ACLU Win; L = ACLU Loss)								
A	B	C	D	E	F	G	H	I	J	K	L	M
				Burger	Stevens	O'Connor	Rehnquist	Powell	Marshall	White	Brennan	Blackmun
526	Heckler v. Mathews	March 5, 1984	465 U.S. 728	L	L	L	L	L	L	L	L	L
527	Blum v. Stenson	March 21, 1984	465 U.S. 886	W	W	W	W	W	W	W	W	W
528	Escambia County v. McMillan	March 27, 1984	466 U.S. 48	L	L	L	L	L	W	L	L	L
529	Oliver v. United States	April 17, 1984	466 U.S. 170	L	W	L	L	L	W	L	W	L
530	Immigration & Naturalization Service v. Delgado	April 17, 1984	466 U.S. 210	L	L	L	L	L	W	L	W	L
531	Justices of Boston Municipal Court v. Lydon	April 18, 1984	466 U.S. 294	L	L	L	L	L	L	L	L	L
532	Palmore v. Sidoti	April 25, 1984	466 U.S. 429	W	W	W	W	W	W	W	W	W
533	Bose Corp. v. Consumers Union, Inc.	April 30, 1984	466 U.S. 485	W	W	L	L	W	W	L	W	W
534	Pulliam v. Allen	May 14, 1984	466 U.S. 522	L	W	L	L	L	W	W	W	W
535	United States v. Cronic	May 14, 1984	466 U.S. 648	L	L	L	L	L	L	L	L	L
536	Welsh v. Wisconsin	May 15, 1984	466 U.S. 740	L	W	W	L	W	W	L	W	W

	Case Name	Date Decided	Case #	Justices and Their Votes (W = ACLU Win; L = ACLU Loss)								
A	B	C	D	E	F	G	H	I	J	K	L	M
				Burger	Stevens	O'Connor	Rehnquist	Powell	Marshall	White	Brennan	Blackmun
537	Members of the City Council of Los Angeles v. Taxpayers for Vincent	May 15, 1984	466 U.S. 789	L	L	L	L	L	W	L	W	W
538	Seattle Times Co. v. Rhinehart	May 21, 1984	467 U.S. 20	L	L	L	L	L	L	L	L	L
539	Hishon v. King & Spalding	May 22, 1984	467 U.S. 69	W	W	W	W	W	W	W	W	W
540	United States v. Gouveia	May 29, 1984	467 U.S. 180	L	L	L	L	L	W	L	L	L
541	New York v. Uplinger	May 30, 1984	467 U.S. 246	L	W	L	L	W	W	L	W	W
542	Immigration & Naturalization Service v. Stevic	June 5, 1984	467 U.S. 407	L	L	L	L	L	L	L	L	L
543	Capital Cities Cable, Inc. v. Crisp	June 18, 1984	467 U.S. 691	W	W	W	W	W	W	W	W	W
544	Secretary of State of Maryland. v. Joseph H. Munson Co.	June 26, 1984	467 U.S. 947	L	W	L	L	L	W	W	W	W
545	Burnett v. Grattan	June 27, 1984	468 U.S. 42	W	W	W	W	W	W	W	W	W
546	Davis v. Scherer	June 28, 1984	468 U.S. 183	L	W	L	L	L	W	L	W	W
547	Clark v. Community for Creative Non-Violence	June 29, 1984	468 U.S. 288	L	L	L	L	L	W	L	W	L

	Case Name	Date Decided	Case #	Justices and Their Votes (W = ACLU Win; L = ACLU Loss)								
A	B	C	D	E	F	G	H	I	J	K	L	M
				Burger	Stevens	O'Connor	Rehnquist	Powell	Marshall	White	Brennan	Blackmun
548	Hobby v. United States	July 2, 1984	468 U.S. 339	L	W	L	L	L	W	L	W	L
549	FCC v. League of Women Voters	July 2, 1984	468 U.S. 364	L	L	W	L	W	W	L	W	W
550	Berkemer v. McCarty	July 2, 1984	468 U.S. 420	W	W	W	W	W	W	W	W	W
551	Roberts v. United States Jaycees	July 3, 1984	468 U.S. 609	Took no part in the decision	W	W	W	W	W	W	W	Took no part in the decision
552	New Jersey v. T.L.O.	January 15, 1985	469 U.S. 325	L	W	L	L	L	W	L	W	L
553	Federal Election Commission v. National Conservative Political Action Committee	March 18, 1985	470 U.S. 480	W	W	W	W	W	L	L	L	W
554	Cleveland Board of Education v. Loudermill	March 19, 1985	470 U.S. 532	W	W	W	L	W	W	W	W	W
555	Anderson v. City of Bessemer	March 19, 1985	470 U.S. 564	W	W	W	W	W	W	W	W	W
556	Lindahl v. Office of Personnel Management	March 20, 1985	470 U.S. 768	L	W	L	L	W	W	L	W	W
557	Tony and Susan Alamo Foundation v. Secretary of Labor	April 23, 1985	471 U.S. 290	W	W	W	W	W	W	W	W	W

	Case Name	Date Decided	Case #	Justices and Their Votes (W = ACLU Win; L = ACLU Loss)								
A	B	C	D	E	F	G	H	I	J	K	L	M
				Burger	Stevens	O'Connor	Rehnquist	Powell	Marshall	White	Brennan	Blackmun
558	Zauderer v. Office of Disciplinary Counsel	May 28, 1985	471 U.S. 626	W	W	W	W	Took no part in the decision	W	W	W	W
559	Oklahoma City v. Tuttle	June 3, 1985	471 U.S. 808	L	W	L	L	Took no part in the decision	L	L	L	L
560	Wallace v. Jaffree	June 4, 1985	472 U.S. 38	L	W	W	L	W	W	L	W	W
561	Lowe v. Securities & Exchange Commission	June 10, 1985	472 U.S. 181	W	W	W	W	Took no part in the decision	W	W	W	W
562	Western Air Lines, Inc. v. Criswell	June 17, 1985	472 U.S. 400	W	W	W	W	Took no part in the decision	W	W	W	W
563	Maryland v. Macon	June 17, 1985	472 U.S. 463	L	L	L	L	L	W	L	W	L
564	McDonald v. Smith	June 19, 1985	472 U.S. 479	L	L	L	L	Took no part in the decision	L	L	L	L
565	In re Snyder	June 24, 1985	472 U.S. 634	W	W	W	W	W	W	W	W	Took no part in the decision
566	United States v. Albertini	June 24, 1985	472 U.S. 675	L	W	L	L	L	W	L	W	L

A	B	C	D	E	F	G	H	I	J	K	L	M
	Case Name	**Date Decided**	**Case #**	**Justices and Their Votes** (W = ACLU Win; L = ACLU Loss)								
				Burger	Stevens	O'Connor	Rehnquist	Powell	Marshall	White	Brennan	Blackmun
567	Jean v. Nelson	June 26, 1985	472 U.S. 846	L	L	L	L	Took no part in the decision	W	L	W	L
568	Atascadero State Hospital v. Scanlon	June 28, 1985	473 U.S. 234	L	W	L	L	L	W	L	W	W
569	Walters v. National Ass'n of Radiation Survivors	June 28, 1985	473 U.S. 305	L	W	L	L	L	W	L	W	L
570	Aguilar v. Felton	July 1, 1985	473 U.S. 402	L	W	L	L	W	W	L	W	W
571	City of Cleburne v. Cleburne Living Center	July 1, 1985	473 U.S. 432	W	W	W	W	W	W	W	W	W
572	Cornelius v. NAACP Legal Defense and Educational Fund, Inc.	July 2, 1985	473 U.S. 788	L	W	L	L	Took no part in the decision	Took no part in the decision	L	W	W
573	Marek v. Chesny	July 27, 1985	473 U.S. 1	L	L	L	L	L	W	L	W	W
574	Miller v. Fenton	December 3, 1985	474 U.S. 104	W	W	W	L	W	W	W	W	W
575	Wainwright v. Greenfield	January 14, 1986	474 U.S. 284	W	W	W	W	W	W	W	W	W

181

	Case Name	Date Decided	Case #	Burger	Stevens	O'Connor	Rehnquist	Powell	Marshall	White	Brennan	Blackmun
A	B	C	D	E	F	G	H	I	J	K	L	M
576	Witters v. Washington Department of Services for the Blind	January 27, 1986	474 U.S. 481	L	L	L	L	L	L	L	L	L
577	City of Renton v. Playtime Theatres, Inc.	February 25, 1986	475 U.S. 41	L	L	L	L	L	W	L	W	L
578	Malley v. Briggs	March 5, 1986	475 U.S. 335	W	W	W	L	L	W	W	W	W
579	Pembaur v. City of Cincinnati	March 25, 1986	475 U.S. 469	L	W	W	L	L	W	W	W	W
580	Goldman v. Weinberger	March 25, 1986	475 U.S. 503	L	L	W	L	L	W	L	W	W
581	Bender v. Williamsport Area School District	March 25, 1986	475 U.S. 534	W	L	L	W	W	L	W	L	L
582	Holbrook v. Flynn	March 26, 1986	475 U.S. 560	L	L	L	L	L	L	L	L	L
583	Evans v. Jeff D.	April 21, 1986	475 U.S. 717	L	L	L	L	L	W	L	W	W
584	Philadelphia Newspapers, Inc. v. Hepps	April 21, 1986	475 U.S. 767	L	L	W	L	W	W	L	W	W
585	Smalis v. Pennsylvania	May 5, 1986	476 U.S. 140	W	W	W	W	W	W	W	W	W
586	California v. Ciraolo	May 19, 1986	476 U.S. 207	L	L	L	L	W	W	L	W	W
587	Bowen v. City of New York	June 2, 1986	476 U.S. 467	W	W	W	W	W	W	W	W	W

	Case Name	Date Decided	Case #	Justices and Their Votes (W = ACLU Win; L = ACLU Loss)								
A	B	C	D	E	F	G	H	I	J	K	L	M
				Burger	Stevens	O'Connor	Rehnquist	Powell	Marshall	White	Brennan	Blackmun
588	City of Los Angeles v. Preferred Communications, Inc.	June 2, 1986	476 U.S. 488	W	W	W	W	W	W	W	W	W
589	Thornburgh v. American College of Obstetricians and Gynecologists	June 11, 1986	476 U.S. 747	L	W	L	L	W	W	L	W	W
590	Memphis Community School District v. Stachura	June 25, 1986	477 U.S. 299	L	L	L	L	L	L	L	L	L
591	Kimmelman v. Morrison	June 26, 1986	477 U.S. 365	W	W	W	W	W	W	W	W	W
592	Murray v. Carrier	June 26, 1986	477 U.S. 478	L	L	L	L	L	W	L	W	L
593	Ohio Civil Rights Commission v. Dayton Christian Schools, Inc.	June 27, 1986	477 U.S. 619	W	W	W	W	W	W	W	W	W
594	New Mexico v. Earnest	June 27, 1986	477 U.S. 648	L	L	L	L	L	L	L	L	L
595	Press-Enterprise Co. v. Superior Court	June 30, 1986	478 U.S. 1	W	L	W	L	W	W	W	W	W
596	Davis v. Bandemer	June 30, 1986	478 U.S. 109	L	W	L	L	W	L	L	L	L

	Case Name	Date Decided	Case #	Justices and Their Votes (W = ACLU Win; L = ACLU Loss)								
A	B	C	D	E	F	G	H	I	J	K	L	M
				Burger	Stevens	O'Connor	Rehnquist	Powell	Marshall	White	Brennan	Blackmun
597	Posadas de Puerto Rico Associates v. Tourism Company of Puerto Rico	July 1, 1986	478 U.S. 328	L	W	L	L	L	W	L	W	W
598	Rose v. Clark	July 2, 1986	478 U.S. 570	L	L	L	L	L	W	L	W	W
599	Arcara v. Cloud Books Inc.	July 7, 1986	478 U.S. 697	L	L	L	L	L	W	L	W	W
600	Munro v. Socialist Workers Party	December 10, 1986	479 U.S. 189	Scalia L	L	L	L	L	W	L	W	L
601	Federal Election Commission v. Massachusetts Citizens For Life, Inc.	December 15, 1986	479 U.S. 238	W	L	W	L	W	W	L	W	L
602	California Federal Savings & Loan Association v. Guerra	January 13, 1987	479 U.S. 272	W	W	W	L	L	W	L	W	W
603	Colorado v. Bertine	January 14, 1987	479 U.S. 367	L	L	L	L	L	W	L	W	L
604	Wimberly v. Labor and Industrial Relations Commission of Missouri	January 21, 1987	479 U.S. 511	L	L	L	L	L	L	L	L	Took no part in the decision
605	California v. Brown	January 27, 1987	479 U.S. 538	L	W	L	L	L	W	L	W	W
606	City of Springfield v. Kibbe	February 25, 1987	480 U.S. 257	W	W	L	L	L	W	L	W	W

A	B	C	D				Justices and Their Votes (W = ACLU Win; L = ACLU Loss)					
	Case Name	Date Decided	Case #	E	F	G	H	I	J	K	L	M
				Scalia	Stevens	O'Connor	Rehnquist	Powell	Marshall	White	Brennan	Blackmun
607	Arizona v. Hicks	March 3, 1987	480 U.S. 321	W	W	L	L	L	W	W	W	W
608	Town of Newton v. Rumery	March 9, 1987	480 U.S. 386	L	W	L	L	L	W	L	W	W
609	Immigration & Naturalization Service v. Cardoza-Fonseca	March 9, 1987	480 U.S. 421	W	W	W	L	L	W	L	W	W
610	Johnson v. Transportation Agency	March 25, 1987	480 U.S. 616	L	W	W	L	W	W	L	W	W
611	O'Connor v. Ortega	March 31, 1987	480 U.S. 709	L	W	L	L	L	W	L	W	W
612	Corp. for the Presiding Bishop of the Church of Jesus Christ of Latter-Day Saints v. Amos	March 31, 1987	483 U.S. 327	L	L	L	L	L	L	L	L	L
613	Arkansas Writers' Project, Inc. v. Ragland	April 22, 1987	481 U.S. 221	L	W	W	L	W	W	W	W	W
614	Meese v. Keene	April 28, 1987	481 U.S. 465	Took no part in the decision	L	L	L	L	W	L	W	W
615	Pope v. Illinois	May 4, 1987	481 U.S. 497	W	L	W	W	W	L	W	L	L

	Case Name	Date Decided	Case #	Justices and Their Votes (W = ACLU Win; L = ACLU Loss)								
A	B	C	D	E	F	G	H	I	J	K	L	M
				Scalia	Stevens	O'Connor	Rehnquist	Powell	Marshall	White	Brennan	Blackmun
616	Board of Directors of Rotary Int'l v. Rotary Club of Duarte	May 4, 1987	481 U.S. 537	W	W	Took no part in the decision	W	W	W	W	W	Took no part in the decision
617	Pennsylvania v. Finley	May 18, 1987	481 U.S. 551	L	W	L	L	L	W	L	W	L
618	United States v. Salerno	May 26, 1987	481 U.S. 739	L	W	L	L	L	W	L	W	L
619	Hilton v. Braunskill	May 26, 1987	481 U.S. 770	L	L	L	L	L	W	L	W	W
620	United States v. Mendoza-Lopez	May 26, 1987	481 U.S. 828	L	W	L	L	W	W	L	W	W
621	United States v. Hohri	June 1, 1987	482 U.S. 64	Took no part in the decision	L	L	L	L	L	L	L	L
622	O'Lone v. Estate of Shabazz	June 9, 1987	482 U.S. 342	L	W	L	L	L	W	L	W	W
623	Miller v. Florida	June 9, 1987	482 U.S. 423	W	W	W	W	W	W	W	W	W
624	City of Houston v. Hill	June 15, 1987	482 U.S. 451	W	W	W	L	W	W	W	W	W
625	Edwards v. Aguillard	June 19, 1987	482 U.S. 578	L	W	W	L	W	W	W	W	W
626	New York v. Burger	June 19, 1987	482 U.S. 691	L	L	W	L	L	W	L	W	L
627	Kentucky v. Stincer	June 19, 1987	482 U.S. 730	L	W	L	L	L	W	L	W	L

	Case Name	Date Decided	Case #	Justices and Their Votes (W = ACLU Win; L = ACLU Loss)								
A	B	C	D	E	F	G	H	I	J	K	L	M
				Scalia	Stevens	O'Connor	Rehnquist	Powell	Marshall	White	Brennan	Blackmun
628	Bowen v. Gilliard	June 25, 1987	483 U.S. 587	L	L	L	L	L	W	L	W	W
629	Anderson v. Creighton	June 25, 1987	483 U.S. 635	L	W	L	L	L	W	L	W	L
630	Greer v. Miller	June 26, 1987	483 U.S. 756	L	L	L	L	L	W	L	W	W
631	Griffin v. Wisconsin	June 26, 1987	483 U.S. 868	L	W	L	L	L	W	L	W	W
632	Church of Scientology of California v. Internal Revenue Service	November 10, 1987	484 U.S. 9	Took no part in the decision	L	L	L	VACANT SEAT	L	L	Took no part in the decision	L
633	Karcher v. May	December 1, 1987	484 U.S. 72	W	W	W	W	VACANT SEAT	W	W	W	W
634	Deakins v. Monaghan	January 12, 1988	484 U.S. 193	W	W	W	W	VACANT SEAT	W	W	W	W
635	Hazelwood School District v. Kuhlmeier	January 13, 1988	484 U.S. 260	L	L	L	L	VACANT SEAT	W	L	W	W
636	Virginia v. American Booksellers Ass'n, Inc.	January 25, 1988	484 U.S. 383	L	L	L	L	VACANT SEAT	L	L	L	L

	Case Name	Date Decided	Case #	Justices and Their Votes (W = ACLU Win; L = ACLU Loss)								
A	B	C	D	E	F	G	H	I	J	K	L	M
				Scalia	Stevens	O'Connor	Rehnquist	Powell	Marshall	White	Brennan	Blackmun
637	Department of the Navy v. Egan	February 23, 1988	484 U.S. 518	L	L	L	L	Kennedy Took no part in the decision	W	W	W	L
638	Pennell v. City of San Jose	February 24, 1988	485 U.S. 1	L	W	L	W	Took no part in the decision	W	W	W	W
639	Hustler Magazine, Inc. v. Falwell	February 24, 1988	485 U.S. 46	W	W	W	W	Took no part in the decision	W	W	W	W
640	Boos v. Barry	March 22, 1988	485 U.S. 312	W	W	W	L	Took no part in the decision	W	L	W	L
641	Lyng v. Northwest Indian Cemetery Protective Ass'n	April 19, 1988	485 U.S. 439	L	L	L	L	Took no part in the decision	W	L	W	W
642	Traynor v. Turnage	April 20, 1988	485 U.S. 535	Took no part in the decision	L	L	L	Took no part in the decision	W	L	W	W

A	B	C	D	E	F	G	H	I	J	K	L	M
	Case Name	**Date Decided**	**Case #**	**Justices and Their Votes** (W = ACLU Win; L = ACLU Loss)								
				Scalia	Stevens	O'Connor	Rehnquist	Kennedy	Marshall	White	Brennan	Blackmun
643	Edward J. DeBartolo Corp. v. Florida Gulf Coast Building & Construction Trades Council	April 20, 1988	485 U.S. 568	W	W	W	W	Took no part in the decision	W	W	W	W
644	United States v. Providence Journal Co.	May 2, 1988	485 U.S. 693	W	L	W	L	Took no part in the decision	W	W	W	W
645	Meyer v. Grant	June 6, 1988	486 U.S. 414	W	W	W	W	W	W	W	W	W
646	Clark v. Jeter	June 6, 1988	486 U.S. 456	W	W	W	W	W	W	W	W	W
647	City of Lakewood v. Plain Dealer Publishing Co.	June 17, 1988	486 U.S. 750	W	L	L	Took no part in the decision	Took no part in the decision	W	L	W	W
648	New York State Club Ass'n v. City of New York	June 20, 1988	487 U.S. 1	W	W	W	W	W	W	W	W	W
649	West v. Atkins	June 20, 1988	487 U.S. 42	W	W	W	W	W	W	W	W	W
650	United States Catholic Conference v. Abortion Rights Mobilization, Inc.	June 20, 1988	487 U.S. 72	L	L	L	L	L	W	L	L	L

	Case Name	Date Decided	Case #	Justices and Their Votes (W = ACLU Win; L = ACLU Loss)								
A	B	C	D	E Scalia	F Stevens	G O'Connor	H Rehnquist	I Kennedy	J Marshall	K White	L Brennan	M Blackmun
651	Ross v. Oklahoma	June 22, 1988	487 U.S. 81	L	W	L	L	L	W	L	W	W
652	Bank of Nova Scotia v. United States	June 22, 1988	487 U.S. 250	L	L	L	L	L	W	L	L	L
653	Schweiker v. Chilicky	June 24, 1988	487 U.S. 412	L	L	L	L	L	W	L	W	W
654	Kadrmas v. Dickinson Public Schools	June 24, 1988	487 U.S. 450	L	W	L	L	L	W	L	W	W
655	Frisby v. Schultz	June 27, 1988	487 U.S. 474	L	W	L	L	L	W	L	W	L
656	Murray v. United States	June 27, 1988	487 U.S. 533	W	L	L	W	Took no part in the decision	L	W	Took no part in the decision	W
657	Bowen v. Kendrick	June 29, 1988	487 U.S. 589	L	W	L	L	L	W	L	W	W
658	Watson v. Fort Worth Bank & Trust	June 29, 1988	487 U.S. 977	W	W	W	W	Took no part in the decision	W	W	W	W
659	Penson v. Ohio	November 29, 1988	488 U.S. 75	W	W	W	L	W	W	W	W	W
660	Carlucci v. Doe	December 6, 1988	488 U.S. 93	L	L	L	L	L	L	L	L	L
661	Owens v. Okure	January 10, 1989	488 U.S. 235	W	W	W	W	W	W	W	W	W
662	Florida v. Riley	January 23, 1989	488 U.S. 445	L	W	L	L	L	W	L	W	W

	Case Name	Date Decided	Case #	Justices and Their Votes (W = ACLU Win; L = ACLU Loss)								
A	B	C	D	E	F	G	H	I	J	K	L	M
				Scalia	Stevens	O'Connor	Rehnquist	Kennedy	Marshall	White	Brennan	Blackmun
663	City of Richmond v. J.A. Croson Co.	January 23, 1989	488 U.S. 469	L	L	L	L	L	W	L	W	W
664	Texas Monthly, Inc. v. Bullock	February 21, 1989	489 U.S. 1	L	W	W	L	L	W	W	W	W
665	Fort Wayne Books, Inc. v. Indiana	February 21, 1989	489 U.S. 46	W	W	W	W	W	W	W	W	W
666	DeShaney v. Winnebago County Department of Social Services	February 22, 1989	489 U.S. 189	L	L	L	L	L	W	L	W	W
667	City of Canton, Ohio v. Harris	February 28, 1989	489 U.S. 378	W	L	W	L	W	L	L	L	L
668	Blanton v. City of North Las Vegas, Nevada	March 6, 1989	489 U.S. 538	L	L	L	L	L	L	L	L	L
669	Graham v. Connor	March 15, 1989	490 U.S. 386	W	W	W	W	W	W	W	W	W
670	Skinner v. Railway Labor Executives' Ass'n	March 21, 1989	489 U.S. 602	L	L	L	L	L	W	L	W	L
671	National Treasury Employees Union v. Von Raab	March 21, 1989	489 U.S. 656	W	W	L	L	L	W	L	W	L
672	Board of Estimate of New York v. Morris	March 22, 1989	489 U.S. 688	W	W	W	W	W	W	W	W	W

A	B Case Name	C Date Decided	D Case #	E Scalia	F Stevens	G O'Connor	H Rehnquist	I Kennedy	J Marshall	K White	L Brennan	M Blackmun
							Justices and Their Votes (W = ACLU Win; L = ACLU Loss)					
673	United States Department of Justice v. Reporters Committee for Freedom of the Press	March 22, 1989	489 U.S. 749	W	W	W	W	W	W	W	W	W
674	Frazee v. Illinois Dep't of Employment Security	March 29, 1989	489 U.S. 829	W	W	W	W	W	W	W	W	W
675	American Foreign Service Ass'n v. Garfinkel	April 18, 1989	490 U.S. 153	W	W	W	W	W	W	W	W	W
676	Frank v. Minnesota Newspaper Ass'n, Inc.	April 25, 1989	490 U.S. 225	L	W	L	L	L	W	W	L	L
677	Price-Waterhouse v. Hopkins	May 1, 1989	490 U.S. 228	W	L	L	W	W	L	L	L	L
678	Maleng v. Cook	May 15, 1989	490 U.S. 488	W	W	W	W	W	W	W	W	W
679	Wards Cove Packing Co. v. Atonio	June 5, 1989	490 U.S. 642	L	W	L	L	L	W	L	W	W
680	Martin v. Wilks	June 12, 1989	490 U.S. 755	L	W	L	L	L	W	L	W	W
681	Will v. Michigan Department of State Police	June 15, 1989	491 U.S. 58	L	W	L	L	L	W	L	W	W
682	Quinn v. Millsap	June 15, 1989	491 U.S. 95	W	W	W	W	W	W	W	W	W
683	Michael H. v. Gerald D.	June 15, 1989	491 U.S. 110	L	L	L	L	L	W	W	W	W

A	B	C	D	E	F	G	H	I	J	K	L	M
	Case Name	**Date Decided**	**Case #**	Scalia	Stevens	O'Connor	Rehnquist	Kennedy	Marshall	White	Brennan	Blackmun
684	Patterson v. McLean Credit Union	June 15, 1989	491 U.S. 164	L	W	L	L	L	W	L	W	W
685	Dellmuth v. Muth	June 15, 1989	491 U.S. 223	L	W	L	L	L	W	L	W	W
686	Texas v. Johnson	June 21, 1989	491 U.S. 397	W	L	L	L	W	W	L	W	W
687	Independent Federation of Flight Attendants v. Zipes	June 22, 1989	491 U.S. 754	L	Took no part in the decision	L	L	L	W	L	W	L
688	Murray v. Giarratano	June 23, 1989	492 U.S. 1	L	W	L	L	L	W	L	W	W
689	Webster v. Reproductive Health Services	July 3, 1989	492 U.S. 490	L	W	L	L	L	W	L	W	W
690	County of Allegheny v. American Civil Liberties Union Greater Pittsburgh Chapter	July 3, 1989	492 U.S. 573	L	W	W	L	L	W	L	W	W
691	Spallone v. United States	January 10, 1990	493 U.S. 265	L	W	L	L	L	W	L	W	W
692	Jimmy Swaggart Ministries v. Board of Equalization of California	January 17, 1990	493 U.S. 378	W	W	W	W	W	W	W	W	W

	Case Name	Date Decided	Case #	Justices and Their Votes (W = ACLU Win; L = ACLU Loss)								
A	B	C	D	E Scalia	F Stevens	G O'Connor	H Rehnquist	I Kennedy	J Marshall	K White	L Brennan	M Blackmun
693	Federal Trade Commission v. Superior Court Trial Lawyers Ass'n	January 22, 1990	493 U.S. 411	W	W	W	W	W	L	W	L	L
694	Holland v. Illinois	January 22, 1990	493 U.S. 474	L	W	L	L	L	W	L	W	W
695	Zinermon v. Burch	February 27, 1990	494 U.S. 113	L	W	L	L	L	W	W	W	W
696	United States v. Verdugo-Urquidez	February 28, 1990	494 U.S. 259	L	L	L	L	L	W	L	W	W
697	Michigan v. Harvey	March 5, 1990	494 U.S. 344	L	W	L	L	L	W	L	W	W
698	Butterworth v. Smith	March 21, 1990	494 U.S. 624	W	W	W	W	W	W	W	W	W
699	Austin v. Michigan Chamber of Commerce	March 27, 1990	494 U.S. 652	W	L	W	L	W	L	L	L	L
700	Employment Division v. Smith	April 17, 1990	494 U.S. 872	L	L	L	L	L	W	L	W	W
701	Keller v. State Bar of California	June 4, 1990	496 U.S. 1	W	W	W	W	W	W	W	W	W
702	Illinois v. Perkins	June 4, 1990	496 U.S. 292	L	L	L	L	L	W	L	L	L
703	United States v. Eichman	June 11, 1990	496 U.S. 310	W	L	L	L	W	W	L	W	W
704	Alabama v. White	June 11, 1990	496 U.S. 325	L	W	L	L	L	W	L	W	L
705	Milkovich v. Lorain Journal Co.	June 21, 1990	497 U.S. 1	L	L	L	L	L	W	L	W	L

	Case Name	Date Decided	Case #	Scalia	Stevens	O'Connor	Rehnquist	Kennedy	Marshall	White	Brennan	Blackmun
A	B	C	D	E	F	G	H	I	J	K	L	M
706	Cruzan v. Director, Missouri Department of Health	June 25, 1990	497 U.S. 261	L	W	L	L	L	W	L	W	W
707	Hodgson v. Minnesota	June 25, 1990	497 U.S. 417	L	W	W	L	L	W	L	W	W
708	Metro Broadcasting, Inc. v. FCC	June 27, 1990	497 U.S. 547	L	W	L	L	L	W	W	W	W
709	Walton v. Arizona	June 27, 1990	497 U.S. 639	L	W	L	L	L	W	L	W	W
710	United States v. Kokinda	June 27, 1990	497 U.S. 720	L	W	L	L	L	W	L	W	W
711	Idaho v. Wright	June 27, 1990	497 U.S. 805	W	W	W	L	L	W	L	W	L
712	Board of Education of Oklahoma City v. Dowell	January 15, 1991	498 U.S. 237	L	W	L	L	L	W	L	Souter Took no part in the decision	W
713	UAW v. Johnson Controls, Inc.	March 20, 1991	499 U.S. 187	W	W	W	W	W	W	W	W	W
714	Equal Employment Opportunity Commission v. Arabian American Oil Co.	March 26, 1991	499 U.S. 244	L	W	L	L	L	W	L	L	W

	Case Name	Date Decided	Case #	Justices and Their Votes (W = ACLU Win; L = ACLU Loss)								
A	B	C	D	E	F	G	H	I	J	K	L	M
				Scalia	Stevens	O'Connor	Rehnquist	Kennedy	Marshall	White	Souter	Blackmun
715	Powers v. Ohio	April 1, 1991	499 U.S. 400	L	W	W	L	W	W	W	W	W
716	County of Riverside v. McLaughlin	May 13, 1991	500 U.S. 44	W	W	L	L	L	W	L	L	W
717	Rust v. Sullivan	May 23, 1991	500 U.S. 173	L	W	W	L	L	W	L	L	W
718	Siegert v. Gilley	May 23, 1991	500 U.S. 226	L	W	L	L	L	W	L	L	W
719	Burns v. Reed	May 30, 1991	500 U.S. 478	W	W	W	W	W	W	W	W	W
720	Edmonson v. Leesville Concrete Co.	June 3, 1991	500 U.S. 614	L	W	L	L	W	W	W	W	W
721	Clark v. Roemer	June 3, 1991	500 U.S. 646	W	W	W	W	W	W	W	W	W
722	Renne v. Geary	June 17, 1991	501 U.S. 312	L	L	L	L	L	W	W	L	W
723	Florida v. Bostick	June 20, 1991	501 U.S. 429	L	W	L	L	L	W	L	L	W
724	Barnes v. Glen Theatre, Inc.	June 21, 1991	501 U.S. 560	L	W	L	L	L	W	W	L	W
725	Harmelin v. Michigan	June 27, 1991	501 U.S. 957	L	W	L	L	L	W	W	L	W
726	Gentile v. State Bar of Nevada	June 27, 1991	501 U.S. 1030	L	W	W	L	W	W	L	L	W

A	B	C	D	E	F	G	H	I	J	K	L	M
	Case Name	**Date Decided**	**Case #**	**Justices and Their Votes** (W = ACLU Win; L = ACLU Loss)								
				Scalia	Stevens	O'Connor	Rehnquist	Kennedy	Marshall	White	Souter	Blackmun
727	Hafer v. Melo	November 5, 1991	502 U.S. 21	W	W	W	W	W	Thomas Took no part in the decision	W	W	W
728	Simon & Schuster, Inc. v. Members of the New York State Crime Victims Board	December 10, 1991	502 U.S. 105	W	W	W	W	W	Took no part in the decision	W	W	W
729	United States Department of State v. Ray	December 16, 1991	502 U.S. 164	L	L	L	L	L	Took no part in the decision	L	L	L
730	Norman v. Reed	January 14, 1992	502 U.S. 279	L	W	W	W	W	Took no part in the decision	W	W	W
731	Immigration & Naturalization Service v. Doherty	January 15, 1992	502 U.S. 314	W	W	L	L	L	Took no part in the decision	L	W	L
732	Rufo v. Inmates of the Suffolk County Jail	January 15, 1992	502 U.S. 367	L	W	L	L	L	Took no part in the decision	L	L	W

A	B	C	D	E	F	G	H	I	J	K	L	M
	Case Name	**Date Decided**	**Case #**	**Justices and Their Votes** (W = ACLU Win; L = ACLU Loss)								
				Scalia	Stevens	O'Connor	Rehnquist	Kennedy	Thomas	White	Souter	Blackmun
733	Hudson v. McMillian	February 25, 1992	503 U.S. 1	L	W	W	W	W	L	W	W	W
734	Collins v. City of Harker Heights, Texas	February 26, 1992	503 U.S. 115	L	L	L	L	L	L	L	L	L
735	Dawson v. Delaware	March 9, 1992	503 U.S. 159	W	W	W	W	W	L	W	W	W
736	Freeman v. Pitts	March 31, 1992	503 U.S. 467	L	L	L	L	L	Took no part in the decision	L	L	L
737	Jacobson v. United States	April 6, 1992	503 U.S. 540	L	W	L	L	L	W	W	W	W
738	Denton v. Hernandez	May 4, 1992	504 U.S. 25	L	W	L	L	L	L	L	L	W
739	United States v. Burke	May 26, 1992	504 U.S. 229	L	L	W	L	L	W	L	L	L
740	Burdick v. Takushi	June 8, 1992	504 U.S. 428	L	W	L	L	W	L	L	L	W
741	Ankenbrandt v. Richards	June 15, 1992	504 U.S. 689	W	W	W	W	W	W	W	W	W
742	Morgan v. Illinois	June 15, 1992	504 U.S. 719	L	W	W	L	W	L	W	W	W
743	Forsyth County v. Nationalist Movement	June 19, 1992	505 U.S. 123	L	W	W	L	W	L	L	W	W
744	Wright v. West	June 19, 1992	505 U.S. 277	L	L	L	L	L	L	L	L	L

A	B Case Name	C Date Decided	D Case #	E Scalia	F Stevens	G O'Connor	H Rehnquist	I Kennedy	J Thomas	K White	L Souter	M Blackmun
				\(W = ACLU Win; L = ACLU Loss\)								
745	R.A.V. v. City of St. Paul	June 22, 1992	505 U.S. 377	W	W	W	W	W	W	W	W	W
746	Lee v. Weisman	June 24, 1992	505 U.S. 577	L	W	W	L	W	L	L	W	W
747	International Society for Krishna Consciousness, Inc. v. Lee	June 26, 1992	505 U.S. 672	L	W	L	L	L	L	L	W	W
748	Planned Parenthood of Southeastern Pennsylvania v. Casey	June 29, 1992	505 U.S. 833	L	W	W	L	W	L	L	W	W
749	Soldal v. Cook County, Illinois	December 8, 1992	506 U.S. 56	W	W	W	W	W	W	W	W	W
750	Crosby v. United States	January 13, 1993	506 U.S. 255	W	W	W	W	W	W	W	W	W
751	Bray v. Alexandria Women's Health Clinic	January 13, 1993	506 U.S. 263	L	W	W	L	L	L	L	L	W
752	Brecht v. Abrahamson	April 21, 1993	507 U.S. 619	L	L	W	L	L	L	W	W	W
753	Withrow v. Williams	April 21, 1993	507 U.S. 680	L	W	L	L	W	L	W	W	W
754	Gilmore v. Taylor	June 7, 1993	508 U.S. 333	L	W	L	L	L	L	L	L	W
755	Minnesota v. Dickerson	June 7, 1993	508 U.S. 366	W	W	W	W	W	W	W	W	W

A	B	C	D	E	F	G	H	I	J	K	L	M
	Case Name	**Date Decided**	**Case #**	**Justices and Their Votes** (W = ACLU Win; L = ACLU Loss)								
				Scalia	Stevens	O'Connor	Rehnquist	Kennedy	Thomas	White	Souter	Blackmun
756	Lamb's Chapel v. Center Moriches Union Free School District	June 7, 1993	508 U.S. 384	W	W	W	W	W	W	W	W	W
757	Wisconsin v. Mitchell	June 11, 1993	508 U.S. 476	W	W	W	W	W	W	W	W	W
758	Church of Lukumi Babalu Aye, Inc. v. City of Hialeah	June 11, 1993	508 U.S. 520	W	W	W	W	W	W	W	W	W
759	Godinez v. Moran	June 24, 1993	509 U.S. 389	L	W	L	L	L	L	L	L	W
760	United States v. Edge Broadcasting Co.	June 25, 1993	509 U.S. 418	L	W	L	L	L	L	L	L	W
761	Alexander v. United States	June 28, 1993	509 U.S. 544	L	W	L	L	W	L	L	W	W
762	Austin v. United States	June 28, 1993	509 U.S. 602	W	W	W	W	W	W	W	W	W
763	Harris v. Forklift Systems, Inc.	November 9, 1993	510 U.S. 17	W	W	W	W	W	W	Ginsburg W	W	W
764	United States v. James Daniel Good Real Property	December 13, 1993	510 U.S. 43	L	W	L	L	W	L	W	W	W
765	Weiss v. United States	January 19, 1994	510 U.S. 163	L	L	L	L	L	L	L	L	L
766	National Organization for Women, Inc. v. Scheidler	January 24, 1994	510 U.S. 249	W	W	W	W	W	W	W	W	W

A	B	C	D	E	F	G	H	I	J	K	L	M
	Case Name	**Date Decided**	**Case #**	Justices and Their Votes (W = ACLU Win; L = ACLU Loss)								
				Scalia	Stevens	O'Connor	Rehnquist	Kennedy	Thomas	Ginsburg	Souter	Blackmun
767	Albright v. Oliver	January 24, 1994	510 U.S. 266	L	W	L	L	L	L	L	L	W
768	Elder v. Holloway	February 23, 1994	510 U.S. 510	W	W	W	W	W	W	W	W	W
769	Campbell v. Acuff-Rose Music, Inc.	March 7, 1994	510 U.S. 569	W	W	W	W	W	W	W	W	W
770	J.E.B. v. Alabama ex rel. T.B.	April 19, 1994	511 U.S. 127	L	W	W	L	W	L	W	W	W
771	Nichols v. United States	June 6, 1994	511 U.S. 738	L	W	L	L	L	L	W	L	W
772	Farmer v. Brennan	June 6, 1994	511 U.S. 825	W	W	W	W	W	W	W	W	W
773	City of Ladue v. Gilleo	June 13, 1994	512 U.S. 43	W	W	W	W	W	W	W	W	W
774	McFarland v. Scott	June 30, 1994	512 U.S. 849	L	W	L	L	W	L	W	W	W
775	Tuilaepa v. California	June 30, 1994	512 U.S. 967	L	L	L	L	L	L	L	L	W
776	Lebron v. National Railroad Passenger Corp.	February 21, 1995	513 U.S. 374	W	W	L	W	W	W	W	W	Breyer W
777	O'Neal v. McAninch	February 21, 1995	513 U.S. 432	L	W	W	L	W	L	W	W	W
778	United States v. National Treasury Employees Union	February 22, 1995	513 U.S. 454	L	W	W	L	W	L	W	W	W
779	Arizona v. Evans	March 1, 1995	514 U.S. 1	L	W	L	L	L	L	W	L	L

	Case Name	Date Decided	Case #	Justices and Their Votes (W = ACLU Win; L = ACLU Loss)								
A	B	C	D	E	F	G	H	I	J	K	L	M
				Scalia	Stevens	O'Connor	Rehnquist	Kennedy	Thomas	Ginsburg	Souter	Breyer
780	Swint v. Chambers County Commission	March 1, 1995	514 U.S. 35	L	L	L	L	L	L	L	L	L
781	McIntyre v. Ohio Elections Commission	April 19, 1995	514 U.S. 334	L	W	W	L	W	W	W	W	W
782	City of Edmonds v. Oxford House, Inc.	May 15, 1995	514 U.S. 725	L	W	W	W	L	L	W	W	W
783	U.S. Term Limits, Inc. v. Thornton	May 22, 1995	514 U.S. 779	L	W	L	L	W	L	W	W	W
784	Wilson v. Arkansas	May 22, 1995	514 U.S. 927	W	W	W	W	W	W	W	W	W
785	Missouri v. Jenkins	June 12, 1995	515 U.S. 70	L	W	L	L	L	L	W	W	W
786	Kimberlin v. Quinlan	June 12, 1995	515 U.S. 321	W	W	W	W	W	W	W	W	W
787	Sandin v. Conner	June 19, 1995	515 U.S. 472	L	W	L	L	L	L	W	W	W
788	Hurley v. Irish-American Gay, Lesbian & Bisexual Group of Boston	June 19, 1995	515 U.S. 557	W	W	W	W	W	W	W	W	W
789	Capitol Square Review & Advisory Board v. Pinette	June 29, 1995	515 U.S. 753	W	L	W	W	W	W	L	W	W
790	Rosenberger v. Rector & Visitors of the University of Virginia	June 29, 1995	515 U.S. 819	L	W	L	L	L	L	W	W	W

A	B	C	D	E	F	G	H	I	J	K	L	M
	Case Name	Date Decided	Case #	— Justices and Their Votes (W = ACLU Win; L = ACLU Loss)								
				Scalia	Stevens	O'Connor	Rehnquist	Kennedy	Thomas	Ginsburg	Souter	Breyer
791	Miller v. Johnson	June 29, 1995	515 U.S. 900	L	W	L	L	L	L	W	W	W
792	National Labor Relations Board v. Town & Country Electric, Inc.	November 28, 1995	516 U.S. 85	W	W	W	W	W	W	W	W	W
793	United States v. Chesapeake & Potomac Telephone Co. of Virginia	February 27, 1996	516 U.S. 415	L	L	L	L	L	L	L	L	L
794	Wisconsin v. City of New York	March 20, 1996	517 U.S. 1	L	L	L	L	L	L	L	L	L
795	Morse v. Republican Party of Virginia	March 27, 1996	517 U.S. 186	L	W	W	L	L	L	W	W	W
796	United States v. Armstrong	May 13, 1996	517 U.S. 456	L	W	L	L	L	L	L	L	L
797	44 Liquormart, Inc. v. Rhode Island	May 13, 1996	517 U.S. 484	W	W	W	W	W	W	W	W	W
798	Romer v. Evans	May 20, 1996	517 U.S. 620	L	W	W	L	W	L	W	W	W
799	Ornelas v. United States	May 28, 1996	517 U.S. 690	L	W	W	W	W	W	W	W	W
800	Loving v. United States	June 3, 1996	517 U.S. 748	L	L	L	L	L	L	L	L	L
801	Whren v. United States	June 10, 1996	517 U.S. 806	L	L	L	L	L	L	L	L	L
802	Shaw v. Hunt	June 13, 1996	517 U.S. 899	L	W	L	L	L	L	W	W	W

	Case Name	Date Decided	Case #	Justices and Their Votes (W = ACLU Win; L = ACLU Loss)								
A	B	C	D	E	F	G	H	I	J	K	L	M
				Scalia	Stevens	O'Connor	Rehnquist	Kennedy	Thomas	Ginsburg	Souter	Breyer
803	Lane v. Pena	June 20, 1996	518 U.S. 187	L	W	L	L	L	L	L	L	W
804	United States v. Ursery	June 24, 1996	518 U.S. 267	L	W	L	L	L	L	L	L	L
805	Lewis v. United States	June 24, 1996	518 U.S. 322	L	W	L	L	L	L	W	L	L
806	Lewis v. Casey	June 24, 1996	518 U.S. 343	L	W	L	L	L	L	L	L	L
807	United States v. Virginia	June 26, 1996	518 U.S. 515	L	W	W	W	W	Took no part in the decision	W	W	W
808	Colorado Republican Federal Campaign Committee v. Federal Election Commission	June 26, 1996	518 U.S. 604	W	L	W	W	W	W	L	W	W
809	Board of County Commissioners, Wabaunsee County, Kansas v. Umbehr	June 28, 1996	518 U.S. 668	L	W	W	W	W	L	W	W	W
810	O'Hare Truck Service, Inc. v. City of Northlake	June 28, 1996	518 U.S. 712	L	W	W	W	W	L	W	W	W
811	Denver Area Educational Telecommunications Consortium, Inc. v. Federal Communications Commission	June 28, 1996	518 U.S. 727	L	W	W	L	W	L	W	W	W

A	B Case Name	C Date Decided	D Case #	E Scalia	F Stevens	G O'Connor	H Rehnquist	I Kennedy	J Thomas	K Ginsburg	L Souter	M Breyer
812	Lopez v. Monterey County, California	November 6, 1996	519 U.S. 9	W	W	W	W	W	W	W	W	W
813	Ohio v. Robinette	November 18, 1996	519 U.S. 33	L	W	L	L	L	L	L	L	L
814	M. L. B. v. S. L. J.	December 16, 1996	519 U.S. 102	L	W	W	L	W	L	W	W	W
815	Robinson v. Shell Oil Co.	February 18, 1997	519 U.S. 337	W	W	W	W	W	W	W	W	W
816	Schenck v. Pro-Choice Network of Western New York	February 19, 1997	519 U.S. 357	L	W	W	W	L	L	W	W	L
817	Arizonans for Official English v. Arizona	March 3, 1997	520 U.S. 43	L	L	L	L	L	L	L	L	L
818	Young v. Harper	March 18, 1997	520 U.S. 143	W	W	W	W	W	W	W	W	W
819	United States v. Lanier	March 31, 1997	520 U.S. 259	W	W	W	W	W	W	W	W	W
820	Young v. Fordice	March 31, 1997	520 U.S. 273	W	W	W	W	W	W	W	W	W
821	Chandler v. Miller	April 15, 1997	520 U.S. 305	W	W	W	L	W	W	W	W	W
822	Blessing v. Freestone	April 21, 1997	520 U.S. 329	L	L	L	L	L	L	L	L	L
823	Timmons v. Twin Cities Area New Party	April 28, 1997	520 U.S. 351	L	W	L	L	L	L	W	W	L

A	B Case Name	C Date Decided	D Case #	E Scalia	F Stevens	G O'Connor	H Rehnquist	I Kennedy	J Thomas	K Ginsburg	L Souter	M Breyer
824	Richards v. Wisconsin	April 28, 1997	520 U.S. 385	L	L	L	L	L	L	L	L	L
825	Edwards v. Balisok	May 19, 1997	520 U.S. 641	L	L	L	L	L	L	L	L	L
826	Reno v. Bossier Parish School Board	May 21, 1997	520 U.S. 471	L	W	L	L	L	L	L	W	L
827	Clinton v. Jones	May 27, 1997	520 U.S. 681	W	W	W	W	W	W	W	W	W
828	McMillian v. Monroe County, Alabama	June 2, 1997	520 U.S. 781	L	W	L	L	L	L	W	W	W
829	Abrams v. Johnson	June 19, 1997	521 U.S. 74	L	W	L	L	L	L	W	W	W
830	Agostini v. Felton	June 23, 1997	521 U.S. 203	L	W	L	L	L	L	W	W	W
831	Idaho v. Coeur d'Alene Tribe of Idaho	June 23, 1997	521 U.S. 261	L	W	L	L	L	L	W	W	W
832	Kansas v. Hendricks	June 23, 1997	521 U.S. 346	L	W	L	L	L	L	W	W	W
833	Richardson v. McKnight	June 23, 1997	521 U.S. 399	L	W	W	L	L	L	W	W	W
834	City of Boerne v. Flores	June 25, 1997	521 U.S. 507	L	L	W	L	L	L	L	W	W
835	Washington v. Glucksberg	June 26, 1997	521 U.S. 702	L	L	L	L	L	L	L	L	L
836	Vacco v. Quill	June 26, 1997	521 U.S. 793	L	L	L	L	L	L	L	L	L

206

	Case Name	Date Decided	Case #	Justices and Their Votes (W = ACLU Win; L = ACLU Loss)								
A	B	C	D	E	F	G	H	I	J	K	L	M
				Scalia	Stevens	O'Connor	Rehnquist	Kennedy	Thomas	Ginsburg	Souter	Breyer
837	Reno v. American Civil Liberties Union	June 26, 1997	521 U.S. 844	W	W	W	W	W	W	W	W	W
838	Oncale v. Sundowner Offshore Services, Inc.	March 4, 1998	523 U.S. 75	W	W	W	W	W	W	W	W	W
839	Ohio Adult Parole Authority v. Woodard	March 25, 1998	523 U.S. 272	L	L	L	L	L	L	L	L	L
840	Texas v. United States	March 31, 1998	523 U.S. 296	W	W	W	W	W	W	W	W	W
841	Miller v. Albright	April 22, 1998	523 U.S. 420	L	L	L	L	L	L	W	W	W
842	Crawford-El v. Britton	May 4, 1998	523 U.S. 574	L	W	L	L	W	L	W	W	W
843	Ricci v. Village of Arlington Heights	May 4, 1998	523 U.S. 613	L	L	L	L	L	L	L	L	L
844	Bousley v. United States	May 18, 1998	523 U.S. 614	L	W	W	W	W	L	W	W	W
845	Stewart v. Martinez-Villareal	May 18, 1998	523 U.S. 637	L	W	W	W	W	L	W	W	W
846	Arkansas Educational Television Commission v. Forbes	May 18, 1998	523 U.S. 666	L	W	L	L	L	L	W	W	L
847	Federal Election Commission v. Akins	June 1, 1998	524 U.S. 11	W	L	W	L	L	W	L	L	L

	Case Name	Date Decided	Case #	Justices and Their Votes (W = ACLU Win; L = ACLU Loss)								
A	B	C	D	E	F	G	H	I	J	K	L	M
				Scalia	Stevens	O'Connor	Rehnquist	Kennedy	Thomas	Ginsburg	Souter	Breyer
848	Pennsylvania Department of Corrections v. Yeskey	June 15, 1998	524 U.S. 206	W	W	W	W	W	W	W	W	W
849	Pennsylvania Board of Probation & Parole v. Scott	June 22, 1998	524 U.S. 357	L	W	L	L	L	L	W	W	W
850	National Endowment for the Arts v. Finley	June 25, 1998	524 U.S. 569	L	L	L	L	L	L	L	W	L
851	Bragdon v. Abbott	June 25, 1998	524 U.S. 624	L	W	L	L	W	L	W	W	W
852	Faragher v. City of Boca Raton	June 26, 1998	524 U.S. 775	L	W	W	W	W	L	W	W	W
853	Wright v. Universal Maritime Service Corp.	November 16, 1998	525 U.S. 70	W	W	W	W	W	W	W	W	W
854	Minnesota v. Carter	December 1, 1998	525 U.S. 83	L	W	L	L	L	L	W	W	L
855	Knowles v. Iowa	December 8, 1998	525 U.S. 113	W	W	W	W	W	W	W	W	W
856	Buckley v. American Constitutional Law Foundation, Inc.	January 12, 1999	525 U.S. 182	W	W	L	L	W	W	W	W	L
857	Roberts v. Galen of Virginia, Inc.	January 13, 1999	525 U.S. 249	W	W	W	W	W	W	W	W	W

A	B	C	D	E	F	G	H	I	J	K	L	M
	Case Name	**Date Decided**	**Case #**	**Justices and Their Votes** (W = ACLU Win; L = ACLU Loss)								
				Scalia	Stevens	O'Connor	Rehnquist	Kennedy	Thomas	Ginsburg	Souter	Breyer
858	Department of Commerce v. United States House of Representatives	January 25, 1999	525 U.S. 316	L	W	L	L	L	L	W	W	W
859	National Collegiate Athletic Ass'n v. Smith	February 23, 1999	525 U.S. 459	L	L	L	L	L	L	L	L	L
860	Reno v. American-Arab Anti-Discrimination Committee	February 24, 1999	525 U.S. 471	L	L	L	L	L	L	L	W	L
861	Saenz v. Roe	May 17, 1999	526 U.S. 489	W	W	W	L	W	L	W	W	W
862	Hunt v. Cromartie	May 17, 1999	526 U.S. 541	W	W	W	W	W	W	W	W	W
863	Wilson v. Layne	May 24, 1999	526 U.S. 603	L	W	L	L	L	L	L	L	L
864	Davis v. Monroe County Board of Education	May 24, 1999	526 U.S. 629	L	W	W	L	L	L	W	W	W
865	City of Chicago v. Morales	June 10, 1999	527 U.S. 41	L	W	W	L	W	L	W	W	W
866	Lilly v. Virginia	June 10, 1999	527 U.S. 116	W	W	W	W	W	W	W	W	W
867	Greater New Orleans Broadcasting Ass'n, Inc. v. United States	June 14, 1999	527 U.S. 173	W	W	W	W	W	W	W	W	W

	Case Name	Date Decided	Case #									
				Scalia	Stevens	O'Connor	Rehnquist	Kennedy	Thomas	Ginsburg	Souter	Breyer
A	B	C	D	E	F	G	H	I	J	K	L	M
868	Martin v. Hadix	June 21, 1999	527 U.S. 343	L	W	L	L	L	L	W	L	L
869	Sutton v. United Air Lines, Inc.	June 22, 1999	527 U.S. 471	L	W	L	L	L	L	L	L	W
870	Kolstad v. American Dental Ass'n	June 22, 1999	527 U.S. 526	W	W	W	L	W	L	W	W	W
871	Olmstead v. L.C. ex rel. Zimring	June 22, 1999	527 U.S. 581	L	W	W	L	W	L	W	W	W
872	United States v. Weatherhead	December 3, 1999	528 U.S. 1042	W	L	L	L	L	L	L	L	L
873	Illinois v. Wardlow	January 12, 2000	528 U.S. 119	L	W	L	L	L	L	W	W	W
874	Reno v. Condon	January 12, 2000	528 U.S. 141	W	W	W	W	W	W	W	W	W
875	Friends of the Earth v. Laidlaw Environmental Services	January 12, 2000	528 U.S. 167	L	W	W	W	W	L	W	W	W
876	Nixon v. Shrink Missouri Government PAC	January 24, 2000	528 U.S. 377	W	L	L	L	W	W	L	L	L
877	Village of Willowbrook v. Olech	February 23, 2000	528 U.S. 562	W	W	W	W	W	W	W	W	W
878	Board of Regents of the University of Wisconsin System v. Southworth	March 22, 2000	529 U.S. 217	W	W	W	W	W	W	W	W	W

	Case Name	Date Decided	Case #	Justices and Their Votes (W = ACLU Win; L = ACLU Loss)								
A	B	C	D	Scalia	Stevens	O'Connor	Rehnquist	Kennedy	Thomas	Ginsburg	Souter	Breyer
				E	F	G	H	I	J	K	L	M
879	Garner v. Jones	March 28, 2000	529 U.S. 244	L	W	L	L	L	L	W	W	L
880	Florida v. J. L.	March 28, 2000	529 U.S. 266	W	W	W	W	W	W	W	W	W
881	Erie v. Pap's A. M.	March 29, 2000	529 U.S. 277	L	W	L	L	L	L	W	W	L
882	Williams v. Taylor	April 18, 2000	529 U.S. 362	L	W	W	L	W	L	W	W	W
883	Troxel v. Granville	June 5, 2000	530 U.S. 57	L	L	W	W	L	W	W	W	W
884	Reeves v. Sanderson Plumbing Products, Inc.	June 12, 2000	530 U.S. 133	W	W	W	W	W	W	W	W	W
885	Santa Fe Independent School District v. Doe	June 19, 2000	530 U.S. 290	L	W	W	L	W	L	W	W	W
886	Miller v. French	June 19, 2000	530 U.S. 327	L	W	L	L	L	L	W	W	W
887	Dickerson v. United States	June 26, 2000	530 U.S. 428	L	W	W	W	W	L	W	W	W
888	Boy Scouts of America v. Dale	June 28, 2000	530 U.S. 640	L	W	L	L	L	L	W	W	W
889	Hill v. Colorado	June 28, 2000	530 U.S. 703	W	L	L	L	W	W	L	L	L
890	Mitchell v. Helms	June 28, 2000	530 U.S. 793	L	W	L	L	L	L	W	W	L

	Case Name	Date Decided	Case #	Justices and Their Votes (W = ACLU Win; L = ACLU Loss)								
A	B	C	D	E	F	G	H	I	J	K	L	M
				Scalia	Stevens	O'Connor	Rehnquist	Kennedy	Thomas	Ginsburg	Souter	Breyer
891	Stenberg v. Carhart	June 28, 2000	530 U.S. 914	L	W	W	L	L	L	W	W	W
892	City of Indianapolis v. Edmond	November 28, 2000	531 U.S. 32	L	W	W	L	W	L	W	W	W
893	Bush v. Palm Beach County Canvassing Board	December 1, 2000	531 U.S. 70	L	L	L	L	L	L	L	L	L
894	Legal Services Corp. v. Velazquez	February 28, 2001	531 U.S. 533	L	W	L	L	W	L	W	W	W
895	Ferguson v. City of Charleston	March 21, 2001	532 U.S. 67	L	W	W	L	W	L	W	W	W
896	Shaw v. Murphy	April 18, 2001	532 U.S. 223	L	L	L	L	L	L	L	L	L
897	Easley v. Cromartie	April 18, 2001	532 U.S. 234	L	W	W	L	L	L	W	W	W
898	Alexander v. Sandoval	April 24, 2001	532 U.S. 275	L	W	L	L	L	L	W	W	W
899	Atwater v. City of Lago Vista	April 24, 2001	532 U.S. 318	L	W	W	L	L	L	W	L	W
900	U.S. v. Oakland Cannabis Buyers' Coop.	May 14, 2001	532 U.S. 483	L	L	L	L	L	L	L	L	Took no part in the decision
901	Bartnicki v. Vopper	May 21, 2001	532 U.S. 514	L	W	W	L	W	L	W	W	W

A	B Case Name	C Date Decided	D Case #	E Scalia	F Stevens	G O'Connor	H Rehnquist	I Kennedy	J Thomas	K Ginsburg	L Souter	M Breyer
	Case Name	**Date Decided**	**Case #**	**Justices and Their Votes** (W = ACLU Win; L = ACLU Loss)								
902	Buckhannon Board & Care Home, Inc. v. West Virginia Department of Health & Human Resources	May 29, 2001	532 U.S. 598	L	W	L	L	L	L	W	W	W
903	Booth v. Churner	May 29, 2001	532 U.S. 731	L	L	L	L	L	L	L	L	L
904	Pollard v. E. I. du Pont de Nemours & Co.	June 4, 2001	532 U.S. 843	W	W	Took no part in the decision	W	W	W	W	W	W
905	Kyllo v. United States	June 11, 2001	533 U.S. 27	W	L	L	L	L	W	W	W	W
906	Nguyen v. INS	June 11, 2001	533 U.S. 53	L	L	W	L	L	L	W	W	W
907	Good News Club v. Milford Central School	June 11, 2001	533 U.S. 98	L	W	L	L	L	L	W	W	L
908	Saucier v. Katz	June 18, 2001	533 U.S. 194	L	L	L	L	L	L	L	L	L
909	INS v. St. Cyr	June 25, 2001	533 U.S. 289	L	W	L	L	W	L	W	W	W
910	Calcano-Martinez v. INS	June 25, 2001	533 U.S. 348	L	W	L	L	W	L	W	W	W
911	FEC v. Colo. Republican Fed. Campaign Comm.	June 25, 2001	533 U.S. 431	W	L	L	W	W	W	L	L	L
912	Lorillard Tobacco Co. v. Reilly	June 28, 2001	533 U.S. 525	W	L	W	W	W	W	L	L	L

A	B Case Name	C Date Decided	D Case #	E Scalia	F Stevens	G O'Connor	H Rehnquist	I Kennedy	J Thomas	K Ginsburg	L Souter	M Breyer
												Justices and Their Votes (W = ACLU Win; L = ACLU Loss)
913	Zadvydas v. Davis	June 28, 2001	533 U.S. 678	L	W	W	L	L	L	W	W	W
914	Correctional Services Corp. v. Malesko	November 27, 2001	534 U.S. 61	L	W	L	L	L	L	W	W	W
915	Adarand Constructors, Inc. v. Mineta	November 27, 2001	534 U.S. 103	W	W	W	W	W	W	W	W	W
916	EEOC v. Waffle House, Inc.	January 15, 2002	534 U.S. 279	L	W	W	L	W	L	W	W	W
917	Kansas v. Crane	January 22, 2002	534 U.S. 407	W	L	L	L	L	W	L	L	L
918	Swierkiewicz v. Sorema N. A.	February 26, 2002	534 U.S. 506	W	W	W	W	W	W	W	W	W
919	Dep't of Hous. & Urban Dev. v. Rucker	March 26, 2002	535 U.S. 125	L	L	L	L	L	L	L	L	Took no part in the decision
920	Hoffman Plastic Compounds, Inc. v. NLRB	March 27, 2002	535 U.S. 137	L	W	L	L	L	L	W	W	W
921	Ashcroft v. Free Speech Coalition	April 16, 2002	535 U.S. 234	L	W	L	L	W	W	W	W	W
922	Ashcroft v. American Civil Liberties Union	May 13, 2002	535 U.S. 564	L	W	L	L	L	L	L	L	L

A	B	Case Name	C	Date Decided	D	Case #	Justices and Their Votes (W = ACLU Win; L = ACLU Loss)								
							E	F	G	H	I	J	K	L	M
							Scalia	Stevens	O'Connor	Rehnquist	Kennedy	Thomas	Ginsburg	Souter	Breyer
923		Verizon Maryland, Inc. v. Pub. Serv. Comm'n of Maryland		May 20, 2002		535 U.S. 635	W	W	Took no part in the decision	W	W	W	W	W	W
924		Bell v. Cone		May 28, 2002		535 U.S. 685	L	W	L	L	L	L	L	L	L
925		Chevron U.S.A., Inc. v. Echazabal		June 10, 2002		536 U.S. 73	L	L	L	L	L	L	L	L	L
926		Watchtower Bible & Tract Soc'y of New York, Inc. v. Village of Stratton		June 17, 2002		536 U.S. 150	W	W	W	L	W	W	W	W	W
927		Gonzaga Univ. v. Doe		June 20, 2002		536 U.S. 273	L	W	L	L	L	L	W	L	L
928		Atkins v. Virginia		June 20, 2002		536 U.S. 304	L	W	W	L	W	L	W	W	W
929		Christopher v. Harbury		June 20, 2002		536 U.S. 403	L	L	L	L	L	L	L	L	L
930		Zelman v. Simmons-Harris		June 27, 2002		536 U.S. 639	L	W	L	L	L	L	W	W	W
931		Hope v. Pelzer		June 27, 2002		536 U.S. 730	L	W	W	L	W	L	W	W	W
932		Republican Party of Minnesota v. White		June 27, 2002		536 U.S. 765	W	L	W	W	W	W	L	L	L

	Case Name	Date Decided	Case #	Justices and Their Votes (W = ACLU Win; L = ACLU Loss)								
A	B	C	D	E	F	G	H	I	J	K	L	M
				Scalia	Stevens	O'Connor	Rehnquist	Kennedy	Thomas	Ginsburg	Souter	Breyer
933	Bd. of Ed. of Indep. Sch. Dist. No. 92 of Pottawatomie Cty. v. Earls	June 27, 2002	536 U.S. 822	L	W	W	L	L	L	W	W	L
934	Connecticut Dep't of Pub. Safety v. Doe	March 5, 2003	538 U.S. 1	L	L	L	L	L	L	L	L	L
935	Lockyer v. Andrade	March 5, 2003	538 U.S. 63	L	W	L	L	L	L	W	W	W
936	Smith v. Doe	March 5, 2003	538 U.S. 84	L	W	L	L	L	L	W	L	W
937	Virginia v. Black	April 7, 2003	538 U.S. 343	L	W	W	W	W	L	W	W	W
938	Medical Board of California v. Hason	April 7, 2003	538 U.S. 958	W	W	W	W	W	W	W	W	W
939	Demore v. Kim	April 29, 2003	538 U.S. 510	L	W	L	L	L	L	W	W	W
940	Nevada Dep't of Human Res. v. Hibbs	May 27, 2003	538 U.S. 721	L	W	W	W	L	L	W	W	W
941	Chavez v. Martinez	May 27, 2003	538 U.S. 760	L	W	L	L	W	L	W	L	L
942	Desert Palace, Inc. v. Costa	June 9, 2003	539 U.S. 90	W	W	W	W	W	W	W	W	W
943	Virginia v. Hicks	June 16, 2003	539 U.S. 113	L	L	L	L	L	L	L	L	L
944	Overton v. Bazzetta	June 16, 2003	539 U.S. 126	L	L	L	L	L	L	L	L	L

	Case Name	Date Decided	Case #	Justices and Their Votes (W = ACLU Win; L = ACLU Loss)								
A	B	C	D	E	F	G	H	I	J	K	L	M
				Scalia	Stevens	O'Connor	Rehnquist	Kennedy	Thomas	Ginsburg	Souter	Breyer
945	Sell v. United States	June 16, 2003	539 U.S. 166	W	L	W	L	L	W	L	L	L
946	U.S. v. American Library Ass'n, Inc.	June 23, 2003	539 U.S. 194	L	W	L	L	L	L	W	W	L
947	Gratz v. Bollinger	June 23, 2003	539 U.S. 244	L	W	L	L	L	L	W	W	L
948	Grutter v. Bollinger	June 23, 2003	539 U.S. 306	L	W	W	L	L	L	W	W	W
949	Georgia v. Ashcroft	June 26, 2003	539 U.S. 461	L	W	L	L	L	L	W	W	W
950	Lawrence v. Texas	June 26, 2003	539 U.S. 558	L	W	W	L	W	L	W	W	W
951	Nike, Inc. v. Kasky	June 26, 2003	539 U.S. 654	L	L	W	L	W	L	L	L	W
952	Arizona v. Gant	October 20, 2003	540 U.S. 963	L	L	L	L	L	L	L	L	L
953	McConnell v. Federal Election Comm'n	December 10, 2003	540 U.S. 93	W	L	L	W	W	W	L	L	L
954	Maryland v. Pringle	December 15, 2003	540 U.S. 366	L	L	L	L	L	L	L	L	L
955	Illinois v. Lidster	January 13, 2004	540 U.S. 419	L	W	L	L	L	L	W	W	L
956	Frew v. Hawkins	January 14, 2004	540 U.S. 431	W	W	W	W	W	W	W	W	W
957	Doe v. Chao	February 24, 2004	540 U.S. 614	L	W	L	L	L	L	W	L	W

A	B Case Name	C Date Decided	D Case #	E Scalia	F Stevens	G O'Connor	H Rehnquist	I Kennedy	J Thomas	K Ginsburg	L Souter	M Breyer
958	Locke v. Davey	February 25, 2004	540 U.S. 712	L	W	W	W	W	L	W	W	W
959	Crawford v. Washington	March 8, 2004	541 U.S. 36	W	W	W	W	W	W	W	W	W
960	Vieth v. Jubelirer	April 28, 2004	541 U.S. 267	L	W	L	L	L	L	W	W	W
961	Thornton v. United States	May 24, 2004	541 U.S. 615	L	W	L	L	L	L	L	W	L
962	Elk Grove United School District v. Newdow	June 14, 2004	542 U.S. 1	Took no part in the decision	L	L	L	L	L	L	L	L
963	Hibbs v. Winn	June 14, 2004	542 U.S. 88	L	W	W	L	L	L	W	W	W
964	Pennsylvania State Police v. Suders	June 14, 2004	542 U.S. 129	L	L	L	L	L	W	L	L	L
965	Hiibel v. Sixth Judicial District Court of Nevada, Humboldt County	June 21, 2004	542 U.S. 177	L	W	L	L	L	L	W	W	W
966	Blakely v. Washington	June 24, 2004	542 U.S. 296	W	W	L	L	L	W	W	W	L
967	Beard v. Banks	June 24, 2004	542 U.S. 406	L	W	L	L	L	L	W	W	W
968	Rumsfeld v. Padilla	June 28, 2004	542 U.S. 426	L	W	L	L	L	L	W	W	W
969	Rasul v. Bush	June 28, 2004	542 U.S. 466	L	W	W	L	W	L	W	W	W

	Case Name	Date Decided	Case #	Justices and Their Votes (W = ACLU Win; L = ACLU Loss)								
A	B	C	D	E	F	G	H	I	J	K	L	M
				Scalia	Stevens	O'Connor	Rehnquist	Kennedy	Thomas	Ginsburg	Souter	Breyer
970	Hamdi v. Rumsfeld	June 28, 2004	542 U.S. 507	L	L	W	W	W	L	W	W	W
971	Missouri v. Seibert	June 28, 2004	542 U.S. 600	L	W	L	L	W	L	W	W	W
972	United States v. Patane	June 28, 2004	542 U.S. 630	L	W	L	L	L	L	W	W	W
973	Ashcroft v. American Civil Liberties Union	June 29, 2004	542 U.S. 656	L	W	L	L	W	W	W	W	L
974	Sosa v. Alvarez-Machain	June 29, 2004	542 U.S. 692	L	L	L	L	L	L	L	L	L
975	Leocal v. Ashcroft	November 9, 2004	543 U.S. 1	W	W	W	W	W	W	W	W	W
976	Kowalski v. Tesmer	December 13, 2004	543 U.S. 125	L	W	L	L	L	L	W	W	L
977	Clark v. Martinez	January 12, 2005	543 U.S. 371	W	W	W	L	W	L	W	W	W
978	Illinois v. Caballes	January 24, 2005	543 U.S. 405	L	L	L	Took no part in the decision	L	L	W	W	L
979	Johnson v. California	February 23, 2005	543 U.S. 499	L	L	W	Took no part in the decision	W	L	W	W	W
980	Roper v. Simmons	March 1, 2005	543 U.S. 551	L	W	L	L	W	L	W	W	W

A	B	C	D		Justices and Their Votes (W = ACLU Win; L = ACLU Loss)							
	Case Name	Date Decided	Case #	E	F	G	H	I	J	K	L	M
				Scalia	Stevens	O'Connor	Rehnquist	Kennedy	Thomas	Ginsburg	Souter	Breyer
981	Ballard v. Commissioner of Internal Revenue	March 7, 2005	544 U.S. 40	W	W	W	L	W	L	W	W	W
982	Muehler v. Mena	March 22, 2005	544 U.S. 93	L	L	L	L	L	L	L	L	L
983	Jackson v. Birmingham Bd. of Educ.	March 29, 2005	544 U.S. 167	L	W	W	L	L	L	W	W	W
984	Cutter v. Wilkinson	May 31, 2005	544 U.S. 709	W	W	W	W	W	W	W	W	W
985	Johnson v. California	June 13, 2005	545 U.S. 162	W	W	W	W	W	L	W	W	W
986	Wilkinson v. Austin	June 13, 2005	545 U.S. 209	L	L	L	L	L	L	L	L	L
987	Halbert v. Michigan	June 23, 2005	545 U.S. 605	L	W	W	L	W	L	W	W	W
988	Town of Castle Rock v. Gonzales	June 27, 2005	545 U.S. 748	L	W	L	L	L	L	W	L	L
989	McCreary County v. American Civil Liberties Union of Kentucky	June 27, 2005	545 U.S. 844	L	W	W	L	L	L	W	W	W
990	Metro-Goldwyn-Mayer Studios, Inc. v. Grokster, Ltd.	June 27, 2005	545 U.S. 913	L	L	L	L	L	L	L	L	L
991	National Cable and Television Communications Ass'n v. Brand X Internet Services	June 27, 2005	545 U.S. 967	W	L	L	L	L	L	W	W	L

	Case Name	Date Decided	Case #	Justices and Their Votes (W = ACLU Win; L = ACLU Loss)								
A	B	C	D	E	F	G	H	I	J	K	L	M
				Scalia	Stevens	O'Connor	Rehnquist	Kennedy	Thomas	Ginsburg	Souter	Breyer
992	U.S. v. Georgia	January 10, 2006	546 U.S. 151	W	W	W	Roberts, J. W	W	W	W	W	W
993	Gonzales v. Oregon	January 17, 2006	546 U.S. 243	L	W	W	L	W	L	W	W	W
994	Ayotte v. Planned Parenthood of Northern New England	January 18, 2006	546 U.S. 320	L	L	L	L	L	L	L	L	L
995	Wisconsin Right to Life, Inc. v. Federal Election Commission	January 23, 2006	546 U.S. 410	W	W	W	W	W	W	W	W	W
996	Gonzales v. O Centro Espírita Beneficente União do Vegetal	February 21, 2006	546 U.S. 418	W	W	Alito Took no part in the decision	W	W	W	W	W	W
997	Rumsfeld v. Forum for Academic & Institutional Rights, Inc.	March 6, 2006	547 U.S. 47	L	L	Took no part in the decision	L	L	L	L	L	L
998	Garcetti v. Ceballos	May 30, 2006	547 U.S. 410	L	W	L	L	L	L	W	W	W
999	Hudson v. Michigan	June 15, 2006	547 U.S. 586	L	W	L	L	L	L	W	W	W
1000	Davis v. Washington	June 19, 2006	547 U.S. 813	L	L	L	L	L	L	L	L	L

	Case Name	Date Decided	Case #	\multicolumn{9}{c}{Justices and Their Votes (W = ACLU Win; L = ACLU Loss)}								
A	B	C	D	E	F	G	H	I	J	K	L	M
				Scalia	Stevens	Alito	Roberts, J.	Kennedy	Thomas	Ginsburg	Souter	Breyer
1001	Samson v. California	June 19, 2006	547 U.S. 843	L	W	L	L	L	L	L	W	W
1002	Fernandez-Vargas v. Gonzales	June 22, 2006	548 U.S. 30	L	W	L	L	L	L	L	L	L
1003	Burlington Northern & Santa Fe Ry. Co. v. White	June 22, 2006	548 U.S. 53	W	W	W	W	W	W	W	W	W
1004	Woodford v. Ngo	June 22, 2006	548 U.S. 81	L	W	L	L	L	L	W	W	L
1005	Randall v. Sorrell	June 26, 2006	548 U.S. 230	W	L	W	W	W	W	L	L	W
1006	Beard v. Banks	June 28, 2006	548 U.S. 521	L	W	Took no part in the decision	L	L	L	W	L	L
1007	Hamdan v. Rumsfeld	June 29, 2006	548 U.S. 557	L	W	L	Took no part in the decision	W	L	W	W	W
1008	Lopez v. Gonzales	December 5, 2006	549 U.S. 47	W	W	W	W	W	L	W	W	W
1009	Jones v. Bock	January 22, 2007	549 U.S. 199	W	W	W	W	W	W	W	W	W
1010	Lawrence v. Florida	February 20, 2007	549 U.S. 327	L	W	L	L	L	L	W	W	W
1011	Gonzales v. Carhart	April 18, 2007	550 U.S. 124	L	W	L	L	L	L	W	W	W

	Case Name	Date Decided	Case #	Justices and Their Votes (W = ACLU Win; L = ACLU Loss)								
A	B	C	D	E	F	G	H	I	J	K	L	M
				Scalia	Stevens	Alito	Roberts, J.	Kennedy	Thomas	Ginsburg	Souter	Breyer
1012	Scott v. Harris	April 30, 2007	550 U.S. 372	L	W	L	L	L	L	L	L	L
1013	Ledbetter v. Goodyear Tire & Rubber Co.	May 29, 2007	550 U.S. 618	L	W	L	L	L	L	W	W	W
1014	Uttecht v. Brown	June 4, 2007	551 U.S. 1	L	W	L	L	L	L	W	W	W
1015	Sole v. Wyner	June 4, 2007	551 U.S. 74	L	L	L	L	L	L	L	L	L
1016	Long Island Care at Home, Ltd. v. Coke	June 11, 2007	551 U.S. 158	L	L	L	L	L	L	L	L	L
1017	Brendlin v. California	June 18, 2007	551 U.S. 249	W	W	W	W	W	W	W	W	W
1018	Morse v. Frederick	June 25, 2007	551 U.S. 393	L	W	L	L	L	L	W	W	W
1019	Federal Election Commission v. Wisconsin Right to Life, Inc.	June 25, 2007	551 U.S. 449	W	L	W	W	W	W	L	L	L
1020	Hein v. Freedom From Religion Foundation, Inc.	June 25, 2007	551 U.S. 587	L	W	L	L	L	L	W	W	W
1021	Parents Involved in Community Schools v. Seattle School Dist. No. 1	June 28, 2007	551 U.S. 701	L	W	L	L	L	L	W	W	W
1022	Kimbrough v. U.S.	December 10, 2007	552 U.S. 85	W	W	L	W	W	L	W	W	W

A	B	C	D	E	F	G	H	I	J	K	L	M
	Case Name	**Date Decided**	**Case #**	**Justices and Their Votes** (W = ACLU Win; L = ACLU Loss)								
				Scalia	Stevens	Alito	Roberts, J.	Kennedy	Thomas	Ginsburg	Souter	Breyer
1023	New York State Bd. of Elections v. Lopez Torres	January 16, 2008	552 U.S. 196	L	L	L	L	L	L	L	L	L
1024	Danforth v. Minnesota	February 20, 2008	552 U.S. 264	W	W	W	L	L	W	W	W	W
1025	Baze v. Rees	April 16, 2008	553 U.S. 35	L	L	L	L	L	L	W	W	L
1026	Virginia v. Moore	April 23, 2008	553 U.S. 164	L	L	L	L	L	L	L	L	L
1027	Crawford v. Marion County Election Bd.	April 28, 2008	553 U.S. 181	L	L	L	L	L	L	W	W	W
1028	Riley v. Kennedy	May 27, 2008	553 U.S. 406	L	W	L	L	L	L	L	W	L
1029	CBOCS West, Inc. v. Humphries	May 27, 2008	553 U.S. 442	L	W	W	W	W	L	W	W	W
1030	Engquist v. Oregon Department of Agriculture	June 9, 2008	553 U.S. 591	L	W	L	L	L	L	W	W	L
1031	Boumediene v. Bush	June 12, 2008	553 U.S. 723	L	W	L	L	W	L	W	W	W
1032	Kennedy v. Louisiana	June 25, 2008	554 U.S. 407	L	W	L	L	W	L	W	W	W
1033	Herring v. U.S.	January 14, 2009	555 U.S. 135	L	W	L	L	L	L	W	W	W
1034	Pearson v. Callahan	January 21, 2009	555 U.S. 223	L	L	L	L	L	L	L	L	L

A	B	C	D	E	F	G	H	I	J	K	L	M
	Case Name	Date Decided	Case #	Justices and Their Votes (W = ACLU Win; L = ACLU Loss)								
				Scalia	Stevens	Alito	Roberts, J.	Kennedy	Thomas	Ginsburg	Souter	Breyer
1035	Fitzgerald v. Barnstable School Comm.	January 21, 2009	555 U.S. 246	W	W	W	W	W	W	W	W	W
1036	Crawford v. Metropolitan Government of Nashville & Davidson County, Tennessee	January 26, 2009	555 U.S. 271	W	W	W	W	W	W	W	W	W
1037	Van de Kamp v. Goldstein	January 26, 2009	555 U.S. 335	L	L	L	L	L	L	L	L	L
1038	Bartlett v. Strickland	March 9, 2009	556 U.S. 1	L	W	L	L	L	L	W	W	W
1039	Vermont v. Brillon	March 9, 2009	556 U.S. 81	L	W	L	L	L	L	L	L	W
1040	Arizona v. Gant	April 21, 2009	556 U.S. 332	W	W	L	L	L	W	W	W	L
1041	Nken v. Holder	April 22, 2009	556 U.S. 418	W	W	L	W	W	L	W	W	W
1042	F.C.C. v. Fox Television Stations, Inc.	April 28, 2009	556 U.S. 502	L	W	L	L	L	L	W	W	W
1043	Montejo v. Louisiana	May 26, 2009	556 U.S. 778	L	W	L	L	L	L	W	W	W
1044	Nijhawan v. Holder	June 15, 2009	557 U.S. 29	L	L	L	L	L	L	L	L	L
1045	District Attorney's Office for the Third Judicial Dist. v. Osborne	June 18, 2009	557 U.S. 52	L	W	L	L	L	L	W	W	W

	Case Name	Date Decided	Case #	Justices and Their Votes (W = ACLU Win; L = ACLU Loss)								
A	B	C	D	E Scalia	F Stevens	G Alito	H Roberts, J.	I Kennedy	J Thomas	K Ginsburg	L Souter	M Breyer
1046	Northwest Austin Mun. Utility Dist. No. One v. Holder	June 22, 2009	557 U.S. 193	L	L	L	L	L	W	L	L	L
1047	Safford Unified School Dist. No. 1 v. Redding	June 25, 2009	557 U.S. 364	W	W	W	W	W	L	W	W	W
1048	Ricci v. DeStefano	June 29, 2009	557 U.S. 557	L	W	L	L	L	L	W	W	W
1049	Alvarez v. Smith	December 8, 2009	558 U.S. 87	L	L	L	L	L	L	L	Sotomayor L	L
1050	Kucana v. Holder	January 20, 2010	558 U.S. 233	W	W	W	W	W	W	W	W	W
1051	Wood v. Allen	January 20, 2010	558 U.S. 290	L	W	L	L	W	L	L	L	L
1052	Citizens United v. Federal Election Com'n	January 21, 2010	558 U.S. 310	W	L	W	W	W	W	L	L	L
1053	Kiyemba v. Obama	March 1, 2010	559 U.S. 131	W	W	W	W	W	W	W	W	W
1054	Berghuis v. Smith	March 30, 2010	559 U.S. 314	L	L	L	L	L	L	L	L	L
1055	U.S. v. Stevens	April 20, 2010	559 U.S. 460	W	W	L	W	W	W	W	W	W
1056	Perdue v. Kenny A.	April 21, 2010	559 U.S. 542	L	W	L	L	L	L	W	W	W

	Case Name	Date Decided	Case #	Justices and Their Votes (W = ACLU Win; L = ACLU Loss)								
A	B	C	D	E	F	G	H	I	J	K	L	M
				Scalia	Stevens	Alito	Roberts, J.	Kennedy	Thomas	Ginsburg	Sotomayor	Breyer
1057	Salazar v. Buono	April 28, 2010	559 U.S. 700	L	W	L	L	L	L	W	W	W
1058	Hui v. Castaneda	May 3, 2010	559 U.S. 799	L	L	L	L	L	L	L	L	L
1059	Lewis v. City of Chicago	May 24, 2010	560 U.S. 205	W	W	W	W	W	W	W	W	W
1060	Berghuis v. Thompkins	June 1, 2010	560 U.S. 370	L	W	L	L	L	L	W	W	W
1061	Barber v. Thomas	June 7, 2010	560 U.S. 474	L	W	L	L	W	L	W	L	L
1062	Holland v. Florida	June 14, 2010	560 U.S. 631	L	W	W	W	W	L	W	W	W
1063	City of Ontario v. Quon	June 17, 2010	560 U.S. 746	L	L	L	L	L	L	L	L	L
1064	Holder v. Humanitarian Law Project	June 21, 2010	561 U.S. 1	L	L	L	L	L	L	W	W	W
1065	Christian Legal Society v. Martinez	June 28, 2010	561 U.S. 661	L	W	L	L	W	L	W	W	W
1066	National Aeronautics and Space Administration v. Nelson	January 19, 2011	562 U.S. 134	L	Kagan Took no part in the decision	L	L	L	L	L	L	L

	Case Name	Date Decided	Case #	Justices and Their Votes (W = ACLU Win; L = ACLU Loss)								
A	B	C	D	E	F	G	H	I	J	K	L	M
				Scalia	Kagan	Alito	Roberts, J.	Kennedy	Thomas	Ginsburg	Sotomayor	Breyer
1067	Thompson v. North American Stainless, LP	January 24, 2011	562 U.S. 170	W	Took no part in the decision	W	W	W	W	W	W	W
1068	FCC v. AT&T Inc.	March 1, 2011	562 U.S. 397	W	Took no part in the decision	W	W	W	W	W	W	W
1069	Snyder v. Phelps	March 2, 2011	562 U.S. 443	W	W	L	W	W	W	W	W	W
1070	Milner v. Dep't of Navy	March 7, 2011	562 U.S. 562	W	W	W	W	W	W	W	W	L
1071	Connick v. Thompson	March 29, 2011	563 U.S. 51	L	W	L	L	L	L	W	W	W
1072	Arizona Christian School Tuition Organization v. Winn	April 4, 2011	563 U.S. 125	L	W	L	L	L	L	W	W	W
1073	Cullen v. Pinholster	April 4, 2011	563 U.S. 170	L	W	L	L	L	L	W	W	W
1074	Sossamon v. Texas	April 20, 2011	563 U.S. 277	L	Took no part in the decision	L	L	L	L	L	W	W
1075	Brown v. Plata	May 23, 2011	563 U.S. 493	L	W	L	L	W	L	W	W	W

A	B	C	D	E	F	G	H	I	J	K	L	M
	Case Name	**Date Decided**	**Case #**	**Justices and Their Votes** (W = ACLU Win; L = ACLU Loss)								
				Scalia	Kagan	Alito	Roberts, J.	Kennedy	Thomas	Ginsburg	Sotomayor	Breyer
1076	Chamber of Commerce of U.S. v. Whiting	May 26, 2011	563 U.S. 582	L	Took no part in the decision	L	L	L	L	W	W	W
1077	Ashcroft v. al-Kidd	May 31, 2011	563 U.S. 731	L	Took no part in the decision	L	L	L	L	L	L	L
1078	Fox v. Vice	June 6, 2011	563 U.S. 826	W	W	W	W	W	W	W	W	W
1079	J.D.B. v. North Carolina	June 16, 2011	564 U.S. 261	L	W	L	L	W	L	W	W	W
1080	Wal-Mart Stores, Inc. v. Dukes	June 20, 2011	564 U.S. 338	L	W	L	L	L	L	W	W	W
1081	Borough of Duryea v. Guarnieri	June 20, 2011	564 U.S. 379	L	L	L	L	L	L	L	L	L
1082	Turner v. Rogers	June 20, 2011	564 U.S. 431	L	W	L	L	W	L	W	W	W
1083	Brown v. Entertainment Merchants Ass'n	June 27, 2011	564 U.S. 786	W	W	W	W	W	L	W	W	L
1084	Hosanna-Tabor Evangelical Lutheran Church and School v. EEOC	January 11, 2012	565 U.S. 171	L	L	L	L	L	L	L	L	L
1085	Maples v. Thomas	January 18, 2012	565 U.S. 266	L	W	W	W	W	L	W	W	W

229

A	B	C	D	E	F	G	H	I	J	K	L	M
	Case Name	**Date Decided**	**Case #**	**Justices and Their Votes** (W = ACLU Win; L = ACLU Loss)								
				Scalia	Kagan	Alito	Roberts, J.	Kennedy	Thomas	Ginsburg	Sotomayor	Breyer
1086	Golan v. Holder	January 18, 2012	565 U.S. 302	L	Took no part in the decision	W	L	L	L	L	L	W
1087	U.S. v. Jones	January 23, 2012	565 U.S. 400	W	W	W	W	W	W	W	W	W
1088	Messerschmidt v. Millender	February 22, 2012	565 U.S. 535	L	W	L	L	L	L	W	W	L
1089	Douglas v. Independent Living Center of Southern California, Inc.	February 22, 2012	565 U.S. 606	W	L	W	W	L	W	L	L	L
1090	Coleman v. Court of Appeals of Maryland	March 20, 2012	566 U.S. 30	L	W	L	L	L	L	W	W	W
1091	Mayo Collaborative Services v. Prometheus Laboratories, Inc.	March 20, 2012	566 U.S. 66	W	W	W	W	W	W	W	W	W
1092	Missouri v. Frye	March 21, 2012	566 U.S. 134	L	W	L	L	W	L	W	W	W
1093	Lafler v. Cooper	March 21, 2012	566 U.S. 156	L	W	L	L	W	L	W	W	W
1094	Florence v. Board of Chosen Freeholders of County of Burlington	April 2, 2012	566 U.S. 318	L	W	L	L	L	L	W	W	W

	Case Name	Date Decided	Case #	Justices and Their Votes (W = ACLU Win; L = ACLU Loss)								
A	B	C	D	E	F	G	H	I	J	K	L	M
				Scalia	Kagan	Alito	Roberts, J.	Kennedy	Thomas	Ginsburg	Sotomayor	Breyer
1095	Reichle v. Howards	June 4, 2012	566 U.S. 658	L	Took no part in the decision	L	L	L	L	L	L	L
1096	FCC v. Fox Television Stations	June 21, 2012	567 U.S. 239	L	L	L	L	L	L	L	Took no part in the decision	L
1097	Dorsey v. U.S.	June 21, 2012	567 U.S. 260	L	W	L	L	W	L	W	W	W
1098	Arizona v. U.S.	June 25, 2012	567 U.S. 387	L	Took no part in the decision	L	W	W	L	W	W	W
1099	National Fed'n of Indep. Business v. Sebelius	June 28, 2012	567 U.S. 519	L	W	L	W	L	L	W	W	W
1100	U.S. v. Alvarez	June 28, 2012	567 U.S. 709	L	W	L	W	W	L	W	W	W
1101	Ryan v. Gonzales	January 8, 2013	568 U.S. 57	L	L	L	L	L	L	L	L	L
1102	Bailey v. U.S.	February 19, 2013	568 U.S. 186	W	W	L	W	W	L	W	W	L
1103	Florida v. Harris	February 19, 2013	568 U.S. 237	L	L	L	L	L	L	L	L	L
1104	Clapper v. Amnesty Int'l USA	February 26, 2013	568 U.S. 398	L	W	L	L	L	L	W	W	W

	Case Name	Date Decided	Case #	Justices and Their Votes (W = ACLU Win; L = ACLU Loss)								
A	B	C	D	E	F	G	H	I	J	K	L	M
				Scalia	Kagan	Alito	Roberts, J.	Kennedy	Thomas	Ginsburg	Sotomayor	Breyer
1105	Kiobel v. Royal Dutch Petroleum Co.	April 17, 2013	569 U.S. 108	L	L	L	L	L	L	L	L	L
1106	Missouri v. McNeely	April 17, 2013	569 U.S. 141	W	W	L	L	W	L	W	W	L
1107	McBurney v. Young	April 29, 2013	569 U.S. 221	L	L	L	L	L	L	L	L	L
1108	Maryland v. King	June 3, 2013	569 U.S. 435	W	W	L	L	L	L	W	W	L
1109	Ass'n for Molecular Pathology v. Myriad Genetics	June 13, 2013	569 U.S. 576	W	W	W	W	W	W	W	W	W
1110	Arizona v. Inter Tribal Council of Arizona	June 17, 2013	570 U.S. 1	W	W	L	W	W	L	W	W	W
1111	Alleyne v. U.S.	June 17, 2013	570 U.S. 99	L	W	L	L	L	W	W	W	W
1112	Salinas v. Texas	June 17, 2013	570 U.S. 178	L	W	L	L	L	L	W	W	W
1113	Agency for Int'l Dev. v. Alliance for Open Society Int'l	June 20, 2013	570 U.S. 205	L	Took no part in the decision	W	W	W	L	W	W	W
1114	Shelby County v. Holder	June 25, 2013	570 U.S. 529	L	W	L	L	L	L	W	W	W
1115	Adoptive Couple v. Baby Girl	June 25, 2013	570 U.S. 637	W	W	L	L	L	L	W	W	L

A	B	C	D	E	F	G	H	I	J	K	L	M
	Case Name	**Date Decided**	**Case #**	**Justices and Their Votes** (W = ACLU Win; L = ACLU Loss)								
				Scalia	Kagan	Alito	Roberts, J.	Kennedy	Thomas	Ginsburg	Sotomayor	Breyer
1116	Hollingsworth v. Perry	June 26, 2013	570 U.S. 693	W	W	L	W	L	L	W	L	W
1117	U.S. v. Windsor	June 26, 2013	570 U.S. 744	L	W	L	L	W	L	W	W	W
1118	Kansas v. Cheever	December 11, 2013	571 U.S. 87	L	L	L	L	L	L	L	L	L
1119	U.S. v. Apel	February 26, 2014	571 U.S. 359	L	L	L	L	L	L	L	L	L
1120	Schuette v. Coalition to Defend Affirmative Action	April 22, 2014	572 U.S. 291	L	Took no part in the decision	L	L	L	L	W	W	L
1121	Town of Greece v. Galloway	May 5, 2014	572 U.S. 565	L	W	L	L	L	L	W	W	W
1122	Wood v. Moss	May 27, 2014	572 U.S. 744	L	L	L	L	L	L	L	L	L
1123	Susan B. Anthony List v. Driehaus	June 16, 2014	573 U.S. 149	W	W	W	W	W	W	W	W	W
1124	Alice Corp. v. CLS Bank Int'l	June 19, 2014	573 U.S. 208	W	W	W	W	W	W	W	W	W
1125	Lane v. Franks	June 19, 2014	573 U.S. 228	W	W	W	W	W	W	W	W	W
1126	Riley v. California	June 25, 2014	573 U.S. 373	W	W	W	W	W	W	W	W	W
1127	McCullen v. Coakley	June 26, 2014	573 U.S. 464	L	L	L	L	L	L	L	L	L
1128	Burwell v. Hobby Lobby Stores, Inc.	June 30, 2014	573 U.S. 682	L	W	L	L	L	L	W	W	W

	Case Name	Date Decided	Case #	Justices and Their Votes (W = ACLU Win; L = ACLU Loss)								
A	B	C	D	E	F	G	H	I	J	K	L	M
				Scalia	Kagan	Alito	Roberts, J.	Kennedy	Thomas	Ginsburg	Sotomayor	Breyer
1129	Heien v. North Carolina	December 15, 2014	574 U.S. 54	L	L	L	L	L	L	L	W	L
1130	Holt v. Hobbs	January 20, 2015	574 U.S. 352	W	W	W	W	W	W	W	W	W
1131	Young v. United Parcel Service, Inc.	March 25, 2015	135 S.Ct. 1338; 575 U.S. –	L	W	W	W	L	L	W	W	W
1132	Armstrong v. Exceptional Child Center, Inc.	March 31, 2015	135 S.Ct. 1378; 575 U.S. –	L	W	L	L	W	L	W	W	L
1133	Williams-Yulee v. Florida Bar	April 29, 2015	135 S.Ct. 1656; 575 U.S. –	W	L	W	L	W	W	L	L	L
1134	City and County of San Francisco v. Sheehan	May 18, 2015	135 S.Ct. 1765; 575 U.S. –	W	W	L	L	L	L	L	L	Took no part in the decision
1135	Elonis v. United States	June 1, 2015	135 S.Ct. 2001; 575 U.S. –	W	W	W	W	W	L	W	W	W

234

	Case Name	Date Decided	Case #	Justices and Their Votes (W = ACLU Win; L = ACLU Loss)								
A	B	C	D	E	F	G	H	I	J	K	L	M
				Scalia	Kagan	Alito	Roberts, J.	Kennedy	Thomas	Ginsburg	Sotomayor	Breyer
1136	E.E.O.C. v. Abercrombie & Fitch Stores	June 1, 2015	135 S.Ct. 2028; 575 U.S. –	W	W	W	W	W	L	W	W	W
1137	Kerry v. Din	June 15, 2015	135 S.Ct. 2128; 576 U.S. –	L	W	L	L	L	L	W	W	W
1138	Walker v. Texas Div., Sons of Confederate Veterans, Inc.	June 18, 2015	135 S.Ct. 2239; 576 U.S. –	W	L	W	W	W	L	L	L	L
1139	Kingsley v. Hendrickson	June 22, 2015	135 S.Ct. 2466; 576 U.S. –	L	W	L	L	W	L	W	W	W
1140	Texas Dept. of Housing and Community Affairs v. Inclusive Communities Project, Inc.	June 25, 2015	135 S.Ct. 2507; 576 U.S. –	L	W	L	L	W	L	W	W	W
1141	Obergefell v. Hodges	June 26, 2015	135 S.Ct. 2584; 576 U.S. –	L	W	L	L	W	L	W	W	W

	Case Name	Date Decided	Case #	Justices and Their Votes (W = ACLU Win; L = ACLU Loss)								
A	B	C	D	E	F	G	H	I	J	K	L	M
				Scalia	Kagan	Alito	Roberts, J.	Kennedy	Thomas	Ginsburg	Sotomayor	Breyer
1142	Arizona State Legislature v. Arizona Indep. Redistricting Comm'n	June 29, 2015	135 S.Ct. 2652; 576 U.S. –	L	W	L	L	W	L	W	W	W
1143	Hurst v. Florida	January 12, 2016	136 S.Ct. 616; 577 U.S. –	W	W	L	W	W	W	W	W	W
1144	Montgomery v. Louisiana	January 25, 2016	136 S.Ct. 718; 577 U.S. –	L	W	L	W	W	L	W	W	W
1145	Evenwel v. Abbott	April 4, 2016	136 S.Ct. 1120; 578 U.S. –	VACANT SEAT	W	W	W	W	W	W	W	W
1146	Zubik v. Burwell	May 16, 2016	136 S.Ct. 1557; 578 U.S. –	VACANT SEAT	L	L	L	L	L	L	L	L
1147	Simmons v. Himmelreich	June 6, 2016	136 S.Ct. 1843; 578 U.S. –	VACANT SEAT	W	W	W	W	W	W	W	W
1148	Williams v. Pennsylvania	June 9, 2016	136 S.Ct. 1899; 579 U.S. –	VACANT SEAT	W	L	L	W	L	W	W	W

	Case Name	Date Decided	Case #	Justices and Their Votes (W = ACLU Win; L = ACLU Loss)								
A	B	C	D	E	F	G	H	I	J	K	L	M
				Scalia	Kagan	Alito	Roberts, J.	Kennedy	Thomas	Ginsburg	Sotomayor	Breyer
1149	Utah v. Strieff	June 20, 2016	136 S.Ct. 2056; 579 U.S. –	VACANT SEAT	W	L	L	L	L	W	W	L
1150	Birchfield v. North Dakota	June 23, 2016	136 S.Ct. 2160; 579 U.S. –	VACANT SEAT	W	W	W	W	L	W	W	W
1151	Fisher v. Univ. of Texas at Austin	June 23, 2016	136 S.Ct. 2198; 579 U.S. –	VACANT SEAT	Took no part in the decision	L	L	W	L	W	W	W
1152	Whole Woman's Health v. Hellerstedt	June 27, 2016	136 S.Ct. 2292; 579 U.S. –	VACANT SEAT	W	L	L	W	L	W	W	W
1153	Fry v. Napoleon Community Schools	February 22, 2017	137 S.Ct. 743; 580 U.S. –	VACANT SEAT	W	W	W	W	W	W	W	W
1154	Pena-Rodriguez v. Colorado	March 6, 2017	137 S.Ct. 855; 580 U.S. –	VACANT SEAT	W	L	L	W	L	W	W	W
1155	Moore v. Texas	March 28, 2017	137 S.Ct. 1039; 581 U.S. –	VACANT SEAT	W	L	L	W	L	W	W	W

	Case Name	Date Decided	Case #	Justices and Their Votes (W = ACLU Win; L = ACLU Loss)								
A	B	C	D	E	F	G	H	I	J	K	L	M
				Scalia	Kagan	Alito	Roberts, J.	Kennedy	Thomas	Ginsburg	Sotomayor	Breyer
1156	Bank of America Corp. v. City of Miami	May 1, 2017	137 S.Ct. 1296; 581 U.S. –	Gorsuch Took no part in the decision	W	L	W	L	L	W	W	W
1157	County of Los Angeles v. Mendez	May 30, 2017	137 S.Ct. 1539; 581 U.S. –	Took no part in the decision	L	L	L	L	L	L	L	L
1158	Advocate Health Care Network v. Stapleton	June 5, 2017	137 S.Ct. 1652; 581 U.S. –	Took no part in the decision	L	L	L	L	L	L	L	L
1159	Sessions v. Morales-Santana	June 12, 2017	137 S.Ct. 1678; 582 U.S. –	Took no part in the decision	W	W	W	W	W	W	W	W
1160	Packingham v. North Carolina	June 19, 2017	137 S.Ct. 1730; 582 U.S. –	Took no part in the decision	W	W	W	W	W	W	W	W
1161	Matal v. Tam	June 19, 2017	137 S.Ct. 1744; 582 U.S. –	Took no part in the decision	W	W	W	W	W	W	W	W

A	B Case Name	C Date Decided	D Case #	E Gorsuch	F Kagan	G Alito	H Roberts, J.	I Kennedy	J Thomas	K Ginsburg	L Sotomayor	M Breyer
						Justices and Their Votes (W = ACLU Win; L = ACLU Loss)						
1162	Ziglar v. Abbasi	June 19, 2017	137 S.Ct. 1843; 582 U.S. _	Took no part in the decision	Took no part in the decision	L	L	L	L	W	Took no part in the decision	W
1163	Weaver v. Massachusetts	June 22, 2017	137 S.Ct. 1899; 582 U.S. _	L	W	L	L	L	L	L	L	W
1164	Hernandez v. Mesa	June 26, 2017	137 S.Ct. 2003; 582 U.S. _	Took no part in the decision	W	W	W	W	L	L	W	L
1165	Trinity Lutheran Church of Columbia, Inc. v. Comer	June 26, 2017	137 S.Ct. 2012; 582 U.S. _	L	L	L	L	L	L	W	W	L
1166	Davila v. Davis	June 26, 2017	137 S.Ct. 2058; 582 U.S. _	L	W	L	L	L	L	W	W	W
1167	Trump v. Int'l Refugee Assistance Project	June 26, 2017	137 S.Ct. 2080; 582 U.S. _	L	L	L	L	L	L	L	L	L
1168	District of Columbia v. Wesby	January 22, 2018	138 S.Ct. 577; 583 U.S. _	L	L	L	L	L	L	L	L	L

A	B	C	D	Justices and Their Votes (W = ACLU Win; L = ACLU Loss)								
	Case Name	Date Decided	Case #	E	F	G	H	I	J	K	L	M
				Gorsuch	Kagan	Alito	Roberts, J.	Kennedy	Thomas	Ginsburg	Sotomayor	Breyer
1169	Class v. United States	February 21, 2018	138 S.Ct. 798; 583 U.S. –	W	W	L	W	L	L	W	W	W
1170	Jennings v. Rodriguez	February 27, 2018	138 S.Ct. 830; 583 U.S. –	L	Took no part in the decision	L	L	L	L	W	W	W
1171	Ayestas v. Davis	March 21, 2018	138 S.Ct. 1080; 584 U.S. –	W	W	W	W	W	W	W	W	W
1172	Byrd v. United States	May 14, 2018	138 S.Ct. 1518; 584 U.S. –	W	W	W	W	W	W	W	W	W
1173	Epic Systems Corp. v. Lewis	May 21, 2018	138 S.Ct. 1612; 584 U.S. –	L	W	L	L	L	L	W	W	W
1174	Masterpiece Cakeshop, Ltd. v. Colorado Civil Rights Comm'n	June 4, 2018	138 S.Ct. 1719; 584 U.S. –	L	L	L	L	L	L	W	W	L

	Case Name	Date Decided	Case #	Justices and Their Votes (W = ACLU Win; L = ACLU Loss)								
A	B	C	D	E	F	G	H	I	J	K	L	M
				Gorsuch	Kagan	Alito	Roberts, J.	Kennedy	Thomas	Ginsburg	Sotomayor	Breyer
1175	Husted v. A. Philip Randolph Institute	June 11, 2018	138 S.Ct. 1833; 584 U.S. –	L	W	L	L	L	L	W	W	W
1176	Gill v. Whitford	June 18, 2018	138 S.Ct. 1916; 585 U.S. –	L	L	L	L	L	L	L	L	L
1177	Benisek v. Lamone	June 18, 2018	138 S.Ct. 1942; 585 U.S. –	L	L	L	L	L	L	L	L	L
1178	Carpenter v. United States	June 22, 2018	138 S.Ct. 2206; 585 U.S. –	L	W	L	W	L	L	W	W	W
1179	Trump v. Hawaii	June 26, 2018	138 S.Ct. 2392; 585 U.S. –	L	W	L	L	L	L	W	W	W
1180	Janus v. American Federation of State, County, and Municipal Employees, Council 31	June 27, 2018	138 S.Ct. 2448; 585 U.S. –	L	W	L	L	L	L	W	W	W

	Case Name	Date Decided	Case #	Justices and Their Votes (W = ACLU Win; L = ACLU Loss)								
A	B	C	D	E	F	G	H	I	J	K	L	M
				Gorsuch	Kagan	Alito	Roberts, J.	Kennedy	Thomas	Ginsburg	Sotomayor	Breyer
1181	Timbs v. Indiana	February 20, 2019	139 S.Ct. 682; 586 U.S. _	W	W	W	W	Kavanaugh W	W	W	W	W
1182	Nielsen v. Preap	March 19, 2019	139 S.Ct. 954; 586 U.S. _	L	W	L	L	L	L	W	W	W
1183	Bucklew v. Precythe	April 1, 2019	139 S.Ct. 1112; 587 U.S. _	L	W	L	L	L	L	W	W	W
1184	Nieves v. Bartlett	May 28, 2019	139 S.Ct. 1715; 587 U.S. _	L	L	L	L	L	L	L	W	L
1185	Manhattan Community Access Corp. v. Halleck	June 17, 2019	139 S.Ct. 1921; 587 U.S. _	L	W	L	L	L	L	W	W	W
1186	Gamble v. United States	June 17, 2019	139 S.Ct. 1960; 587 U.S. _	W	L	L	L	L	L	W	L	L

A	B	C	D				Justices and Their Votes (W = ACLU Win; L = ACLU Loss)					
	Case Name	Date Decided	Case #	E	F	G	H	I	J	K	L	M
				Gorsuch	Kagan	Alito	Roberts, J.	Kavanaugh	Thomas	Ginsburg	Sotomayor	Breyer
1187	American Legion v. American Humanist Ass'n	June 20, 2019	139 S.Ct. 2067; 588 U.S. –	L	L	L	L	L	L	W	W	L
1188	Gundy v. United States	June 20, 2019	139 S.Ct. 2116; 588 U.S. –	W	L	L	W	Took no part in the decision	W	L	L	L
1189	McDonough v. Smith	June 20, 2019	139 S.Ct. 2149; 588 U.S. –	L	L	W	W	W	L	W	W	W
1190	Iancu v. Brunetti	June 24, 2019	139 S.Ct. 2294; 588 U.S. –	W	W	W	L	W	W	W	L	L
1191	Rucho v. Common Cause	June 27, 2019	139 S.Ct. 2484; 588 U.S. –	L	W	L	L	L	L	W	W	W
1192	Mitchell v. Wisconsin	June 27, 2019	139 S.Ct. 2525; 588 U.S. –	W	W	L	L	L	L	W	W	L
1193	Dep't of Commerce v. New York	June 27, 2019	139 S.Ct. 2551; 588 U.S. –	L	W	L	W	L	L	W	W	W

VI.

A Summary of the Voting Record of Each U.S. Supreme Court Justice in ACLU Cases From 1925 to 2019

The following chart ranks the 51 U.S. Supreme Court justices in accordance with the percentage that each voted in favor of the position taken by the ACLU in the cases before them, with the caveat that such listed percentages should be considered given the total number of cases each justice voted on.

Some examples:

- While Justice William J. Brennan, Jr. voted in favor of the ACLU position in 83.36% of the 607 cases he voted on. Justice Benjamin Nathan Cardozo voted with the ACLU 100%, but only voted on four cases.

- 28 of the justices voted in favor of the ACLU positions more than 50% of the time; 22 of the justices voted with the ACLU less than 50% of the time (Justice Fred Moore Vinson was not included in the 50 justices because he voted with the ACLU 50% of the time).

- Of the 28 justices who sided with the ACLU in more than 50% of the cases, 57.14% were nominated by Democratic presidents and 42.86% by Republican presidents. Of the 22 justices who sided with the ACLU in less than 50% of the cases, 22.73% were nominated by Democratic presidents, 77.27% by Republican presidents.

- Of the justices voting in at least 10 ACLU cases, Justice Arthur Joseph Goldberg was the most supportive of the ACLU's side, voting 97.14% with them in 35 cases, while Justice James Clark McReynolds was the least supportive, voting with the ACLU 18.18% of the time in 11 cases.

In addition, 29 or 56.86% of the 51 justices were nominated by Republican presidents, while 22 or 43.14% were nominated by Democratic presidents.

Chart: *The 51 U.S. Supreme Court Justices[12] from 1925 to 2019; Their Terms; Votes on the ACLU's Cases; Related Information* [13]

	U.S. Supreme Court Justice[14] / Dates Served on Court	# of Votes on ACLU Cases	# of Votes on the ACLU's Side	% of Votes on the ACLU's side	Political Party of President		President Who Nominated Justice[15]
					Dem.	Rep.	
	A	B	C	D	E	F	G
1	Benjamin Nathan Cardozo 1932–1938	4	4	100%		R	Herbert Hoover

---

[12] The images of the justices are courtesy of "Collection of the Supreme Court of the United States," and we are especially grateful to the Office of the Curator, Supreme Court of the United States, for providing them.

[13] These cases are listed from highest percent total (in Column D) to lowest. While the two justices, #23 and #24, Willis Van Devanter and George Sutherland, had the same percent totals, Devanter is listed first because he joined the Court before Sutherland.

[14] Justice names as shown on the supremecourt.gov page "Justices 1789 to Present: Chief Justices."

[15] Spelling of presidents' names from whitehouse.gov "Presidents" page.

	U.S. Supreme Court Justice[14] / Dates Served on Court	# of Votes on ACLU Cases	# of Votes on the ACLU's Side	% of Votes on the ACLU's side	Political Party of President		President Who Nominated Justice[15]
					Dem.	Rep.	
	A	B	C	D	E	F	G
2	Arthur Joseph Goldberg 1962–1965	35	34	97.14%	D		John F. Kennedy
3	Charles Evans Hughes 1930–1941	10	9	90.00%		R	Herbert Hoover[16]

---

[16] "On April 25, 1910, President William H. Taft nominated Hughes to the Supreme Court of the United States, and the Senate confirmed the appointment on May 2, 1910. Hughes resigned from the court (as an associate justice) on June 10, 1916 … On February 3, 1930, President Herbert Hoover nominated Hughes Chief Justice of the United States, and the Senate confirmed the appointment on February 13, 1930." (Associate Justice: 1910-1916, Chief Justice: 1930-1941) ("The History of the Courts." The Supreme Court Historical Society. Accessed January 7, 2021. https://supremecourthistory.org/history-of-the-courts/.)

	U.S. Supreme Court Justice[14] / Dates Served on Court	# of Votes on ACLU Cases	# of Votes on the ACLU's Side	% of Votes on the ACLU's side	Political Party of President		President Who Nominated Justice[15]
					Dem.	Rep.	
	A	B	C	D	E	F	G
4	William Orville Douglas 1939–1975	347	305	87.90%	D		Franklin D. Roosevelt
5	Louis Dembitz Brandeis 1916–1939	8	7	87.50%	D		Woodrow Wilson
6	Thurgood Marshall 1967–1991	522	446	85.44%	D		Lyndon B. Johnson

	U.S. Supreme Court Justice[14] / Dates Served on Court	# of Votes on ACLU Cases	# of Votes on the ACLU's Side	% of Votes on the ACLU's side	Political Party of President		President Who Nominated Justice[15]
					Dem.	Rep.	
	A	B	C	D	E	F	G
7	Earl Warren 1953–1969	143	122	85.31%		R	Dwight D. Eisenhower
8	Abe Fortas 1965–1969	47	40	85.11%	D		Lyndon B. Johnson
9	William J. Brennan, Jr. 1956–1990	607	506	83.36%		R	Dwight D. Eisenhower

	U.S. Supreme Court Justice[14] / Dates Served on Court	# of Votes on ACLU Cases	# of Votes on the ACLU's Side	% of Votes on the ACLU's side	Political Party of President Dem. Rep.		President Who Nominated Justice[15]
	A	B	C	D	E	F	G
10	Frank Murphy 1940–1949	48	37	77.08%	D		Franklin D. Roosevelt
11	Wiley Blount Rutledge 1943–1949	39	30	76.92%	D		Franklin D. Roosevelt
12	Elena Kagan 2010– Present	114	85	74.56%	D		Barack Obama

	U.S. Supreme Court Justice[14] / Dates Served on Court	# of Votes on ACLU Cases	# of Votes on the ACLU's Side	% of Votes on the ACLU's side	Political Party of President		President Who Nominated Justice[15]
					Dem.	Rep.	
	A	B	C	D	E	F	G
13	Sonia Sotomayor 2009– Present	143	106	74.13%	D		Barack Obama
14	Hugo Lafayette Black 1937–1971	246	182	73.98%	D		Franklin D. Roosevelt
15	Ruth Bader Ginsburg 1993–d. 9/18/2020	431	312	72.39%	D		William J. Clinton

	U.S. Supreme Court Justice[14] / Dates Served on Court	# of Votes on ACLU Cases	# of Votes on the ACLU's Side	% of Votes on the ACLU's side	Political Party of President		President Who Nominated Justice[15]
					Dem.	Rep.	
	A	B	C	D	E	F	G
16	John Paul Stevens 1975–2010	693	488	70.42%		R	Gerald R. Ford
17	David H. Souter 1990–2009	336	232	69.05%		R	George H. W. Bush
18	Oliver Wendell Holmes, Jr. 1902–1932	3	2	66.67%		R	Theodore Roosevelt

U.S. Supreme Court Justice[14] / Dates Served on Court	# of Votes on ACLU Cases	# of Votes on the ACLU's Side	% of Votes on the ACLU's side	Political Party of President		President Who Nominated Justice[15]
				Dem.	Rep.	
A	B	C	D	E	F	G
19 Stephen G. Breyer 1994–present	415	268	64.58%	D		William J. Clinton
20 Harry A. Blackmun 1970–1994	533	326	61.16%		R	Richard M. Nixon
21 Harlan Fiske Stone 1925–1946	40	24	60.00%		R	Calvin Coolidge

	U.S. Supreme Court Justice[14] / Dates Served on Court	# of Votes on ACLU Cases	# of Votes on the ACLU's Side	% of Votes on the ACLU's side	Political Party of President		President Who Nominated Justice[15]
					Dem.	Rep.	
	A	B	C	D	E	F	G
22	Harold Hitz Burton 1945–1958	69	41	59.42%	D		Harry S. Truman
23	Willis Van Devanter 1911–1937	7	4	57.14%		R	William Howard Taft
24	George Sutherland 1922–1938	7	4	57.14%		R	Warren G. Harding

	U.S. Supreme Court Justice[14] / Dates Served on Court	# of Votes on ACLU Cases	# of Votes on the ACLU's Side	% of Votes on the ACLU's side	Political Party of President		President Who Nominated Justice[15]
					Dem.	Rep.	
	A	B	C	D	E	F	G
25	Potter Stewart 1958–1981	372	211	56.72%		R	Dwight D. Eisenhower
26	Robert Houghwout Jackson 1941–1954	55	29	52.73%	D		Franklin D. Roosevelt
27	Stanley Forman Reed 1938–1957	81	41	50.62%	D		Franklin D. Roosevelt

	U.S. Supreme Court Justice[14] / Dates Served on Court	# of Votes on ACLU Cases	# of Votes on the ACLU's Side	% of Votes on the ACLU's side	Political Party of President		President Who Nominated Justice[15]
					Dem.	Rep.	
	A	B	C	D	E	F	G
28	Felix Frankfurter 1939–1962	121	61	50.41%	D		Franklin D. Roosevelt
29	Fred Moore Vinson 1946–1953	34	17	50.00%	D		Harry S. Truman
30	Byron Raymond White 1962–1993	623	300	48.15%	D		John F. Kennedy

	U.S. Supreme Court Justice[14] / Dates Served on Court	# of Votes on ACLU Cases	# of Votes on the ACLU's Side	% of Votes on the ACLU's side	Political Party of President		President Who Nominated Justice[15]
					Dem.	Rep.	
	A	B	C	D	E	F	G
31	Thomas Campbell Clark 1949–1967	132	63	47.73%	D		Harry S. Truman
32	John Marshall Harlan 1955–1971	174	80	45.98%		R	Dwight D. Eisenhower
33	Owen Josephus Roberts 1930–1945	35	16	45.71%		R	Herbert Hoover

	U.S. Supreme Court Justice[14] / Dates Served on Court	# of Votes on ACLU Cases	# of Votes on the ACLU's Side	% of Votes on the ACLU's side	Political Party of President		President Who Nominated Justice[15]
					Dem.	Rep.	
	A	B	C	D	E	F	G
34	Sherman Minton 1949–1956	29	13	44.83%	D		Harry S. Truman
35	Anthony M. Kennedy 1988–2018	533	238	44.65%		R	Ronald Reagan
36	Sandra Day O'Connor 1981–2006	511	224	43.84%		R	Ronald Reagan

	U.S. Supreme Court Justice[14] / Dates Served on Court	# of Votes on ACLU Cases	# of Votes on the ACLU's Side	% of Votes on the ACLU's side	Political Party of President		President Who Nominated Justice[15]
					Dem.	Rep.	
	A	B	C	D	E	F	G
37	Lewis F. Powell, Jr. 1972–1987	354	155	43.79%		R	Richard M. Nixon
38	Warren Earl Burger 1969–1986	375	126	33.60%		R	Richard M. Nixon
39	Pierce Butler 1923–1939	9	3	33.33%		R	Warren G. Harding

	U.S. Supreme Court Justice[14] / Dates Served on Court	# of Votes on ACLU Cases	# of Votes on the ACLU's Side	% of Votes on the ACLU's side	Political Party of President		President Who Nominated Justice[15]
					Dem.	Rep.	
	A	B	C	D	E	F	G
40	John G. Roberts, Jr. 2005–Present	201	67	33.33%		R	George W. Bush
41	Antonin Scalia 1986–d. 2/13/2016	540	174	32.22%		R	Ronald Reagan
42	Charles Evans Whittaker 1957–1962	35	11	31.43%		R	Dwight D. Eisenhower

	U.S. Supreme Court Justice[14] / Dates Served on Court	# of Votes on ACLU Cases	# of Votes on the ACLU's Side	% of Votes on the ACLU's side	Political Party of President		President Who Nominated Justice[15]
					Dem.	Rep.	
	A	B	C	D	E	F	G
43	Neil M. Gorsuch 2017– Present	30	8	26.67%		R	Donald Trump
44	Clarence Thomas 1991– present	459	122	26.58%		R	George H. W. Bush
45	Samuel A. Alito, Jr. 2006– Present	195	51	26.15%		R	George W. Bush

	U.S. Supreme Court Justice[14] / Dates Served on Court	# of Votes on ACLU Cases	# of Votes on the ACLU's Side	% of Votes on the ACLU's side	Political Party of President		President Who Nominated Justice[15]
					Dem.	Rep.	
	A	B	C	D	E	F	G
46	William H. Rehnquist	718	186	25.91%		R	Richard M. Nixon
	1972–2005						
47	James Francis Byrnes	4	1	25.00%	D		Franklin D. Roosevelt
	1941–1942						
48	Brett M. Kavanaugh	12	3	25.00%		R	Donald Trump
	2018–Present						

	U.S. Supreme Court Justice[14] / Dates Served on Court	# of Votes on ACLU Cases	# of Votes on the ACLU's Side	% of Votes on the ACLU's side	Political Party of President		President Who Nominated Justice[15]
					Dem.	Rep.	
	A	B	C	D	E	F	G
49	James Clark McReynolds 1914–1941	11	2	18.18%	D		Woodrow Wilson
50	William Howard Taft 1921–1930	2	0	0		R	Warren G. Harding
51	Edward Terry Sanford 1923–1930	2	0	0		R	Warren G. Harding
	Totals	10,510	5,819	55.37%	22	29	

VII.

Presidents and the Favorable ACLU Voting Percentage of the Justice(s) They Nominated[17]

This chart shows, in order from earliest to most recent by the 19 presidents who nominated them, the percentage of each justice's votes on the side of the ACLU and how many ACLU/SCOTUS cases on which they voted.

For example, Theodore Roosevelt, No. 1 in Column A below, nominated one justice to the Court, Oliver Wendell Holmes, Jr. He voted on three ACLU cases and was on the side of the ACLU in two of those cases, or 66.67% of the time.

Warren G, Harding, president No. 4, put four justices on the U.S. Supreme Court. Those four justices collectively voted on 20 ACLU/SCOTUS cases. Seven of those votes, or 35%, were on the same side as the ACLU.

Chart: *Presidents and the Favorable ACLU Voting Percentage of the Justice(s) They Nominated* [18]

	President Nominating Justice(s)	Number of U.S. Supreme Court Justice(s) Nominated by President	# of Votes by the Justice(s) on ACLU Cases	# of Votes on the ACLU's Side	% of Votes on the ACLU's side (D/E)	Political Party of Nominating President Dem. Rep.	
	A	**B**	**C**	**D**	**E**	**F**	**G**
1	**Theodore Roosevelt**						R
	- Oliver Wendell Holmes, Jr.	3	2	66.67%			
	Totals	**3**	**2**	**66.67%**			

---

[17] Presidents were not considered to have nominated a new justice when they elevated a sitting justice to chief justice.

[18] The presidents named in Column A are listed from earliest elected president to most recent.

	President Nominating Justice(s)	Number of U.S. Supreme Court Justice(s) Nominated by President	# of Votes by the Justice(s) on ACLU Cases	# of Votes on the ACLU's Side	% of Votes on the ACLU's side (D/E)	Political Party of Nominating President Dem. Rep.	
	A	B	C	D	E	F	G
2	**William Howard Taft**						R
		- Willis Van Devanter	7	4	57.14%		
		Totals	**7**	**4**	**57.14%**		
3	**Woodrow Wilson**					D	
		- Louis Dembitz Brandeis	8	7	87.50%		
		- James Clark McReynolds	11	2	18.18%		
		Totals	**19**	**9**	**47.37%**		
4	**Warren G. Harding**						R
		- George Sutherland	7	4	57.14%		
		- Pierce Butler	9	3	33.33%		
		- William Howard Taft	2	0	0		
		- Edward Terry Sanford	2	0	0		
		Totals	**20**	**7**	**35.00%**		
5	**Calvin Coolidge**						R
		- Harlan Fiske Stone	40	24	60.00%		
		Totals	**40**	**24**	**60.00%**		

	President Nominating Justice(s)	Number of U.S. Supreme Court Justice(s) Nominated by President	# of Votes by the Justice(s) on ACLU Cases	# of Votes on the ACLU's Side	% of Votes on the ACLU's side (D/E)	Political Party of Nominating President Dem.	Rep.
	A	B	C	D	E	F	G
6	Herbert Hoover						R
		- Benjamin Nathan Cardozo	4	4	100%		
		- Charles Evans Hughes	10	9	90.00%		
		- Owen Josephus Roberts	35	16	45.71%		
		Totals	**49**	**29**	**59.18%**		
7	Franklin D. Roosevelt						D
		- William Orville Douglas	347	305	87.90%		
		- Frank Murphy	48	37	77.08%		
		- Wiley Blount Rutledge	39	30	76.92%		
		- Hugo Lafayette Black	246	182	73.98%		
		- Robert Houghwout Jackson	55	29	52.73%		
		- Stanley Forman Reed	81	41	50.62%		
		- Felix Frankfurter	121	61	50.41%		
		- James Francis Byrnes	4	1	25.00%		
		Totals	**941**	**686**	**72.90%**		

	President Nominating Justice(s)	Number of U.S. Supreme Court Justice(s) Nominated by President	# of Votes by the Justice(s) on ACLU Cases	# of Votes on the ACLU's Side	% of Votes on the ACLU's side (D/E)	Political Party of Nominating President Dem. Rep.	
	A	B	C	D	E	F	G
8	Harry S. Truman					D	
	- Harold Hitz Burton	69	41	59.42%			
	- Fred Moore Vinson	34	17	50.00%			
	- Thomas Campbell Clark	132	63	47.73%			
	- Sherman Minton	29	13	44.83%			
	Totals	**264**	**134**	**50.76%**			
9	Dwight D. Eisenhower						R
	- Earl Warren	143	122	85.31%			
	- William J. Brennan, Jr.	607	506	83.36%			
	- Potter Stewart	372	211	56.72%			
	- John Marshall Harlan	174	80	45.98%			
	- Charles Evans Whittaker	35	11	31.43%			
	Totals	**1,331**	**930**	**69.87%**			

	President Nominating Justice(s)	Number of U.S. Supreme Court Justice(s) Nominated by President	# of Votes by the Justice(s) on ACLU Cases	# of Votes on the ACLU's Side	% of Votes on the ACLU's side (D/E)	Political Party of Nominating President Dem. Rep.	
	A	B	C	D	E	F	G
10	**John F. Kennedy**					D	
	- Arthur Joseph Goldberg	35	34	97.14%			
	- Byron Raymond White	623	300	48.15%			
	Totals	**658**	**334**	**50.76%**			
11	**Lyndon B. Johnson**					D	
	- Thurgood Marshall	522	446	85.44%			
	- Abe Fortas	47	40	85.11%			
	Totals	**569**	**486**	**85.41%**			
12	**Richard M. Nixon**						R
	- Harry A. Blackmun	533	326	61.16%			
	- Lewis F. Powell, Jr.	354	155	43.79%			
	- Warren Earl Burger	375	126	33.60%			
	- William H. Rehnquist	718	186	25.91%			
	Totals	**1,980**	**793**	**40.05%**			

	President Nominating Justice(s)	Number of U.S. Supreme Court Justice(s) Nominated by President	# of Votes by the Justice(s) on ACLU Cases	# of Votes on the ACLU's Side	% of Votes on the ACLU's side (D/E)	Political Party of Nominating President Dem. Rep.	
	A	**B**	**C**	**D**	**E**	**F**	**G**
13	**Gerald R. Ford**						R
		- John Paul Stevens	693	488	70.42%		
		Totals	**693**	**488**	**70.42%**		
14	**Ronald Reagan**						R
		- Anthony M. Kennedy	533	238	44.65%		
		- Sandra Day O'Connor	511	224	43.84%		
		- Antonin Scalia	540	174	32.22%		
		Totals	**1,584**	**636**	**40.15%**		
15	**George H. W. Bush**						R
		- David H. Souter	336	232	69.05%		
		- Clarence Thomas	459	122	26.58%		
		Totals	**795**	**354**	**44.53%**		
16	**William J. Clinton**					D	
		- Ruth Bader Ginsburg	431	312	72.39%		
		- Stephen G. Breyer	415	268	64.58%		
		Totals	**846**	**580**	**68.56%**		

	President Nominating Justice(s)	Number of U.S. Supreme Court Justice(s) Nominated by President	# of Votes by the Justice(s) on ACLU Cases	# of Votes on the ACLU's Side	% of Votes on the ACLU's side (D/E)	Political Party of Nominating President Dem. Rep.	
	A	B	C	D	E	F	G
17	George W. Bush						R
		- John G. Roberts, Jr.	201	67	33.33%		
		- Samuel A. Alito, Jr.	195	51	26.15%		
		Totals	396	118	29.80%		
18	Barack Obama					D	
		- Elena Kagan	114	85	74.56%		
		- Sonia Sotomayor	143	106	74.13%		
		Totals	257	191	74.32%		
19	Donald Trump						R
		- Neil M. Gorsuch	30	8	26.67%		
		- Brett M. Kavanaugh	12	3	25.00%		
		Totals	42	11	26.19%		

VIII.

The Number and Percentage of Votes on the ACLU's Side by the Justice(s) Nominated by Each of the 19 Presidents

This chart shows how many justices were nominated by a president to the U.S. Supreme Court, how many ACLU cases each "President's Justice(s)" voted on, and the percentages of cases in which each president's justice(s) sided with the ACLU, from highest to lowest voting percentage.

For example, the chart shows that Lyndon B. Johnson put two justices on the U.S. Supreme Court (Thurgood Marshall and Abe Fortas), and those two justices voted on 569 ACLU cases, siding with the ACLU 486 times. Therefore, Johnson's justices voted on the side of the ACLU at 85.41%, the highest percentage of presidential justice votes on the ACLU's side.

The last president, Donald Trump, put two justices on the U.S. Supreme Court (Neil M. Gorsuch and Brett M. Kavanaugh). Those two justices voted 42 times on ACLU cases, siding with the ACLU 11 times, or 26.19% of the time, the lowest percentage of presidential justice votes on the ACLU's side.

Chart: *The Number and Percentage of Votes on the ACLU's Side by the Justice(s) Nominated by Each of the 19 Presidents, sorted by Column E.*[19]

	President Nominating Justice(s)	Number of U.S. Supreme Court Justice(s) Nominated by President	# of Votes by the Justice(s) on ACLU Cases	# of Votes on the ACLU's Side	% of Votes on the ACLU's side (D/E)	Political Party of Nominating President	
						Dem.	Rep.
	A	**B**	**C**	**D**	**E**	**F**	**G**
1	Lyndon B. Johnson	2	569	486	85.41%	D	
2	Barack Obama	2	257	191	74.32%	D	
3	Franklin D. Roosevelt	8	941	686	72.90%	D	
4	Gerald R. Ford	1	693	488	70.42%		R
5	Dwight D. Eisenhower	5	1,331	930	69.87%		R
6	William J. Clinton	2	846	580	68.56%	D	
7	Theodore Roosevelt	1	3	2	66.67%		R
8	Calvin Coolidge	1	40	24	60.00%		R
9	Herbert Hoover	3	49	29	59.18%		R
10	William Howard Taft	1	7	4	57.14%		R

[19] The percent totals in Column E are from highest to lowest. When there are two presidents with the same percent total, they will be listed in order from earliest elected president to most recent.

	President Nominating Justice(s)	Number of U.S. Supreme Court Justice(s) Nominated by President	# of Votes by the Justice(s) on ACLU Cases	# of Votes on the ACLU's Side	% of Votes on the ACLU's side (D/E)	Political Party of Nominating President	
						Dem.	Rep.
	A	B	C	D	E	F	G
11	Harry S. Truman	4	264	134	50.76%	D	
12	John F. Kennedy	2	658	334	50.76%	D	
13	Woodrow Wilson	2	19	9	47.37%	D	
14	George H. W. Bush	2	795	354	44.53%		R
15	Ronald Reagan	3	1,584	636	40.15%		R
16	Richard M. Nixon	4	1,980	793	40.05%		R
17	Warren G. Harding	4	20	7	35.00%		R
18	George W. Bush	2	396	118	29.80%		R
19	Donald Trump	2	42	11	26.19%		R
		51	10,494	5,816	55.42%	7	12

IX.

The Executive Directors of the ACLU from 1920 to 2020

1.

1920—1950

Roger Nash Baldwin, co-founder of the ACLU, was the first ACLU Executive Director, and he served in that capacity for 30 years. His books include *Liberty Under the Soviets*, 1928, and *Juvenile Courts and Probation*, in 1914 as co-writer. He received a master's degree in social work from Harvard.

2.

1950—1962

Patrick Murphy Malin was the second ACLU Executive Director and served for 12 years after Roger Baldwin. Malin was an economics professor at Swarthmore College from 1930 to 1950.

3.

1962—1970

Jack Pemberton served as ACLU Executive Director through most of the 1960s. He graduated from Harvard Law School, became a law professor, and was regional counsel of the U.S. Equal Employment Opportunity Commission in San Francisco.

4.	 1970—1978	Aryeh Neier served as the ACLU Executive Director for eight years in the '70s. Some of his books include *Dossier: The Secret Files They Keep on You*, 1978, and *Taking Liberties: Four Decades in the Struggle for Rights*, 2003. He received his JD from Cornell University.
5.	 1978—2001	Ira Glasser served as ACLU Executive Director for nearly a quarter of a century. In 1991, Glasser published *Visions of Liberty: The Bill of Rights for All Americans*. Glasser taught mathematics at City University in New York and Sarah Lawrence College, and was editor of a monthly magazine of public affairs titled *Current*.
6.	 2001—Present	Anthony D. Romero has been the executive director of the ACLU since the week before Sept. 11, 2001. According to the ACLU website, he is the "first Latino and openly gay man to serve in that capacity."[20] With NPR correspondent Dina Temple-Raston, he published *In Defense of Our America: The Fight for Civil Liberties in the Age of Terror*.

[20] "Anthony D. Romero." American Civil Liberties Union. Accessed January 7, 2021. https://www.aclu.org/bio/anthony-d-romero.

X.

Questions & Conclusion

While putting together the information in these pages, I have come to think of the work as similar to that of an armorer. The armorer produces weapons (information, facts, and data in this case) and is often agnostic as to who buys their weapons or how they are used. One difference from many armorers is that I do care about how the information in these pages is used. I hope pieces or sections of this work will not be taken out of context or used to mislead.

Regardless of how readers think about or use the information herein, I believe a few percentages, perhaps as looked at through the eyes of an accountant, deserve special thought. Each covers a lot of ground and will surely be seen and interpreted differently. On the positive side, studying, analyzing, and even arguing about the meaning of the numbers below (and the information in these pages) could bring new and interesting thoughts, theories, and conclusions about the ACLU.

- **53.65% — The ACLU's batting average was on the winning side** (on page 29): In the 1,193 ACLU/SCOTUS cases, the ACLU was on the winning side 53.65% of the time during the 94 years of the Union's first 100 years. What does that number say about the ACLU, if anything? Before you read or skimmed this work, did you think about what the Union's batting average over so many years might be? Does the 53.65% seem high, low, or about what you thought? Do you think, perhaps, that the 53.65% number might be high because the Union only got involved in easy cases (assuming there is such a thing) or that number is low because you question the ACLU's competency? Does 53.65% suggest anything about its political agenda over time?

- **25.98% —The percentage of 4–5, 5–4, 4–3 and 3–4 decisions of the 1,193 cases** (on page 29): There were 310 such cases.[21] Given that all the voting justices saw the same facts, data, and arguments on each case, why was there such a difference of opinions on more than a quarter of the 1,193 cases and during so many years? Given that the justices (and all federal judges) essentially have a job for life, shouldn't there be less politics and less reason to feel pressure to vote one way or another on a case (because they can't be fired for their vote on any case)? Given that the justices have all sworn to uphold the Constitution and were presented with the same facts and evidence of each case, would you expect so many cases decided by one vote? What do such close votes say about the clarity of the facts and law in those cases? How much did each justice's personal views and legal philosophy affect their votes, if at all?

- **56.86% of justices who decided these cases were put on the Court by Republican presidents** (on page 246): Of the 51 SCOTUS justices who opined on the 1,193 cases, 29 or 56.86% of those justices were nominated by Republican presidents. Twenty-two or 43.14 % of the justices were put on by Democratic presidents. If those numbers had been reversed, with 56.86% of the justices having been nominated by Democratic presidents, would the batting average of the ACLU have changed, or changed much? If the batting average had changed, how would those changed decisions have affected our country? Would our country be better or worse off today? How could one define "better" between often competing political, societal, and other interests?

---

[21] Of the 310 cases, eight were 3–4 and 4–3 decisions. Those cases are: 1. *United States ex rel. Knauff v. Shaughnessy* (338 U.S. 537); 2. *Hoffa v. United States* (385 U.S. 293); 3. *Fein v. Selective Service System Local Board No. 7* (405 U.S. 365); 4. *Cornelius v. NAACP Legal Defense and Educational Fund, Inc.* (473 U.S. 788); 5. *Traynor v. Turnage* (485 U.S. 535); 6. *City of Lakewood v. Plain Dealer Publishing Co.* (486 U.S. 750); 7. *Murray v. United States* (487 U.S. 533); and 8. *Fisher v. Univ. of Texas at Austin* (136 S.Ct. 2198; 579 U.S. _).

In sum, after reviewing the ACLU/SCOTUS cases over so many years, the votes of the justices (on page 125), and the divergent pros and cons about the ACLU (on page 16), this complex organization is difficult if not impossible to pigeonhole. It becomes obvious that in trying to understand this organization from its SCOTUS cases, just as many questions as answers arise. What is clear, however, is the ACLU has been involved in many cases at the U.S. Supreme Court that have had impactful effects on our country.

Appendix A.

Methodology

The following methodology has been used in compiling this work:

1. The criteria for inclusion of an ACLU/SCOTUS case are when the ACLU was *involved* in the case when it went before the U.S. Supreme Court and the Court issued an opinion between January 19, 1920, and January 19, 2020, the first 100 years of the ACLU.

   "ACLU involvement" in a SCOTUS case includes when the ACLU was a party, filed (or is on) an amicus brief, and/or when an ACLU attorney argued the case or was listed on a brief in the case. An ACLU attorney's involvement includes an ACLU attorney being listed on a party's brief, whether or not the attorney's affiliation with the ACLU is noted on the brief itself.[22]

   Such involvement of an ACLU attorney also includes instances where the ACLU partnered with one or more outside attorneys not necessarily employed by the ACLU but who worked with the ACLU on the case. Involvement also includes cases where the ACLU has made public statements referencing the case as an ACLU case (because the ACLU has deeper records of its involvement in cases than is often available through SCOTUS documents and other public records).

   This criterion excludes cases where the ACLU was only involved when the case was before a lower court, and cases where the writ of

---

[22] Attorney involvement includes an ACLU attorney who was noted on a brief before the U.S. Supreme Court but who may not have been noted as being affiliated with the ACLU. For example, Osmond K. Fraenkel, ACLU chief counsel 1954 to 1977; Melvin Wulf, ACLU legal director 1962 to 1977; or Steven R. Shapiro, ACLU associate legal director 1987 to 1993 and legal director 1993 to 2016 were listed on a party's brief before the U.S. Supreme Court, even though their ACLU affiliation was not always mentioned on the brief itself.

certiorari was denied or granted but then later dismissed (meaning the [U.S. Supreme] Court never issued an opinion deciding the case itself), or where the ACLU's request to file an amicus was denied or withdrawn.

Also excluded from this work are nine split decision *per curiam* cases.[23] Those cases are composed of one 3–3 and eight 4–4 votes. Those nine cases are excluded because it's not clear which justices voted on which side of those cases, and because the U.S. Supreme Court didn't come to a clear decision on any of them. A split decision has a similar effect as cert in those cases being denied. Those nine split decisions leave the lower court ruling in place.

Cases are cited by the party names as listed in the U.S. Supreme Court's decision. Party names sometimes changed during the course of litigation.

Occasionally, I have been told a particular SCOTUS case was an ACLU case but our research could not verify that claim. When that happened, such cases have not been listed in this work although it is possible with more research, we might have discovered other ACLU connections.

2. Win/Loss Definition

This work defines "winning" or "losing" by whether or not the ruling of the U.S. Supreme Court was "with" or "against" the side the ACLU was on, even though in some instances the ACLU was on the "winning side" but some considered it an ACLU loss. Conversely, at times the Union was on the "losing side" but some considered the Union to receive a net benefit from the decision.

---

[23] See footnote 10 on page 125.

Therefore, the above definition of wins and losses may not account for some nuanced or argued results.

For example, this work records the case win/loss definitions count *Staats v. ACLU*, 422 U.S. 1030 (1975) as a loss for the ACLU because in *Staats*, the U.S. Supreme Court voted 8–0 against the side the ACLU was on. However, Ira Glasser, former executive director of the ACLU, considered the *Staats* decision a victory for the ACLU on the merits, because the practical effect of the case achieved the ACLU's goal in bringing it.

Although such nuanced or argued effects about certain case results are interesting and important to some, second guessing or arguing about the outcome of such cases would add a subjectiveness that I chose to avoid.

I have no reason to believe there are many such *Staats* cases, where a loss could reasonably be considered an ACLU win, or a win could be considered a loss. Even if there were, I don't believe the ACLU's win/loss ratio would be changed in any significant way.

For example, if there were, say, a net difference of 20 such cases in this work, and if all those 20 cases increased or decreased the ACLU's wins or losses by that amount, its win ratio of 53.65% in its first 100 years[24] would only increase to 55.32% or decrease to 51.97%.[25]

In the case of ties by the U.S. Supreme Court, where the lower court's ruling was affirmed by an equally divided U.S. Supreme Court (except the split *per curiam* cases), "winning" or "losing" is recorded as to whether or not the divided decision had the effect of ending the issue "with" or "against" the side the ACLU was on.

---

[24] On page 30, 640 wins of 1,193 cases is 53.65%.

[25] 660 wins of 1,193 is 55.32%; 620 wins of 1,193 is 51.97%.

3. The Supporting Data

    Supporting data for the cases came from ACLU websites and
    reports; GALE's U.S. Supreme Court Records and Briefs 1832—
    1978 online; Oyez Project at IIT Chicago-Kent College of Law
    (oyez.org), which was useful in determining the votes of the
    justices; FindLaw (findlaw.com); and Westlaw (westlaw.com).

    Where minor errors were found or when questions arose, and for
    some clarification, the print version of the *United States Supreme
    Court Reports, Lawyer's Edition,* was used to ensure the most
    accurate quotation possible when copies of the *United States
    Reports*, the official record for SCOTUS cases, were not available.

    Quotations without citation come directly from the cases.
    Quotations from other sources, such as prior opinions from lower
    courts or party briefs, are noted with a footnote citing the source of
    the quotation.

    Citations to cases or statutes within the quoted material are omitted,
    without notation, although single quotation marks designate
    quotations from another source.

    Please refer to the print version of the *United States Reports* for a
    complete reporting of each case in its entirety, as the print version of
    the United States Reports is the official source of SCOTUS cases.

4. [sic]—*intentionally so written*—Used after a printed word or
    passage to indicate that it is intended exactly as printed or to
    indicate that it exactly reproduces an original <said he seed [sic] it
    all> [26]

---

[26] "sic," Merriam-Webster, Accessed January 7, 2021, https://www.merriam-webster.com/.

5. Regarding rounding of percentages for the wins/losses, if the extra number is a 5, 6, 7, 8 or 9, the preceding number has been raised by one. Example: if we want one decimal point, the number 45.55 would become 45.6; if we want two decimal points, the number 56.574 would become 56.57.

6. Editing style—This work uses a combination of styles based mainly on Chicago Manual of Style standard style, but AP Style is used for numbers, where numbers nine and under are written out unless they are part of a vote count.

7. Abbreviations Used

   Definitions for O, CO and DO below were taken from *Black's Law Dictionary; Revised Fourth Edition*; published 1968.

   A. W   = Voting with the ACLU

   B. L   = Voting against the ACLU

   C. Oth = Other—Vacant seat; abstention from vote; etc.

   D. O   = Opinion—The statement by the U.S. Supreme Court of the decision reached in regard to the case, setting forth the law as applied to the case, and detailing the reasoning upon which the decision is based.

   E. CO = Concurring Opinion—An opinion separate from that which embodies the view and decision of the majority, prepared and filed by a justice who agrees with the general result of the decision, and which either reinforces the majority opinion or voices disapproval with the reasoning behind the opinion but approves of its final result.

F. DO = Dissenting Opinion—An opinion separate from that which embodies the views and decision of the majority, prepared and filed by a justice who disagrees with the decision of the U.S. Supreme Court and who expresses his or her own views/reasoning on the case.

G. CDO = Concurring/Dissenting Opinion—An opinion separate from that which embodies the views and decision of the majority, prepared and filed by a justice who agrees with only a portion of the decision of the majority (usually in cases involving more than one issue).

Appendix B.

General Categories of the ACLU/SCOTUS Cases

The ACLU/SCOTUS cases generally fit the four main categories below (with the subcategories added), but given the nature of the law and litigation, a case may fit into more than one category and subcategory. For that reason, I have not attempted to organize the cases in the following categories.

1. 1st Amendment

   A. Obscenity: Cases in this category deal with the limits of the freedom to engage in "obscene" and offensive speech.
   B. Defamation: Cases involving libelous publication and slanderous utterances against individuals.
   C. Religion: Cases involving the free exercise of religion and the prohibition of the establishment of an official religion.
   D. Press, Speech, Association: Cases in this category involve the freedoms of speech, the press, and association.

2. Criminal Justice

   A. 4th Amendment: Cases involving the limits of protection against unwarranted searches and seizures.
   B. Criminal Procedure: Includes the 5th and 6th Amendments, as well as criminal trial procedure under the 14th Amendment.
   C. 8th Amendment: Cases involving the prohibition against cruel and unusual punishment.
   D. Death Penalty: Cases involving a sentence to death.
   E. Drugs: Cases where narcotics are the issue or cause of the arrest.
   F. Prison: Cases involving inmate rights, prison conditions, and the parole process.

3. Civil Rights

   A. Race: Cases dealing with both state and federal racial discrimination.
   B. Gender: Cases dealing with both state and federal gender discrimination.
   C. Federal: Cases involving civil rights protected by federal law.
   D. State: Cases dealing with civil rights protected under the 14th Amendment.
   E. Voting Rights: Cases dealing with the right to vote, right against vote dilution, and redistricting.
   F. Privacy: Cases mainly dealing with reproductive rights (abortion, contraception) and the individual's right to privacy.

4. Governmental Authority

   A. Union: Cuts across categories, but generally cases dealing with government regulation of labor unions.
   B. Immigration/Citizenship: Cases dealing with people immigrating to this country and citizens living abroad.
   C. Communism: Cuts across categories, but generally cases dealing with government statutes and acts, and agencies created to deal with communism.
   D. Census: Cases dealing with census count.
   E. Federalism: Cases dealing with controversy between state government and the federal government.
   F. Civil Procedure: Cases where the issue is a matter of civil trial procedure.
   G. Regulation: Cases dealing with government regulatory agencies.
   H. Immunity: Cases dealing with immunity from damages under the 11th Amendment.
   I. Military: Cases dealing with military personnel or cases under military jurisdiction.

Appendix C.

Three Examples of the ACLU/ SCOTUS Cases from the Three-Volume Set of Cases

Here are cases No. 1, No. 341 and No. 893 from the three-volume set.
Note: The analysis of any case is subjective.

1. Gitlow v. New York
(Decided June 8, 1925; 268 U.S. 652)

I. ISSUE

A. Issues Discussed: First Amendment, Fourteenth Amendment, freedom of speech and of the press

B. Legal Question Presented: Does a state statute regulating speech by prohibiting advocacy of criminal anarchy deprive the defendant of freedom of speech or of the press in violation of the due process clause of the Fourteenth Amendment?

C. Supreme Court's Answer: The state statute is constitutional. However, fundamental rights federally protected under the First Amendment, such as freedom of speech and press, are protected from state impairment by the due process clause of the Fourteenth Amendment.

II. CASE SUMMARY

A. Background

"The defendant [was] a member of the Left Wing Section of the Socialist Party [which] was organized nationally at a conference in New York City in June, 1919 . . . . The conference elected a National Council, of which the defendant was member, and left to it the adoption of a 'Manifesto.' This was published in The Revolutionary Age, the official organ of the Left Wing. . . . Sixteen thousand copies were printed [and] paid for by the defendant, as business manager of the paper . . . . [D]efendant signed a card subscribing to the Manifesto and Program of the Left Wing [and] went to different parts of the State to speak to branches of the Socialist Party about the principles of the Left Wing and advocated their adoption.

[The Manifesto] advocated, in plain and unequivocal language, the necessity of accomplishing the 'Communist Revolution' by a militant and 'revolutionary Socialism,' based on 'the class struggle' and mobilizing the 'power of the proletariat in action,' through mass industrial revolts developing into mass political strikes and 'revolutionary mass action,' for the purpose of conquering and destroying the parliamentary state and establishing in its place, through a 'revolutionary dictatorship of the proletariat,' the system of Communist Socialism."

Defendant was "convicted and sentenced to imprisonment" by the trial court. "The Court of Appeals held that the Manifesto 'advocated the overthrow of [the] government by violence, or by unlawful means.' . . . And both the Appellate Division and the Court of Appeals held the statute constitutional."

The Supreme Court granted certiorari to review the case and affirmed the judgment of the Court of Appeals.

B. Counsel of Record / ACLU Attorney:

ACLU Side (Petitioner/Appellant):	Opposing Side (Respondent/Appellee):
Walter H. Pollak and Walter Nelles argued the cause for appellant.	John Caldwell Myers and W. J. Wetherbee argued the cause for appellee.

III. AMICI CURIAE

ACLU Side (Petitioner/Appellant):	Opposing Side (Respondent/Appellee):
No briefs of amici curiae were filed in support of appellant.	No briefs of amici curiae were filed in support of appellee.

IV. THE SUPREME COURT'S DECISION

A. In upholding the statute and affirming the Court of Appeals decision, the Court determined "[t]he statute does not penalize the utterance or publication of abstract 'doctrine' or academic discussion having no quality of incitement to any concrete action. . . . What it prohibits is language advocating, advising or teaching the overthrow of organized government by unlawful means. [The Manifesto] advocates and urges in fervent language mass action which shall progressively foment industrial disturbances and through political mass strikes and revolutionary mass action overthrow and destroy organized parliamentary government."

The Court "assume[d] that freedom of speech and of the press—which are protected by the First Amendment from abridgment by Congress—are among the fundamental personal rights and 'liberties' protected by the due process clause of the Fourteenth Amendment from impairment by the States." However, "[i]t is a fundamental principle, long established, that the freedom of speech and of the press which is secured by the Constitution, does not confer an absolute right to speak or publish, without responsibility. . . ."

State "'statutes may only be declared unconstitutional where they are arbitrary or unreasonable attempts to exercise authority vested in the State in the public interest.' That utterances inciting to the overthrow of organized government by unlawful means, present a sufficient danger of substantive evil to bring their punishment within the range of legislative discretion, is clear. Such utterances, by their very nature, involve danger to the public peace and to the security of the State."

The Court ultimately found "that the statute is not in itself unconstitutional, and that it has not been applied in the present case in derogation of any constitutional right . . . ."

B. Justice Vote: 2 Pro ACLU Side vs. 7 Con Opposing Side

ACLU Side (Petitioner/Appellant):	Opposing Side (Respondent/Appellee):
1. Holmes, O.—Wrote dissenting opinion 2. Brandeis, L.—Joined dissenting opinion	1. Sanford, E.—Wrote majority opinion 2. Taft, W.—Joined majority opinion 3. Van Devanter, W.—Joined majority opinion 4. McReynolds, J.—Joined majority opinion 5. Sutherland, G.—Joined majority opinion 6. Butler, P.—Joined majority opinion 7. Stone, H.—Joined majority opinion

V. A WIN OR LOSS FOR THE ACLU?

The ACLU, as attorney of record, urged reversal of the judgment of the Court of Appeals; the Supreme Court affirmed in a 7–2 vote, giving the ACLU an apparent **loss**.

(Some believe that this case should be viewed as a win overall because the Court established in *Gitlow* that fundamental rights, such as freedom of speech and press, must not be impaired by the states, incorporating these rights under the due process clause of the Fourteenth Amendment.)

341. Miami Herald Publishing Co. v. Tornillo

(Decided June 25, 1974; 418 U.S. 241)

I. ISSUE

A. **Issues Discussed:** First Amendment, freedom of the press

B. **Legal Question Presented:** "[W]hether a state statute granting a political candidate a right to equal space to reply to criticism and attacks on his record by a newspaper violates the guarantees of a free press."

C. **Supreme Court's Answer:** The state statute violates the First Amendment freedom of the press.

II. CASE SUMMARY

A. Background:

"In the fall of 1972, appellee, Executive Director of the Classroom Teachers Association, . . . was a candidate for the Florida House of Representatives. On September 20, 1972, and again on September 29, 1972, appellant printed editorials critical of appellee's candidacy. In response to these editorials appellee demanded that appellant print verbatim his replies, defending the role of the Classroom Teachers Association and the organization's accomplishments for the citizens of Dade County. Appellant declined to print the appellee's replies and appellee brought suit in Circuit Court, Dade County, seeking declaratory and injunctive relief and actual and punitive damages in excess of $5,000. The action was premised on Florida Statute §104.38 (1973), a 'right of reply' statute which provides that if a candidate for nomination or election is assailed regarding his personal character or official record by any newspaper, the candidate has the right to demand that the newspaper print, free of cost to the candidate, any reply the candidate may make to the newspaper's charges. The reply must appear in as conspicuous a place, and in the same size of type, as the charges which prompted the reply, provided it does not take up more space than the charges. Failure to comply with the statute constitutes a first-degree misdemeanor.

Appellee sought a declaration that §104.38 was unconstitutional. After an emergency hearing requested by appellee, the circuit court denied injunctive relief and held that §104.38 was unconstitutional as an infringement on the freedom of the press under the First and Fourteenth Amendments to the Constitution. The Circuit Court concluded that dictating what a newspaper must print was no different from dictating what it must not print. The Circuit Judge viewed the statute's vagueness as serving 'to restrict and stifle protected expression.' Appellee's cause was dismissed with prejudice.

On direct appeal, the Florida Supreme Court reversed, holding that § 104.38 did not violate constitutional guarantees. It held that free speech was enhanced and not abridged by the Florida right-of-reply statute, which in that court's view, furthered the 'broad societal interest in the free flow of information to the public.' It also held that the statute is not impermissibly vague; the statute informs 'those who are subject to it as to what conduct on their part will render them liable to its penalties.' Civil remedies, including damages, were held to be available under this statute and the case was remanded to the trial court for further proceedings not inconsistent with the Florida Supreme Court's opinion."

The Supreme Court granted certiorari to review the case and reversed.

B. Counsel of Record:

ACLU Side (Petitioner/Appellant):	Opposing Side (Respondent/Appellee):
Daniel P. S. Paul argued the cause for appellant.	Jerome A. Barron argued the cause for appellee.

III. AMICI CURIAE

ACLU Side (Petitioner/Appellant):	Opposing Side (Respondent/Appellee):
Brief of amici curiae filed on behalf of the ACLU of Florida by Jonathan L. Alpert, Irma Robbins Feder, and Richard Yale Feder. Additional briefs of amici curiae were filed on behalf of the Washington Post Co., the Times Mirror Co., New York News Inc., the Chicago Tribune Co., et al., the Florida Publishing Co., the Times Publishing Co., the Gannett Florida Corporation, et al., the American Newspaper Publishers Association, the National Newspaper Association, the American Society of Newspaper Editors, et al., the Reporters Committee for Freedom of the Press Legal Defense and Research Fund, et al., the National Association of Broadcasters, the Radio Television News Directors Association, the National Broadcasting Co., Inc., and Dow Jones & Co., Inc., et al.	Briefs of amici curiae were filed on behalf of the National Citizens Committee for Broadcasting by Albert H. Kramer and Thomas R. Asher; and by Donald U. Sessions, pro se.

IV. THE SUPREME COURT'S DECISION:

A. "The challenged statute creates a right to reply to press criticism of a candidate for nomination or election. The statute was enacted in 1913, and this is only the second recorded case decided under its provisions. . .
.

Appellee's argument that the Florida statute does not amount to a restriction of appellant's right to speak because 'the statute in question here has not prevented the *Miami Herald* from saying anything it wished' begs the core question. Compelling editors or publishers to publish that which 'reason' tells them should not be published is what is at issue in this case. The Florida statute operates as a command in the same sense as a statue or regulation forbidding appellant to publish specified matter. Governmental restraint on publishing need not fall into familiar or traditional patterns to be subject to constitutional limitations on governmental powers. The Florida statute exacts a penalty on the basis of the content of a newspaper. The first phase of the penalty resulting from the compelled printing of a reply is exacted in terms of the cost in printing and composing time and materials and in taking up space that could be devoted to other material the newspaper may have preferred to print. [A] newspaper is not subject to the finite technological limitations of time that confront a broadcaster but it is not correct to say that, as an economic reality, a newspaper can proceed to infinite expansion of its column space to accommodate the replies that a government agency determines or a statute commands the readers should have available.

Faced with the penalties that would accrue to any newspaper that published news or commentary arguably within the reach of the right-of-access statute, editors might well conclude that the safe course is to avoid controversy. Therefore, under the operation of the Florida statute, political and electoral coverage would be blunted or reduced. Government-enforced right of access inescapably 'dampens the vigor and limits the variety of public debate.' . . .

'[T]here is practically universal agreement that a major purpose of [the First] Amendment was to protect the free discussion of governmental affairs. This of course includes discussions of candidates . . . .'

Even if a newspaper would face no additional costs to comply with a compulsory access law and would not be forced to forgo publication of news or opinion by the inclusion of a reply, the Florida statute fails to clear the barriers of the First Amendment because of its intrusion into the function of editors. A newspaper is more than a passive receptacle or conduit for news, comment, and advertising. The choice of material to go into a newspaper, and the decisions made as to limitations on the size and content of the paper, and treatment of public issues and public officials whether fair or unfair - constitute the exercise of editorial control and judgment. It has yet to be demonstrated how governmental regulation of this crucial process can be exercised consistent with First Amendment guarantees of a free press as they have evolved to this time. Accordingly, the judgment of the Supreme Court of Florida is reversed."

C. Justice Vote: 9 Pro ACLU Side vs. 0 Con Opposing Side

ACLU Side (Petitioner/Appellant):	Opposing Side (Respondent/Appellee):
1. Burger, W.—Wrote majority opinion	
2. Blackmun, H.—Joined majority opinion	
3. Powell, L.—Joined majority opinion	
4. Douglas, W.—Joined majority opinion	
5. Brennan, W.—Wrote concurring opinion	
6. Rehnquist, W.—Joined Brennan's concurrence	

ACLU Side (Petitioner/Appellant):	Opposing Side (Respondent/Appellee):
7. White, B.—Wrote concurring opinion	
8. Marshall, T.—Joined majority opinion	
9. Stewart, P.—Joined majority opinion	

V. A WIN OR LOSS FOR THE ACLU?

The ACLU filed as amicus curiae urging reversal of the judgment of the Supreme Court of Florida; the U.S. Supreme Court reversed in a 9–0 vote, giving the ACLU an apparent **win**.

893. Bush v. Palm Beach County Canvassing Board

(Decided December 1, 2000; 531 U.S. 70)

I. ISSUE

A. Issues Discussed: Voting

B. Legal Question Presented: "[W]hether the decision of the Florida Supreme Court, by effectively changing the State's elector appointment procedures after election day, violated the Due Process Clause or 3 U. S. C. § 5, and whether the decision of that court changed the manner in which the State's electors are to be selected, in violation of the legislature's power to designate the manner for selection under Art. II, § 1, cl. 2, of the United States Constitution."

C. Supreme Court's Answer: "After reviewing the opinion of the Florida Supreme Court, we find 'that there is considerable uncertainty as to the precise grounds for the decision.' This is sufficient reason for us to decline at this time to review the federal questions asserted to be present."

II. CASE SUMMARY

A. Background:

"On November 8, 2000, the day following the Presidential election, the Florida Division of Elections reported that Governor Bush had received 2,909,135 votes, and respondent Democrat Vice President Albert Gore, Jr., had received 2,907,351, a margin of 1,784 in Governor Bush's favor. Under Fla. Stat. §102.141(4) (2000), because the margin of victory was equal to or less than one-half of one percent of the votes cast, an automatic machine recount occurred. The recount resulted in a much smaller margin of victory for Governor Bush. Vice President Gore then exercised his statutory right to submit written requests for manual recounts to the canvassing board of any county. He requested recounts in four counties: Volusia, Palm Beach, Broward, and Miami-Dade.

The parties urged conflicting interpretations of the Florida Election Code respecting the authority of the canvassing boards, the Secretary of State (hereinafter Secretary), and the Elections Canvassing Commission. On November 14, in an action brought by Volusia County, and joined by the Palm Beach County Canvassing Board, Vice President Gore, and the Florida Democratic Party, the Florida Circuit Court ruled that the statutory 7-day deadline was mandatory, but that the Volusia board could amend its returns at a later date. The court further ruled that the Secretary, after 'considering all attendant facts and circumstances,' could exercise her discretion in deciding whether to include the late amended returns in the statewide certification.

The Secretary responded by issuing a set of criteria by which she would decide whether to allow a late filing. The Secretary ordered that, by 2 p.m. the following day, November 15, any county desiring to forward late returns submit a written statement of the facts and circumstances justifying a later filing. Four counties submitted statements, and, after reviewing the submissions, the Secretary determined that none justified an extension of the filing deadline. On November 16, the Florida Democratic Party and Vice President Gore filed an emergency motion in the state court, arguing that the Secretary had acted arbitrarily and in contempt of the court's earlier ruling. The following day, the court denied the motion, ruling that the Secretary had not acted arbitrarily and had exercised her discretion in a reasonable manner consistent with the court's earlier ruling. The Democratic Party and Vice President Gore appealed to the First District Court of Appeal, which certified the matter to the Florida Supreme Court. That court accepted jurisdiction and *sua sponte* entered an order enjoining the Secretary and the Elections Canvassing Commission from finally certifying the results of the election and declaring a winner until further order of that court.

The Supreme Court, with the expedition requisite for the controversy, issued its decision on November 21. As the court saw the matter, there were two principal questions: whether a discrepancy between an original machine return and a sample manual recount resulting from the way a ballot has been marked or punched is an 'error in vote tabulation' justifying a full manual recount; and how to reconcile what it spoke of as two conflicts in Florida's election laws: (a) between the timeframe for conducting a manual recount under Fla. Stat. §102.166 (2000) and the timeframe for submitting county returns under §§102.111 and 102.112, and (b) between §102.111, which provides that the Secretary 'shall . . . ignor[e]' late election returns, and §102.112, which provides that she 'may . . . ignor[e]' such returns.

With regard to the first issue, the court held that, under the plain text of the statute, a discrepancy between a sample manual recount and machine returns due to the way in which a ballot was punched or marked did constitute an 'error in vote tabulation' sufficient to trigger the statutory provisions for a full manual recount.

With regard to the second issue, the court held that the 'shall . . . ignor[e]' provision of §102.111 conflicts with the 'may . . . ignor[e]' provision of §102.112, and that the 'may . . . ignor[e]' provision controlled. The court turned to the questions whether and when the Secretary may ignore late manual recounts. The court relied in part upon the right to vote set forth in the Declaration of Rights of the Florida Constitution in concluding that late manual recounts could be rejected only under limited circumstances. The court then stated: '[B]ecause of our reluctance to rewrite the Florida Election Code, we conclude that we must invoke the equitable powers of this Court to fashion a remedy . . . .' The court thus imposed a deadline of November 26, at 5 p.m., for a return of ballot counts. The 7-day deadline of §102.111, assuming it would have applied, was effectively extended by 12 days. The court further directed the Secretary to accept manual counts submitted prior to that deadline."

The Supreme Court granted certiorari to review the case, vacated the decision below, and remanded the case.

B. Counsel of Record:

ACLU Side (Respondent/Appellee):	Opposing Side (Petitioner/Appellant):
Paul F. Hancock, Deputy Attorney General of Florida, argued the cause for appellee Butterworth, Attorney General of Florida. Laurence H. Tribe argued the cause for appellees Gore, et al.	Theodore B. Olson argued the cause for appellant. Joseph P. Klock, Jr. argued the cause for Katherine Harris, et al., appellees under Supreme Court Rule 12.6, in support of appellant.

III. AMICI CURIAE

ACLU Side (Respondent/Appellee):	Opposing Side (Petitioner/Appellant):
Brief of amici curiae filed on behalf of the ACLU by Steven R. Shapiro, Laughlin McDonald, and James K. Green. Brief of amici curiae filed on behalf of the State of Iowa, et al., by Thomas J. Miller, Attorney General of Iowa, Dennis W. Johnson, Solicitor General, and Tam B. Ormiston, Deputy Attorney General, and	Brief of amici curiae filed on behalf of the State of Alabama, et al., by Bill Pryor, Attorney General of Alabama, and Margaret L. Fleming, John J. Park, Jr., Charles B. Campbell, Scott L. Rouse, A. Vernon Barnett IV, and Richard E. Trewhella, Jr., Assistant Attorneys General.

ACLU Side (Respondent/Appellee):	Opposing Side (Petitioner/Appellant):
by the Attorneys General for their respective States as follows: Bill Lockyer of California, Richard Blumenthal of Connecticut, Earl I. Anzai of Hawaii, Karen M. Freeman-Wilson of Indiana, Andrew Ketterer of Maine, J. Joseph Curran, Jr., of Maryland, Thomas F. Reilly of Massachusetts, Joseph P. Mazurek of Montana, Frankie Sue Del Papa of Nevada, Patricia A. Madrid of New Mexico, Drew Edmondson of Oklahoma, Hardy Myers of Oregon, and Sheldon Whitehouse of Rhode Island.	Brief of amici curiae filed on behalf of the Commonwealth of Virginia, et al., by Mark L. Earley, Attorney General of Virginia, Randolph A. Beales, Chief Deputy Attorney General, William Henry Hurd, Solicitor General, Judith Williams Jagdmann, Deputy Attorney General, Siran S. Faulders and Maureen Riley Matsen, Senior Assistant Attorneys General, Eleanor Anne Chesney, Anthony P. Meredith, and Valerie L. Myers, Assistant Attorneys General, Charlie Condon, Attorney General of South Carolina, and Don Stenberg, Attorney General of Nebraska.
Brief of amici curiae filed on behalf of the Coalition for Local Sovereignty by Kenneth B. Clark, in support of neither party.	
Brief of amici curiae filed on behalf of the Florida Senate, et al., by Charles Fried, Einer Elhauge, and Roger J. Magnuson, in support of neither party.	Brief of amici curiae filed on behalf of William H. Haynes, et al., by Jay Alan Sekulow, Thomas P. Monaghan, Stuart J. Roth, Colby M. May, James M. Henderson, Sr., David A. Cortman, Griffin B. Bell,
Brief of amici curiae filed on behalf of the Disenfranchised	

ACLU Side (Respondent/Appellee):	Opposing Side (Petitioner/Appellant):
Voters in the USA, et al., by Ilise Levy Feitshans, in support of neither party.	Paul D. Clement, and Jeffrey S. Bucholtz. Brief of amici curiae filed on behalf of the American Civil Rights Union by John C. Armor and Peter Ferrara.

IV. THE SUPREME COURT'S DECISION:

A. "As a general rule, this Court defers to a state court's interpretation of a state statute. But in the case of a law enacted by a state legislature applicable not only to elections to state offices, but also to the selection of Presidential electors, the legislature is not acting solely under the authority given it by the people of the State, but by virtue of a direct grant of authority made under Art. II, §1, cl. 2, of the United States Constitution. That provision reads:

'Each State shall appoint, in such Manner as the Legislature thereof may direct, a Number of Electors, equal to the whole Number of Senators and Representatives to which the State may be entitled in the Congress . . . .'

Although we did not address the same question petitioner raises here, in *McPherson* v. *Blacker,* 146 U. S. 1, 25 (1892), we said:

'[Art. II, §1, cl. 2,] does not read that the people or the citizens shall appoint, but that 'each State shall'; and if the words 'in such manner as the legislature thereof may direct,' had been omitted, it would seem that the legislative power of appointment could not have been successfully questioned in the absence of any provision in the state constitution in that regard. Hence the insertion of those words, while operating as a limitation upon the State in respect of any attempt to circumscribe the legislative power, cannot be held to operate as a limitation on that power itself.'

There are expressions in the opinion of the Supreme Court of Florida that may be read to indicate that it construed the Florida Election Code without regard to the extent to which the Florida Constitution could, consistent with Art. II, §1, cl. 2, 'circumscribe the legislative power.' The opinion states, for example, that '[t]o the extent that the Legislature may enact laws regulating the electoral process, those laws are valid only if they impose no 'unreasonable or unnecessary' restraints on the right of suffrage' guaranteed by the State Constitution. The opinion also states that '[b]ecause election laws are intended to facilitate the right of suffrage, such laws must be liberally construed in favor of the citizens' right to vote . . . .'

In addition, 3 U. S. C. § 5 provides in pertinent part:

'If any State shall have provided, by laws enacted prior to the day fixed for the appointment of the electors, for its final determination of any controversy or contest concerning the appointment of all or any of the electors of such State, by judicial or other methods or procedures, and such determination shall have been made at least six days before the time fixed for the meeting of the electors, such determination made pursuant to such law so existing on said day, and made at least six days prior to said time of meeting of the electors, shall be conclusive, and shall govern in the counting of the electoral votes as provided in the Constitution, and as hereinafter regulated, so far as the ascertainment of the electors appointed by such State is concerned.'

The parties before us agree that whatever else may be the effect of this section, it creates a 'safe harbor' for a State insofar as congressional consideration of its electoral votes is concerned. If the state legislature has provided for final determination of contests or controversies by a law made prior to election day, that determination shall be conclusive if made at least six days prior to said time of meeting of the electors. The Florida Supreme Court cited 3 U. S. C. §§ 1–10 in a footnote of its opinion, but did not discuss § 5. Since § 5 contains a principle of federal law that would assure finality of the State's determination if made pursuant to a state law in effect before the election, a legislative wish to take advantage of the 'safe harbor' would counsel against any construction of the Election Code that Congress might deem to be a change in the law.

After reviewing the opinion of the Florida Supreme Court, we find 'that there is considerable uncertainty as to the precise grounds for the decision.' This is sufficient reason for us to decline at this time to review the federal questions asserted to be present.

'It is fundamental that state courts be left free and unfettered by us in interpreting their state constitutions. But it is equally important that ambiguous or obscure adjudications by state courts do not stand as barriers to a determination by this Court of the validity under the federal constitution of state action. Intelligent exercise of our appellate powers compels us to ask for the elimination of the obscurities and ambiguities from the opinions in such cases.'

Specifically, we are unclear as to the extent to which the Florida Supreme Court saw the Florida Constitution as circumscribing the legislature's authority under Art. II, §1, cl. 2. We are also unclear as to the consideration the Florida Supreme Court accorded to 3 U. S. C. § 5. The judgment of the Supreme Court of Florida is therefore vacated, and the case is remanded for further proceedings not inconsistent with this opinion."

B. Justice Vote: 0 Pro ACLU Side vs. 9 Con Opposing Side

ACLU Side (Respondent/Appellee):	Opposing Side (Petitioner/Appellant):
	1. Stevens, J.—Per curiam decision
	2. Souter, D.—Per curiam decision
	3. Ginsburg, R.—Per curiam decision
	4. Breyer, S.—Per curiam decision
	5. Rehnquist, W.—Per curiam decision
	6. O'Connor, S.—Per curiam decision
	7. Scalia, A.—Per curiam decision
	8. Kennedy, A.—Per curiam decision
	9. Thomas, C.—Per curiam decision

V.   A WIN OR LOSS FOR THE ACLU?

The ACLU, as amicus curiae, urged affirmance of the judgment of the Florida Supreme Court; the U.S. Supreme Court vacated the judgment and remanded the case in a *per curiam* decision, giving the ACLU an apparent **loss**.

Acknowledgments

I gratefully acknowledge the many friends, associates, researchers, and those interested in this project who have helped me gather, compile, write and, with others, edit this work. Their interest and efforts have made this project possible.

Along the way, many case summaries, metrics and corrections entailing many hundreds of hours of work were put in by Kamy Akhavan, Erica Bianco, Elena Colle, Fiona Connell, Tracey DeFrancesco, Rachel Espana, David Fetterman, Jeannie Gorman, Grant Hubbard, Michael Kelley, Monica Kline, Justin LaMort, Ian Li, Christopher Lippi, Johnny Lo, Jamie Lowry, Allison Martins, Melanie McClinnis, Dillon McGrew, Verica Mitic-Mitchem, Pavan Nagavelli, Robyn Nolan, Lindsey Phoenix, Kimberlee Ray, Tracey Resetar, Ariella Rosenberg, Jonathan Saine, Relic Sun, Hanna Terhaar, Jeff Yablan, Sigrid Hsiju Yang, and Gulcin Yilmazer. Manny Vejar and my daughter Emily Markoff helped fill in data for the U.S. Supreme Court justice votes.

Erwin Chemerinsky was dean of the Irvine School of Law at the University of California, Irvine, when he suggested the need for a lawyer to overview this work, then ending at cases decided by December 31, 2000, and prepare it for publication. Following his suggestion, the A-Mark Foundation that I chair hired Jessica L. Pierucci, a recent law school graduate at that time, to edit and help format the style of the case summaries.

Then in 2015, at the urging of Dean Chemerinsky (then founding dean and distinguished professor of law, and Raymond Pryke Professor of First Amendment Law, at University of California, Irvine School of Law), I decided to expand the project through the ACLU's centennial by including all cases decided by January 19, 2020. I contacted Ms. Pierucci again and she researched and put together the case summaries for the ACLU/SCOTUS

21st century cases. With that work completed, Dean Chemerinsky graciously wrote the foreword for this work.

At the suggestion of Alex Kozinski, in September 2020, Haller Jackson edited my words and cleaned up some of this book's legal methodology and definitions.

My special thanks go to A.R. Hawarden, my consultant and assistant, who was invaluable tying all the pieces of this project together and redoing parts of the project again and again to suit my evolving views of my written words and the presentation of the cases.

Lastly, special thanks to my wife Jadwiga who has suffered through this project for all of the 35 years of our marriage, and who helped finish off some of the metrics and polished some of my words.

Given the 40 years it has taken to complete this project, and my aging memory and imperfect records, I apologize to those who helped with this project but who have been inadvertently left off of this acknowledgment.

About the Author

Los Angeles native Steven C. Markoff is a successful entrepreneur who has produced nonpartisan educational information through various venues since his first published work in 1985, *Should Chief Justice Rose Bird Be Re-confirmed in the Upcoming November 4, 1986, California Election?*

In 1997, Mr. Markoff founded the nonprofit A-Mark Foundation (www.AmarkFoundation.org). The foundation produces reports on various policy issues, including historical research and analysis on our individual rights to bear arms, special investigations involving U.S. presidents, and Benghazi.

STEVEN C. MARKOFF

In 2004, Mr. Markoff founded the nonprofit website ProCon.org (www.ProCon.org), which researched and produced information in a mostly pro/con format on almost 100 socially important topics such as Obamacare, the death penalty, and the Israeli-Palestinian conflict. ProCon.org reached 200 million users before it was acquired by Encyclopædia Britannica in 2020.

Between 2002 and 2010, Mr. Markoff received producer credits on various theatrical films including *Alpha Dogs*, *Next Day Air*, and *Stander*.

His SexEd.net website (www.SexEd.net), which began in 2018, gives diverse third-party opinions on more than 100 topics related to sex.

Mr. Markoff has served on the board of the nonprofit UCLA Management Education Associates and as a member of the Washington, DC-based Federal Task Force on Judicial Selection. He has been a member of the Board of Directors of the nonprofit ACLU Foundation of Southern California from 1979 to 2020.

In late 2020, Mr. Markoff published his first nonfiction book, *The Case Against George W. Bush,* for which he won the Best of Los Angeles award "Best Political Book—2020."

For more information about Steven Markoff, see his online biography at www.stevencmarkoff.com.